Qualitative Comparative Analysis Using R

A comprehensive introduction and teaching resource for state-of-the-art Qualitative Comparative Analysis (QCA) using R software. This guide facilitates the efficient teaching, independent learning, and use of QCA with the best available software, reducing the time and effort required when encountering not just the logic of a new method, but also new software. With its applied and practical focus, the book offers a genuinely simple and intuitive resource for implementing the most complete protocol of QCA. To make the lives of students, teachers, researchers, and practitioners as easy as possible, the book includes learning goals, core points, empirical examples, and tips for good practices. The freely available online material provides a rich body of additional resources to aid users in their learning process. Beyond performing core analyses with the R package QCA, the book also facilitates a close integration with the R package SetMethods, allowing for a host of additional protocols for building a more solid and well-rounded QCA.

Ioana-Elena Oana is a research fellow at the European University Institute (EUI) in Florence. She is the developer of the R package SetMethods and has extensive experience in teaching QCA at various international methods schools and universities across the world. Beyond QCA, her substantive work focuses on collective mobilization, public opinion, and party competition dynamics in the multiple crises that have hit the European Union (EU) since 2008.

Carsten Schneider is professor at the Political Science Department, Central European University (CEU). His research in comparative politics and social science methodology has been published by leading international journals and publishing houses. He is the 2019 awardee of the David Collier Mid-Career Achievement Award of the Qualitative and Multi-Method Research section of the American Political Science Association (APSA).

Eva Thomann is professor at the Department of Policy and Public Administration at the University of Konstanz. She teaches QCA and comparative research design at various international method schools. Her monograph *Customized Implementation of European Union Food Safety Policy: United in Diversity?* (2019) received the 2019 best book award by the International Public Policy Association. She coedits the journal *Regulation & Governance*.

Methods for Social Inquiry

Editors

Colin Elman, Syracuse University
Diana Kapiszewski, Georgetown University
James Mahoney, Northwestern University

The Methods for Social Inquiry series comprises compact texts offering practical instructions for qualitative and multi-method research. Each book is accompanied by pedagogical data and exercises.

The books in the series offer clear, straightforward and concrete guidance for teaching and using methods. While grounded in their relevant prescriptive logics, the books focus on the "how-to" of the methods they discuss – the practical tasks that must be undertaken to effectively employ them. The books should be useful for instruction at both the advanced undergraduate and graduate levels.

The books are tightly integrated with digital content and online enhancements through the Qualitative Data Repository (QDR). QDR is a new NSF-funded repository housing digital data used in qualitative and multi-method social inquiry. The pedagogical data (and related documentation) that accompany the books in the series will be housed in QDR.

Books in the series
Cyr, Jennifer, *Focus Groups for the Social Science Researcher*

Qualitative Comparative Analysis Using R

A Beginner's Guide

Ioana-Elena Oana
European University Institute

Carsten Q. Schneider
Central European University

Eva Thomann
University of Konstanz

CAMBRIDGE
UNIVERSITY PRESS

University Printing House, Cambridge CB2 8BS, United Kingdom

One Liberty Plaza, 20th Floor, New York, NY 10006, USA

477 Williamstown Road, Port Melbourne, VIC 3207, Australia

314–321, 3rd Floor, Plot 3, Splendor Forum, Jasola District Centre, New Delhi – 110025, India

103 Penang Road, #05–06/07, Visioncrest Commercial, Singapore 238467

Cambridge University Press is part of the University of Cambridge.

It furthers the University's mission by disseminating knowledge in the pursuit of education, learning, and research at the highest international levels of excellence.

www.cambridge.org
Information on this title: www.cambridge.org/9781316518724
DOI: 10.1017/9781009006781

© Ioana-Elena Oana, Carsten Q. Schneider and Eva Thomann 2021

First published 2021

Printed in the United Kingdom by TJ Books Limited, Padstow Cornwall

A catalogue record for this publication is available from the British Library.

ISBN 978-1-316-51872-4 Hardback
ISBN 978-1-009-00993-5 Paperback

Contents

Figures

Tables

Acknowledgments

This book has been in the making even when we did not yet know that we would write it. All three of us have been spending many years on learning and teaching QCA. These two activities often went hand in hand. While teaching QCA, we ourselves continued learning. Our thanks therefore go to all the participants of the QCA courses we have taught in so many different places, from courses at our home institutions, to the ECPR Summer and Winter Schools in Methods and Techniques, the Institute for Qualitative and Multi-Method Research (IQMR), the International Political Science Association (IPSA) Methods schools in Mexico City and Sao Paolo, the Winter School of the International Public Policy Association (IPPA) in Aussois, the University of Exeter's Penryn Methods Summer School, and workshops in universities literally all across Europe and beyond. A special note of thanks goes to all of our teaching assistants in these courses. In particular, Giulia Bazzan, Dominik Brenner, Johanna Kuenzler, Ekatarina Paustyan, Kirill Shamiev, Martyna Swiatczak, and Barbora Valikova have provided us with invaluable assistance in drafting and testing many of the exercises and empirical applications used throughout the book.

We are also grateful to the organizers of the QCA International Workshops in Zurich and Antwerp, who provided us with a platform for sharing ideas on some of the topics covered in this book. The COMPASSS website and its leadership and organizers have been a crucial element in communicating among scholars and students interested in QCA and its development. Eva Thomann also gratefully acknowledges everyone who provided her with feedback on her manual to performing QCA with R. A first draft of the book received valuable input during the IQMR 2019 author's workshop in Syracuse. Our discussants at the workshop, Gary Goertz, Markus Kreutzer, and Laura Garcia Montoya, have helped us straighten out the direction of the manuscript in its early stages.

One of the main pitches of the book is that readers learn not only QCA but also its implementation in R. All this would not be possible without the enormous amount of effort put in by countless programmers who provide the software environment – and all free of charge. A particular note of thanks goes to Adrian Dusa, author of the QCA package and constant source of feedback in questions related to the development of the SetMethods package.

This book is a truly collaborative effort, and all authors contributed equally to it. While the three of us had been thinking about the idea of writing this book, it would have remained at the level of an idea if it had not been for the encouragement and support of the editors of the Methods for Social Inquiry series of Cambridge University Press – Colin Elman, Diana Kapiszewksi, and James Mahoney. We are grateful for their trust and for their choice of excellent reviewers, whose comments have helped us to improve our book.

Part I

Getting Started

1 Introduction

QCA in a Nutshell

1.1 Introduction and Learning Goals

This book offers a hands-on introduction and teaching resource for students, users, and teachers of Qualitative Comparative Analysis (QCA; Ragin, 1987, 2000, 2008b). Given its superior ability to model certain aspects of complexity, QCA has made inroads into virtually every social science discipline and beyond. Software solutions for QCA have also been developing at a fast pace. This book seeks to reduce the time and effort required when we first encounter the logic of not just a new method but also new software. It offers a genuinely simple, intuitive, and hands-on resource for implementing the state-of-the-art protocol of QCA using R, the most advanced software environment for QCA. Our book has an applied and practical focus.

In this introductory chapter, we use an empirical example to explain what QCA is and how it works. In the subsequent chapters, we will treat these features and steps in more depth. Using simple language and illustrations, our aim is to familiarize the reader with the basic analytic goals and steps of QCA and illustrate what kind of results this method produces. We then sketch the empirical spread of QCA and related software. Finally, we explain how this book is structured and how the reader can best use it.

Box 1.1 Learning Goals – QCA in a Nutshell

- Familiarity with the general analytic goals and motivations underlying the use of QCA.
- Basic understanding of the main analytic steps involved in doing a QCA.
- Basic understanding and interpretation of QCA results.

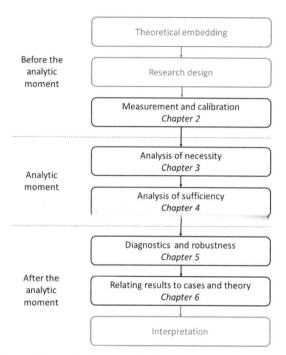

Figure 1.1 Steps of QCA and relevant book chapters

Note: Gray indicates an aspect not specific to QCA.

1.2   QCA in a Nutshell

We start by explaining what kind of research question and motivation would lead us to use QCA in the first place. Then, we introduce the example study that helps us to illustrate the basics of QCA – a study by Freyburg and Garbe (2018), who seek to explain internet shutdowns during elections in sub-Saharan Africa. Based on this example, we guide the reader through the different steps of QCA. We divide this process in the stages *before*, *during*, and *after* the analytic moment – a distinction that we also use for structuring our book into different parts. We conclude by summarizing these steps, and point to the subsequent chapters that cover their technical details (see Figure 1.1).

As Figure 1.1 highlights, some of the analytic steps, though essential, are not specific to QCA, but rather generic aspects of research design and interpretation. We do not cover these aspects in depth in this book, but illustrate them with the specific study by Freyburg and Garbe described in Box 1.2.

Box 1.2 Empirical example: Explaining internet shutdowns in sub-Saharan Africa (Freyburg and Garbe, 2018)

Research question: Why do even Africa's most stable democracies intentionally restrict public internet access during election periods?

Outcome: The occurrence or non-occurrence of internet shutdowns during election periods.

Cases: 33 presidential and parliamentary elections in sub-Saharan African (SSA) countries from 2014 to 2016.

Conditions: State ownership of the internet service providers (ISP); government is an autocracy (AUTOCRACY); occurrence of electoral violence (VIOLENCE).

Sets: Crisp.

Source: Freyburg, Tina, and Garbe, Lisa. 2018. Blocking the bottleneck: Internet shutdowns and ownership at election times in sub-Saharan Africa. *International Journal of Communication,* 12, 3896–3916.

1.2.1 General Goal and Motivation for Using QCA

We can think of empirical research methods as tools in a toolbox. Deciding on which tool to use depends on how suitable it is for performing a given task. For instance, we use a screwdriver to tighten a screw, but not to cut a board. Similarly, the choice of an empirical research method depends on its suitability to answer a given research question. In this section, we introduce four characteristics of QCA: its orientation toward explaining outcomes, case orientation, its set-theoretic foundation, and its approach to modeling causal complexity.[1]

Causes-of-Effects Research Questions

QCA helps us address so-called causes-of-effects type of research questions that ask for the reasons why certain phenomena occur (Mahoney and Goertz, 2006). For example, the study by Freyburg and Garbe (2018) starts with a

---

[1] In this chapter, we use causal language in line with the extant literature, such as 'causes-of-effects' and 'causal complexity'. However, we advise caution in simply taking the results of applied QCA as indicating causality. Whether or under which circumstances the solutions generated with QCA can be interpreted in causal terms is subject to a debate that goes beyond the scope of this book. We hold the position that with QCA one can come closer to a causal interpretation if the cross-case evidence generated with QCA is combined with within-case analyses on the causal mechanisms; see Rohlfing and Schneider (2018). In Chapter 6 on set-theoretic multi-method research (SMMR), we spell out the principles of how to combine QCA with case studies.

particular puzzle: why do even Africa's most stable democracies intentionally restrict public internet access during election periods? Accordingly, their study asks for the conditions that explain why internet shutdowns at election times occur in sub-Saharan Africa. Conversely, we would not use QCA to identify, say, how much a change in leadership affects internet shutdowns. That would be a so-called effects-of-causes question asking for the effect of a specific variable. QCA does not help us identify the magnitude of the effect of a single factor in isolation. Instead, its core motivation is to account for the complex interplay of different factors in bringing about the outcome of interest.

Formalized Comparative Case Studies

QCA is often presented as a method specifically designed for comparing small numbers of cases. However, the number of cases itself is not a good reason for choosing QCA as a method. When Charles Ragin initially introduced QCA (1987), he intended it to be a method for researchers who wish to combine the best features of both qualitative and quantitative methods. QCA is particularly suitable for addressing causes-of-effects questions because it combines formalized comparison with a strong focus on the complexity and individuality of cases. Thus, QCA enables systematic comparisons of relatively small to large numbers of cases (as a rule of thumb, $N \geq 10$). For example, Freyburg and Garbe (2018) use QCA to compare the occurrence or non-occurrence of internet shutdowns in 33 elections in sub-Saharan African (SSA) countries. The use of QCA can only make sense if the phenomenon of interest has two features: it is plausible to frame it in terms of set relations and of causal complexity.

A Set-Analytic Approach

QCA is a set-theoretic method that has its foundations in Boolean algebra and its fuzzy sets extensions (see Chapter 2). This means, first, that we analyze social phenomena as sets. For example, Freyburg and Garbe examine the set of elections during which the state shut down the internet. In their analysis, 10 elections are members of this set, while 23 elections did not resort to internet shutdown. Second, we analyze how different phenomena relate to each other in terms of set relations. Essentially, we want to know whether specific sets of cases are subsets of other sets of cases. For example, Freyburg and Garbe (2018, p. 3901) assert that the set of elections in SSA countries with internet shutdown is a subset of elections in SSA countries where the state has a majority ownership of the internet service provider:

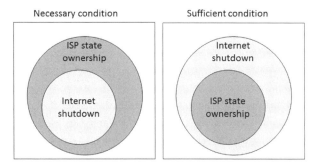

Figure 1.2 Necessary and sufficient conditions as set relations

> We expect a company's commitment to comply with a government's request to shut down its services to be decisively determined by its ownership, notably, facilitated by state majority ownership and hindered otherwise.

This, in fact, is just another way of saying that state majority ownership is a *necessary condition* for internet shutdowns. The left-hand side of the Euler diagram in Figure 1.2 illustrates this.[2] A condition (here: state majority ownership) is a superset of an outcome (here: internet shutdowns) if the outcome is 'hindered' when the condition is not present. This is why on the left-hand side of Figure 1.2, the set of cases with internet shutdowns is fully inside the set of cases with state majority ownership.

Another subset relation that we want to explore with QCA is when a condition is sufficient for an outcome. For instance, state majority ownership would be a *sufficient condition* for internet shutdowns if, whenever the company in charge has state majority ownership, the internet is being shut down during elections. As the right-hand side of Figure 1.2 shows, this is another way of saying that the set of cases with state majority ownership (the condition) is a subset of those cases where the internet was shut down (the outcome). Usually, however, we are less interested in the necessity or sufficiency of single

---

[2] A Euler diagram allows us to visualize the relationship between various sets by displaying them as overlapping circles (or other shapes) surrounded by a box. Each circle in such a diagram denotes one of the sets included in the analysis. Cases that are situated within the circle are members of that particular set, while cases situated outside the circle are non-members. The box around the circles represents the set of all possible cases that are situated within the scope conditions of a particular research or, in other words, the 'universal' set.

conditions. Instead, we are interested in how social phenomena are often the result of combinations of different conditions. QCA helps us explore just that.

Causal Complexity

Indeed, a core feature underlying QCA that distinguishes it from many other methods is that it acknowledges that we can rarely understand social phenomena by focusing on the role of a single factor on its own. Instead, usually complex combinations of conditions bring about a specific outcome. Thus, when we use QCA we can model the presence of three core elements of *causal complexity*, where different sets combine with the logical operations AND, OR, and NOT (Schneider and Wagemann, 2012, pp. 76–99). For example, internet shutdowns might only occur when there is both state ownership of ISPs AND the government in power is authoritarian (Freyburg and Garbe, 2018). This means that we assume *conjunctural causation*: a given factor might only perform its causal role together with another condition. Second, there might be more than one scenario in which internet shutdowns occur. For instance, internet shutdowns might either occur under conditions of state ownership and authoritarian government OR in order to prevent escalation when there is a high level of electoral violence. In other words, many roads may lead to Rome. The assumption of *equifinality* captures that a given event may have several mutually non-exclusive explanations.

Finally, as we shall see later, the occurrence of internet shutdowns in elections in SSA countries has reasons that do not simply mirror the factors that explain its non-occurrence (Freyburg and Garbe, 2018). Instead, the occurrence of an event – such as internet shutdowns – may have different explanations than its non-occurrence – such as when the internet was NOT shut down during an election. In QCA, we call this phenomenon *asymmetric causation*. In real life, there are many examples of this: for instance, while money alone may not make you happy, its absence can be enough to make you unhappy (Thomann et al., 2018).

In summary, we use QCA when research questions ask for the causes of a given effect, when we are interested in the prevalence of set relations and when we assume that empirical relations are complex. If this is the case, then QCA can serve a variety of uses, some of them more theory driven, others more exploratory (see Berg-Schlosser et al., 2008; Schneider and Wagemann, 2010a; Thomann and Maggetti, 2020). We discuss more assumptions underlying QCA and its implementation within a variety of research approaches in the concluding Chapter 7.

Box 1.3 Core points – Goal and motivation for QCA

- The rationale for using QCA should be based on the affinities between the method and characteristics of the research question and phenomena at hand, rather than number of cases alone.
- QCA is suited for addressing 'causes-of-effects' types of questions that ask for the reasons why a certain phenomenon occurs, rather than 'effects-of-causes' questions that ask for the effect of a specific variable on the outcome.
- QCA should be used when the phenomenon under study is best understood in terms of set relation of necessity and sufficiency.
- QCA should be used when the phenomenon under study is assumed to be causally complex in terms of conjunctural causation, equifinality, and asymmetry.

1.2.2   Before the Analytic Moment

Before we actually analyze data with QCA, that is, before the 'analytic moment', we have to make several decisions related to research design[3] and then assign set membership scores to our cases, the so-called process of calibration.

Research Design

Based on the research question that we have formulated, we can define what the outcome is that we want to explain. For instance, Freyburg and Garbe (2018) seek to explain the occurrence of internet shutdowns during elections in sub-Saharan Africa. As a next step, we will need to select and define a set of conditions that should be relevant in explaining this outcome. This step is called *model specification*. To avoid complications during the analysis, most QCA studies include between three and seven conditions for explaining an outcome of interest.[4] Just as with any other quantitative or qualitative method, we will choose the conditions that we include in our study based on the existing body of relevant theory and empirical findings related to the given research question.

---

[3] Further useful literature on research design includes Brady and Collier (2010), Gerring (2011) and Goertz and Mahoney (2012).

[4] This is due to problems of theoretical interpretation, on the one hand, and problems related to limited diversity, on the other (i.e., combinations of conditions for which there is not enough empirical evidence; see Chapter 4). The number of conditions can be larger in two-step QCA; see Section 5.4.1, and Schneider (2019).

In our example, Freyburg and Garbe (2018) chose three conditions to analyze internet shutdowns during elections in SSA. The first condition is state ownership of the ISP because strategies of repression, more generally, are particularly effective if the government has control over that particular resource or infrastructure. The second condition is whether the government is an autocracy. Previous studies claim the manipulation of internet access is more prevalent in autocracies. Finally, electoral violence is an important condition because it is thought to trigger protests by opposition forces. Internet shutdown would make it harder for these forces to organize and communicate. After selecting the conditions and the outcome, we will carefully conceptualize these as sets, and think about how we can observe (measure) them in our analysis.[5]

Another step in designing the research is *case selection*. Case selection involves a set of decisions about defining cases (Ragin, 1987), the universe of cases, scope conditions, and the set of cases we include in the analysis. First, we need to define what constitutes a case, and hence what our unit of analysis is (Ragin and Becker, 1992). The *unit of analysis* is the entity of interest which we study as a whole, at the level of which we draw inferences. For instance, Freyburg and Garbe (2018) look at elections as the unit of analysis for studying whether internet shutdowns occur during elections.[6] Choosing an appropriate unit of analysis is a theoretical question: we need to determine at what level we expect the phenomenon of interest – here, internet shutdowns – to take place. Next, we will think about the scope of our research. Freyburg and Garbe (2018) define the scope of their research to involve elections after decolonialization and since the introduction of internet and social media in Africa. The scope conditions help us define the entire universe of possible cases which would in principle be relevant to analyze the research question.

Finally, we always choose cases within the boundaries of the scope we defined. We can either work with the entire universe of cases (or the population), or select a specific set of cases (or a sample) from it. Freyburg and Garbe (2018) apply several selection criteria to choose cases from this universe, both in order to ensure comparability and due to considerations of data availability. Applying temporal criteria, they focus on the period 2014–2016. In spatial terms, they include only SSA countries. Conceptually, they focus on national elections only. This leads them to compare all the 33 presidential and parliamentary elections in SSA between 2014 and 2016, with the exception of

---

[5] Further literature on conceptualization and measurement includes Adcock and Collier (2001) and Goertz (2012).

[6] The unit of analysis is different from the unit of observation, which is the unit at the level of which we collect data. For example, one can collect individual-level data on public opinion (unit of observation) to obtain a measure of public opinion in a country (unit of analysis) for explaining a country-level phenomenon, for instance, party change.

the ones in Sao Tome and Mauritius, for which data were not available. We will return to the question of case selection in Section 7.2.[7]

Measurement and Calibration

Before we can proceed to the analytic moment, we need to prepare the empirical material – the 'data' – that we can use to compare the cases in the QCA. We have already seen that, in QCA, we think of conditions and outcomes as sets to which cases belong or not. We now need to determine, for each case, the extent to which it belongs to these different sets. The first step in doing so is *measurement*: we need to think about how we can observe the concept that this set stands for in the real world (Adcock and Collier, 2001). For example, to determine the set of elections with ISP state ownership, Freyburg and Garbe (2018) use the percentage of outstanding shares that the state has in ISP in the country. Once we have collected the qualitative and/or quantitative empirical information to measure the conditions and the outcome, we have obtained the 'raw data' for our QCA. In a next step, we need to transform the available data on the cases so that they reflect the sets we are interested in. We call the process of transforming raw data into set membership scores, in order to determine whether and to what extent cases belong to a particular set, *calibration*. For example, Freyburg and Garbe (2018) consider elections in countries where the state has more than 51 per cent of the shares in at least one ISP in the country as members of the set of ISP state ownership, whereas the rest of the elections are not considered members of this set.

In QCA, there are different types of sets. *Crisp sets* are binary: they only distinguish between cases that are members of a set (membership score of 1) and cases that are not members of a set (membership score of 0). Freyburg and Garbe (2018) calibrate crisp-set data on three conditions (ISP state ownership, autocracy, and electoral violence) and the outcome (internet shutdowns) so that each election in SSA countries has a membership score of 1 or 0 in all these sets. However, sometimes we are also interested in the different degrees to which cases belong to a set. For example, we could be interested in different intensities of electoral violence. To this end, we can use *fuzzy sets*, where cases can also belong or not belong to a set to various degrees. Fuzzy-set membership scores vary from 0 to 1 (see Section 2.2.1). For the moment, we stick with so-called crisp sets, that is, sets that only allow membership scores of 1 and 0, to explain the QCA.

---

[7] Issues of case selection, condition selection and research design with QCA more broadly are also discussed in Berg-Schlosser and De Meur (2009), Rihoux and Ragin (2009, chapter 2) and Mello (2021, chapter 3).

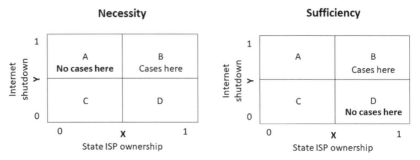

Figure 1.3 Necessity and sufficiency for crisp sets

1.2.3   During the Analytic Moment

After calibrating the raw data into set membership scores, we are ready to proceed to the data analysis in QCA. During the analytic moment, we want to identify whether there are necessary and/or sufficient combinations of conditions for the outcome of interest.

Analyses of Necessity and Sufficiency

As we have seen in Section 1.2.1, to analyze necessity (see Chapter 3), we usually focus on whether each condition or a specific combination of conditions is a superset of the outcome. In other words, we check whether the outcome only occurs in the presence of that condition or that combination of conditions. For us to declare that a condition is necessary, there should not be instances where the outcome occurs but the necessary condition is missing. For example, ISP state majority ownership is necessary for internet shutdowns, if there is no election without ISP state majority where the internet is shut down. Figure 1.3 visualizes this: we do not want to observe cases in quadrant A in the upper-left side. These are the cases that would contradict the statement of necessity, because here the internet was shut down even though the state was not the majority ISP holder. More generally, we write necessity relations as $X \leftarrow Y$. We can read this as 'outcome Y implies condition X', because outcome Y cannot occur in the absence of condition X.[8]

For the analysis of sufficiency (see Chapter 4), we look at conditions that always lead to the outcome. Earlier, we saw in Section 1.2.1 that a sufficient condition is a subset of the outcome. In other words, we want to identify (combinations of) conditions which do not occur together with the absence of

---

[8] Note that Freyburg and Garbe (2018) did not find any necessary conditions for internet shutdowns in their study. We use this example for illustrative purposes.

the outcome. In the Freyburg and Garbe (2018) example, if ISP state ownership is sufficient for internet shutdown, this means that there must not be cases with ISP state ownership that do not result in internet shutdowns. In Figure 1.3, we thus do not want to see cases in the lower-right quadrant D. We generally write sufficiency relations as $X \rightarrow Y$. We can read this as 'condition X implies outcome Y', because there are no cases with condition X but without outcome Y. To analyze sufficiency, we start by looking at all possible combinations of conditions. We then evaluate which of these combinations are subsets of – in other words, sufficient for – the outcome. To reveal all logically possible configurations of conditions, in QCA we have the *truth table* as a useful analytic tool.

Table 1.1 shows the truth table for the occurrence of internet shutdowns in the study by Freyburg and Garbe (2018). Each row of the truth table represents a specific combination of conditions. And all truth table rows together display all the possible logical AND combinations of conditions. The conditions are either present (1) or absent (0). We observe these configurations in one or several cases. We then determine sufficiency by checking the membership of these cases in the outcome set. If all cases with the same configuration also display the outcome, so-called consistency takes on the value 1. In this case, the configuration is considered sufficient for the outcome (OUTPUT 1). In Chapter 4, we expand on how to perform an analysis of sufficiency by constructing and analyzing truth tables.

To put it in very simple terms, the goal of the truth table analysis is to find the shortest possible expressions of those combinations of conditions that are sufficient for the outcome by eliminating irrelevant (redundant) conditions. For example, if we compare the first two sufficient rows in Table 1.1, we can see that they are identical except the condition AUTOCRACY once being absent and once being present. From this we can conclude that the combination of state ISP ownership in a setting of electoral violence is sufficient for internet shutdowns, irrespective of the presence or absence of an autocratic regime. Similarly, the third and fourth row only differ in the condition VIOLENCE; we can hence 'minimize away' this condition as irrelevant through a pairwise comparison of two otherwise identical sufficient truth table rows.

Performing a truth table analysis in this manner, Freyburg and Garbe (2018) find the following sufficient solution for the occurrence of internet shutdowns (S1). In this expression, the negation of a condition is denoted with a $\sim$. The multiplication sign * reads as logical 'AND', and the plus sign + reads as logical 'OR'.

$$S1 : ISP * AUTOCRACY + \sim\!ISP * VIOLENCE \rightarrow SHUTDOWN \quad (1.1)$$

In plain words, this means that there are two scenarios that have typically resulted in internet shutdowns in recent elections in SSA countries. In the first scenario, an autocratic state that holds the majority in ISP ownership shuts

Table 1.1 Truth table, outcome 'Internet Shutdown'

ISP ownership	Conditions Electoral violence	Autocracy	Output	Number of cases	Consistency	Cases
0	1	0	1	1	1	Gabon_16
0	1	1	1	3	1	Republic of Congo_16, Sudan, North_15, Uganda_16
1	0	1	1	4	1	Equatorial Guinea_16, Ethiopia_15, Gambia_16, Togo_15
1	1	1	1	2	1	Burundi_15, Chad_16
0	0	0	0	7	0	Burkina Faso_15, CAR_15, Ghana_16, Guinea_15, Ivory Coast_16,Lesotho_15, Malawi_14
0	0	1	0	2	0	CAR_15, Mauritania_14
1	0	0	0	11	0	Benin_15, Benin_16, Botswana_14, Djibouti_16, Guinea_Bissau_16, Ivory Coast_16, Namibia_14, Niger_16, Nigeria_15, Zambia_15, South Africa_14
1	1	0	0	3	0	Mozambique_14, Tanzania_15, Zambia_16

down the internet during elections. In the second configuration, ISP ownership is not public and there were significant incidents of electoral violence. The authors then discuss the cases that display these specific configurations. This helps them to illustrate the underlying mechanisms behind why private ISP owners may be willing to temporarily shut down their services.

We are not only interested in why the outcome occurs, but we also usually want to analyze why the outcome does *not* occur. For example, it is not only interesting to know under what conditions governments in SSA countries shut the internet down, we also want to learn about the conditions under which they do *not* shut the internet down. We call this the 'negation' of the outcome. Accordingly, the QCA often involves four distinct analyses: necessary conditions for the outcome, necessary conditions for the non-occurrence of the outcome, sufficient conditions for the outcome, and sufficient conditions for the negated outcome. For example, Freyburg and Garbe (2018) find that different configurations of conditions are sufficient for the non-occurrence of the outcome (S2) 'No internet shutdown' (see S2):

$$S2 : {\sim}ISP * {\sim}VIOLENCE + ISP * {\sim}AUTOCRACY \rightarrow {\sim}SHUTDOWN$$

$$(1.2)$$

They find two paths that do not result in an internet shutdown: private ISP ownership when there is no electoral violence, or state ISP ownership in non-authoritarian governments. These QCA results reflect all the different aspects of causal complexity. Firstly, we have evidence of conjunctural causality: the single conditions do not produce internet shutdowns (or their absence) on their own, but only in combination with others. For example, autocratic government is only a factor leading to shutting the internet down if the government also has the majority ownership of ISP. Secondly, the results also reflect equifinality: there is more than just one way the outcome can occur. For example, internet shutdowns during elections can happen when there is state ownership of an ISP in an autocracy; but shutdowns also happen when there is violence during the election combined with no state ownership of an ISP. Thirdly, these results reflect asymmetric causality: the sufficient conditions for no internet shutdowns (S2) are not just the 'opposite' of the sufficient conditions for internet shutdowns (S1).

Less-than-Perfect Set Relations

We should note that social science data tend to be considerably more noisy than the examples we presented so far in Figure 1.3, which depicts perfect subset relations. In practice, we often allow for small deviations from perfect patterns of necessity and sufficiency. In other words, we want these deviations not to

Quasi-necessity   Quasi-sufficiency

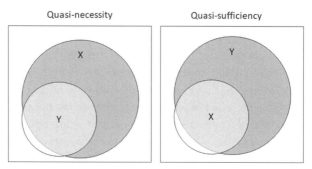

Figure 1.4 Less-than-perfect set relations

exceed a certain, still acceptable, degree. Figure 1.4 illustrates this. For this purpose, with QCA several parameters of fit for necessity and sufficiency allow us to quantify the extent to which set relations deviate from being 'perfect'. In Figure 1.4, these parameters would tell us the relative size of the area where the condition set and the outcome set do not overlap. We introduce the parameters of fit for necessity and sufficiency in Chapters 3 and 4, respectively.

Set Relations with Fuzzy Sets

It is easy to grasp set relations with crisp sets where we only deal with the occurrence or non-occurrence of conditions and the outcome. In the case of fuzzy sets, cases are members in sets to different degrees. In principle, the analyses of necessity and sufficiency for fuzzy sets work in a very similar manner as with crisp sets: we identify supersets (necessity) or subsets (sufficiency) of the outcome. The main difference is that we also take into account the more fine-grained differences 'in degree' in set membership, not only binary differences 'in kind'. In practice, the way this plays out is that we analyze whether the condition set is greater than (necessity) or smaller than (sufficiency) the outcome set. For example, a condition is a superset of the outcome (necessary) if the membership scores of cases in that condition are greater than or equal to their membership in the outcome set.

In the left part of Figure 1.5, we illustrate how this looks when we plot the condition and the outcome. The cases that cluster below the diagonal conform to a pattern of necessity because their membership in the condition set is always greater than or equal to their membership in the outcome set. Conversely, the cases above the diagonal are inconsistent with the statement of necessity. For sufficiency, it is the other way around: as the right part of Figure 1.5 illustrates, the set of cases that are a subset of the outcome (sufficiency) is the set of cases whose membership in the condition set is smaller than or equals their membership in the outcome set. For sufficiency, the cases that weaken the sufficiency statement are hence those that cluster below the diagonal.

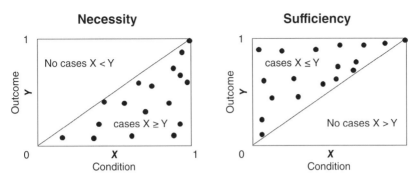

Figure 1.5 Necessity and sufficiency for fuzzy sets

1.2.4 After the Analytic Moment

Once we have identified necessary and sufficient (combinations of) conditions for the outcome, we can apply several procedures for increasing the confidence in our results, for clarifying the extent to which our findings can 'travel' to other contexts, and for deriving more abstract conclusions. Figure 1.6 illustrates how we usually draw inferences at three distinct levels with QCA: the actual set of cases we analyzed, the universe of cases, and the body of theory or abstract knowledge to which we seek to contribute with our research (Thomann and Maggetti, 2020).

On the one hand, we will perform a variety of diagnostics and check the robustness of the results within our sample. Readers will learn more details about this in Chapter 5. Moreover, after the QCA analysis, we often bring individual cases back to the forefront. For instance, we would perform case studies in order to analyze the mechanisms that underlie the different sufficient paths toward the outcome. The rules governing the choice of cases based on a QCA result are spelled out in the framework of set-theoretic multi-method research (SMMR) and we discuss them in more detail in Section 6.3. Freyburg and Garbe (2018), for example, discuss the cases of the Republic of Congo and Uganda in depth, arguing that they are especially relevant because they involve internet shutdowns by private companies. We will also want to learn from cases that deviate from the perfect necessity or sufficiency pattern. This can help us identify potential limitations of our research.

On the other hand, there will also be an element of abstraction 'upwards' (see Figure 1.6), where we relate the results to existing theories and concepts or draw other abstract conclusions on policy recommendations. The detailed procedure for how this can be done in QCA is explained in Section 6.2 and Chapter 7. For instance, Freyburg and Garbe (2018) conclude from their analysis that ISP ownership is critical to understanding authoritarian practices violating citizens'

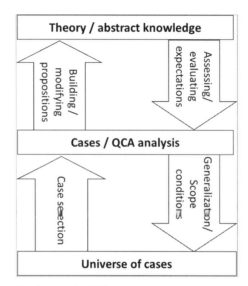

Figure 1.6 Levels of inference in QCA research
Note: Own illustration inspired by Thomann and Maggetti (2020).

freedom of expression in the digital sphere. Finally, we draw inferences 'downwards' toward the relevant universe of cases (see Figure 1.6). This process often involves defining *scope conditions*. Scope conditions represent the conceptual and empirical boundaries within which the theory we use applies or where we expect the phenomenon of interest to take place. They are directly related to how we have earlier defined the relevant universe of cases. When discussing scope conditions, we reflect on the extent to which the results can 'travel' in spatial and temporal terms, but also in terms of the types of cases we might be able to generalize to (Goertz and Mahoney, 2009). In this vein, Freyburg and Garbe (2018) call for more research that accounts for temporally and spatially varying levels of internet penetration and the effects of different ownership structures.

1.3 Spread of QCA and Related Software

While still not considered a 'mainstream' method, QCA has established itself as a methodological tool in the social sciences and beyond. Between 1994 and 2019, in the Web of Science Core Collection database, we find 611 publications describing or using QCA (see Figure 1.7).[9]

---

[9] Search terms were QCA AND 'Qualitative Comparative Analysis' in the title, abstract, author keywords, and Keywords Plus. The Web of Science Core Collection includes sciences, social

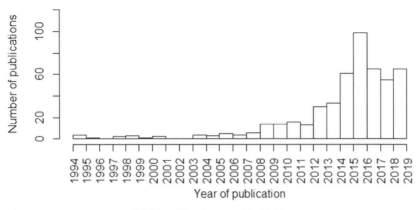

Figure 1.7 Development of QCA publications, 1994–2019

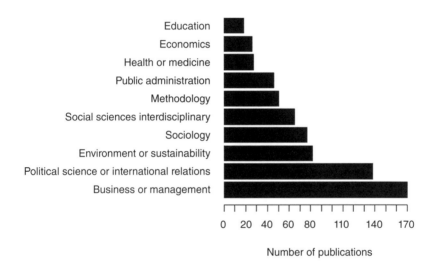

Figure 1.8 QCA-related publications per discipline, 1994–2019

Source: Own illustration based on Web of Science including the 10 most frequent disciplines. Publications can be classified under more than one discipline.[10]

As Figure 1.8 shows, QCA is used prominently in four fields: political science and international relations, sociology, environment and sustainability, and particularly business and management (Wagemann et al., 2016).

sciences, and arts and humanities. The figures include publications between 1987 and 2019, and no publications before 1994 are recorded in the database. Date of search: November 11, 2019.

[10] Combined categories as follows (double counts are possible): Environment or Sustainability = ENVIRONMENTAL STUDIES, ENVIRONMENTAL SCIENCES, PUBLIC

Table 1.2 Top 10 journals publishing QCA-related research, 1987–2019

Journal name	N
Journal of Business Research	61
Sociological Methods & Research	21
Quality & Quantity	17
International Journal of Social Research Methodology	11
European Journal of Political Research	7
Journal of European Public Policy	7
Political Analysis	7
Political Research Quarterly	6
Comparative Political Studies	5
Field Methods	5

Source: Web of Science.

Table 1.2 identifies the top 10 academic outlets with a strong record of publishing QCA-related research. They cover the disciplines of sociology and business research and include some of the most prestigious political science journals. It is notable that five out of the 10 journals are methodological outlets: *Sociological Methods and Research, Quality and Quantity,* the *International Journal of Social Research Methodology, Political Analysis,* and *Field Methods.* These figures reflect that QCA has become an increasingly robust, sophisticated, and attractive tool for empirical social research.

In parallel, Figure 1.9 shows how the use of R packages has increased exponentially in recent years (see also Thiem and Dusa, 2013; Verweij and Trell, 2019) and are catching up in numbers with more widely used 'traditional' software, fs/QCA (Ragin and Davey, 2016), and Tosmana (Cronqvist, 2019).[11] The latter rely on 'point-and-click' style graphical user interfaces, whereas R is a command-line software environment. Once users master R to a sufficient degree – something our book is meant to help with – it provides several advantages. First, analytic flexibility is much higher, as one can customize very precise analytic steps, rather than relying on a few standardized options. The R packages `SetMethods` (Oana and Schneider, 2018) and `QCA` (Dusa, 2018) offer superior functionality compared to other QCA-specific software (see Table 7.4 for details). Second, and related, because R is open-source, methodological innovations continue to quickly find their way to QCA practitioners via the

ENVIRONMENTAL OCCUPATIONAL HEALTH and GREEN SUSTAINABLE SCIENCE TECHNOLOGY; Methodology = SOCIAL SCIENCES MATHEMATICAL METHODS and STATISTICS PROBABILITY; Health or Medicine= HEALTH CARE SCIENCES SERVICES, HEALTH POLICY SERVICES and MEDICINE GENERAL INTERNAL.

[11] See http://compasss.org/software/ for a more complete list of QCA-related software.

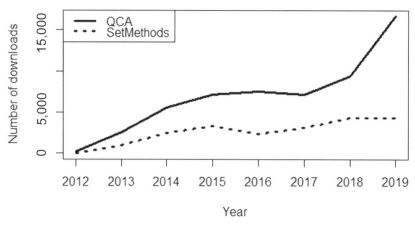

Figure 1.9 Downloads of R packages QCA and SetMethods, 2012–2019

Source: CRAN repository, retrieved November 27, 2019. The figure does not include downloads from github, therefore underrepresentation of the use of SetMethods is likely.

dedicated R packages. Third, QCA analyses in R are easier to replicate, as one can write down and store every analytic step that was performed in order to obtain the results. This is useful not only for others, but also for organizing one's own research project, especially bigger ones that last for longer periods of time and entail many analyses.

Increased computational sophistication may come with practical hurdles for QCA users of the R software. This book serves a simple purpose: to facilitate the efficient teaching, use, and independent learning of state-of-the-art QCA with the best available technology. As readers will see, learning QCA with R is actually a didactic advantage rather than a burden. The use of command lines helps to better understand the logic of the analytic steps performed during QCA. Additionally, in order to aid users in their R learning process, this book is complemented by two resources available in the online appendix, which can be found at https://doi.org/10.7910/DVN/S9QPM5. First, we provide readers with an 'Intro to R' chapter to kickstart the software induction. Second, we offer a series of datasets and template files containing all the basic R commands used through the different steps of a QCA which can be directly customized and copied into R scripts.

1.4 Summary and Logic of the Book

In this chapter, we have introduced QCA as a method that helps us identify necessary and sufficient conditions for an outcome of interest. QCA allows us to model three core aspects of causal complexity. First, conjunctural causation means that different conditions combine to produce an outcome. Second, equifinality means that one outcome may have several, mutually non-exclusive explanations. Finally, asymmetric causation prevails as the occurrence of the outcome has a different explanation than its non-occurrence. QCA is a set-theoretic method. This means that we attribute cases to sets that represent the outcome we want to explain and the conditions we assume to be relevant for this outcome, and we analyze necessary and sufficient conditions as set relations.

1.4.1   Structure of the Book

The book guides the reader through the different analytic steps of QCA before, during, and after the truth table analysis. In the phase before the analytic moment, we design our research, conceptualize cases and sets, and transform them into 'data'. The process of attributing cases to sets is called 'calibration'. Chapter 2 further develops the notions of sets and describes several available procedures for calibrating raw data into set-membership scores. This chapter also discusses in more depth the logical operators that we use to combine sets and their negation. Based on this, we introduce different ways of forming the concepts at the heart of our set-analytic procedure. While we return to the question of case selection in Section 7.2, our book does not aim to provide an extensive theoretical treatment of general research design issues. Issues of case selection, condition selection, and research design with QCA more broadly are discussed in Berg-Schlosser and De Meur (2009), Rihoux and Ragin (2009, chapter 2), and Mello (2021, chapter 3).

The 'analytic moment' refers to the actual analyses of necessity and sufficiency. Chapter 3 introduces the analysis of necessity, when the condition is a superset of the outcome and the respective parameters of fit. Chapter 4 is about analyzing sufficient conditions that are subsets of the outcome set with the help of truth tables and parameters of fit. In this chapter, we also expand on the problem of 'limited empirical diversity', when our cases do not populate all the rows in our truth table. We present various strategies to deal with this problem. For a more in-depth theoretical discussion on issues pertaining to the analytic moment, especially regarding pitfalls in the analysis of necessity and sufficiency, we point the reader to Schneider and Wagemann (2012, chapters 8 and 9).

After the analytic moment, we need to interpret the results and check how 'good' they are. In Chapters 5 and 6, we discuss advanced analytic tools that can – or even should – be used after a QCA result has been obtained. Finally, in Chapter 7 we discuss the steps and options involved in interpreting QCA results more generally, and outline standards of good practice. Throughout the book, we highlight how case knowledge informs QCA at the various stages of the analysis. We use a rich body of examples, some fictitious, some based on real data, to illustrate the different concepts and steps.

1.4.2 How to Use This Book

With this book, we seek to make the lives of students, teachers, researchers, and practitioners as easy as possible when performing the most complete QCA protocol with R. For this, we adopt an applied and practical focus. For recent comprehensive theoretical introductions to QCA, we point the reader to, among others, Rihoux and Ragin (2009) and Schneider and Wagemann (2012). These books provide in-depth theoretical discussions of many of the issues treated in this book, but without the focus on hands-on implementation using R. Dusa (2018) provides a more advanced guide to QCA with R, focused particularly on the QCA package, but less accessible for readers without prior knowledge of the method and software. Mello (2021) also provides a beginner-oriented introduction to QCA, including an appendix of the main R functions, but does not include the state-of-the-art techniques treated in the later chapters of this book, particularly those to be performed after the analytic moment.

All the chapters in the book follow the same structure. We first introduce the topic of the chapter and specify learning goals. This is followed by a very brief conceptual description of the analytic procedure treated in the chapter. Most often, we construct some hypothetical examples to illustrate this conceptual introduction. Next, we show how to implement this procedure in R using RStudio (RStudio Team, 2019) with packages QCA and SetMethods, sometimes using an empirical example from a published QCA study. We explain the structure of the R outputs and how to interpret them. Each chapter concludes with a summary of take-home points. Throughout the book, we use boxes to highlight learning goals, core points, empirical examples, and tips for good practices.

In addition, the freely available online appendix to this book provides a rich body of additional resources. First, it contains additional guidance on implementing specific parts of the analysis in R, including a hands-on introduction to using R and handling datasets in RStudio. Second, the online appendix features all datasets and R scripts to replicate all analyses performed in this book. Third, users can find ready-made template commands with explanations of the most important options online, structured along the analytic steps of QCA. Fourth, the online appendix contains test questions (and answers), as well as exercises (and solutions) which readers and instructors can use as learning resources.

We suggest that readers start the book from page 1 and follow thoroughly the material in Chapters 1–4, as well as Section 5.2 and Chapter 7. In later chapters, we assume that readers know the material introduced in preceding chapters.

In order to test whether or not readers have mastered the material covered in a chapter, we suggest trying our online test questions. Sections 5.3 and 5.4 and Chapter 6 are catered to more advanced users and contain analytic steps that can be used after the analytic moment in order to make more out of the QCA results obtained. We wish the reader an enjoyable reading and learning experience!

Part II

Before the Analytic Moment

2 Calibrating and Combining Sets

In the previous chapter, we learned that QCA is a set-theoretic method in three ways. First, we conceive of social phenomena as sets in which the cases have membership. Second, we look at social phenomena as complex combinations of different sets. Third, we identify necessary and/or sufficient conditions for an outcome as superset or subset relations between sets. In this chapter, we cover the first two aspects.

2.1 Introduction and Learning Goals

When using QCA, we compare cases according to their membership in sets. For example, let us say we want to explain why some students perform particularly well. Thus, we compare students according to their membership in the set of 'good students'. A set is a collection of objects or cases (here: students) that share a common property (here: performing well). To allocate students to this set, we will need to define clear criteria for distinguishing 'good' from 'not good' students. As soon as there is more than one such criterion, we will also need to think about how these criteria combine to indicate that a student is 'good'.

In the first section on set calibration, we discuss how to attribute cases to sets. We start with different types of sets and ways to measure them, then go on to different approaches to calibrating sets and the ways to implement them in R. We then introduce good practices and practical tips for performing calibration, as well as some diagnostic tools for calibration. In the second section on Boolean operations, we discuss how to combine sets with the logical AND, OR, and NOT. We connect the dots and discuss how these techniques help us conceptualize the social phenomena that inform our analysis. This section includes useful rules for combining and presenting set-theoretic expressions. In this way, this chapter prepares the reader for the analysis of set relations, which we will then introduce in Chapters 3 and 4.

Box 2.1 Learning Goals – Calibration

- Basic understanding of the notion of calibration and different calibration techniques.
- Familiarity with good practices and diagnostic tools for set calibration.
- Familiarity with basic Boolean operations on sets and the rules for attributing cases to combined sets.
- Familiarity with different techniques of aggregating sets into higher-order concepts.
- Ability to implement these calibration and concept formation tools in R.

2.2   Sets and Set Calibration

Sets always represent concepts. For example, to decide whether or not a given student belongs to the set of good students, we have to ask: what is a 'good student'? Generally, the properties that characterize the set establish boundaries that define zones of inclusion and exclusion (Schneider and Wagemann, 2012). This involves four main questions. The first is about *definition*: what constitutes a 'good student'? Intuitively, student performance is quite a multi-faceted phenomenon. For instance, we often equate good students with students who perform well academically. However, we could also say that good students are students who attend classes regularly, participate in class, engage with the readings, or help their peers. We will need to spell out the different aspects of student performance that matter for attributing a student to our set of 'good students', and how they matter. After having conceptualized the 'good student', we will need to think about how we can actually recognize a good student in the real world. For instance, how can we capture academic performance? This is a question of *measurement*. For example, it is common to measure academic performance through marks. The third question is then: when do we say that a student is 'good'? For instance, what is the mark that a student needs to have for us to say that their academic performance is good? In QCA, we answer this question in the phase of *calibration*. The fourth issue to address is: what are the empirical properties of the calibrated sets? Here, we are particularly interested in whether most of our cases hold high or low membership in a set and, for fuzzy sets, whether there are cases that hold a set membership of exactly 0.5. Sometimes, such empirical features are unavoidable. Yet, researchers are well advised to be aware of them because, as we show in Chapters 3 and 4, running QCA with skewed sets triggers some analytic challenges that need to be attended to. Figure 2.1 illustrates the different analytic steps involved when calibrating sets.

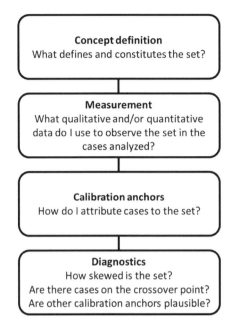

Figure 2.1 Steps of set calibration

In order to determine which students are members of the set of 'good students', we need to answer all questions. The important analytic exercise is to define the boundaries of sets. This essentially means defining the concepts that are at the heart of the empirical analysis. The last section of this chapter is dedicated specifically to some more advanced questions of conceptualization, when concepts have complex structures. For now, for the sake of illustration we will define a 'good student' as a student who performs well academically. We ignore temporarily other aspects of what might be good student performance.

Box 2.2 Mock Example – The 'Good' Student

- *Research question*: What is a good student?
- *Cases*: 17 students in Britain.
- *Variables (raw data)*: Student mark (MARK); Quality and correctness of the student's comments in class (PARTICIPATION); Extent to which the student engages with and helps peers during interactive in-class teaching exercises (PEERS).
- *Sets (calibrated data)*: The good student (GOOD), of which we calibrate five (crisp and fuzzy) versions; Good in-class performance (CLASS); The excellent student (EXCELLENT); The talented student (TALENT); Active in-class participation (PART); Student who supports peers in class (PEER); The high-performing student (PERF).

2.2.1   From Measurement to Calibration

Basically, *measurement* refers to the choices researchers make about linking concepts to observations, that is, about connecting ideas with facts (Lazarsfeld and Barton, 1957). If we think about measurement this way, then there are many ways of measuring social phenomena in both qualitative and quantitative ways (Adcock and Collier, 2001). For example, marks are usually a numerical – that is, quantitative – way of measuring academic performance. At the same time, marks differ between countries. For instance, in the United Kingdom, marks range from 0 to 100, while in Germany, they range from 6 to 1 and in Switzerland, from 1 to 6. However, it could also be plausible to argue that academic performance is more meaningfully thought of as a more qualitative phenomenon; we would need to engage, for instance, with the content of student essays, the students' ability to reflect critically on concepts taught in class, the quality of comments they make in class, and so on.

Raw Data and Measurement Validity

When we calibrate sets, the *raw data* that we use for measurement can come in any form. Data can be qualitative or quantitative, standardized or not, numerical or not, and so on. In fact, using a variety of different raw data sources strengthens our confidence in the resulting set membership scores (Toth et al., 2017; de Block and Vis, 2019).[1] The important point to keep in mind at this stage is that our measurement must be valid. That is, we need to ensure that our observations meaningfully capture the ideas contained in the concepts we are using (Adcock and Collier, 2001; Lazarsfeld and Barton, 1957; Mahoney, 2010). If, for instance, we find that marks do not tell us about important, more nuanced, and meaningful ways in which different students perform academically, then we have a problem with measurement validity and we would need to find a better way of capturing student performance empirically. However, for the time being, we will assume that marks are a valid measure of academic performance.

Defining Calibration

We have already seen that measuring our concepts is only a preparation for the actual calibration process. In fact, we can think of sets as 'boxes' which we can

---

[1] Whether or not our raw data are of a more qualitative nature or involve fine-grained numerical measures can affect the choice of calibration technique. For example, we can use the direct method of calibration (which we introduce in the next subsection) only on numerical data.

assign the cases to – such as the box of 'good students'. Set calibration is the process of assigning set membership scores to cases. We assign cases to sets based on the raw data we have chosen and collected to measure the sets. For instance, let us say we have a class of 17 undergraduate students in Britain, and we use their final marks from year three in order to measure their performance; this is our raw dataset (later in this chapter). Set membership scores tell us whether (and with fuzzy sets also how much) a case fits inside the box. The most important analytic decision we need to take is whether a given student belongs in this box or not. In other words, we establish which empirical score – in our example, which mark – establishes the qualitative 'difference in kind' between good students and other students. We also call this score the 'crossover point', or 'point of indifference' (Ragin, 2008a; Schneider and Wagemann, 2012, chapter 1).

Finding Calibration Anchors

Establishing the difference in kind is not only a highly consequential, but often also quite a tricky question. In addition to empirical information (raw data), we also need a conceptual definition of the set we want to calibrate. For instance, having a list of marks for each of our 17 students (measurement) is all very well, but now we need to define which of these marks actually indicate that these are 'good students' (calibration). We may now ask (again): what constitutes a 'good' student? Do we apply a restrictive definition, where only excellent or outstanding students are considered 'good'? Or is it enough for a student to have a more-than-average performance to count as a good student? Partly, our decision will depend on our research question: are we more interested in explaining the academic trajectories of 'geniuses', in which case really high marks are needed? Or is our study about the conditions that enable students to be competitive on the labour market, which in this case the decisive criterion would be what marks enable competitiveness?

   Sometimes, obvious facts can help us make these decisions. For instance, it is fairly obvious that a fail is never a sign of good academic performance. At other times, we can rely on generally accepted notions in the social sciences. For example, there might be decades of research indicating that a safe way of recognizing academic geniuses is that they generally achieve the highest possible category of marks. Or we can use accumulated field- or case-specific knowledge to inform calibration decisions (Schneider and Wagemann, 2012, chapter 1). For instance, although marks formally range from 0 to 100 in the United Kingdom, having engaged with the context of the British education system, we will know that these days students will generally want to achieve at least a 2:1, which is typically a mark in the range between 60 and 69.

Below that, it is difficult for them to get invited to job interviews or to access postgraduate programmes.

At this stage, two things have hopefully become clear. First, there is often more than one possible way of calibrating a set. Second, calibration is fundamentally a conceptual exercise, not just an empirical one. We need to justify our calibration decisions. Finding rules for assigning valid set membership values requires us to make'[…] the calibration process transparent and to make it lead to a set that has high content validity for the concept of interest.' (Schneider and Wagemann, 2012, p. 32).

Types of Sets

Let us now use the 'good student' example to discuss the calibration of different types of sets. We conceive the good student as a student who is competitive on the British (non-academic) labor market. When calibrating sets, one decision we need to take is which type of set to choose. In QCA, we deal with three basic types of sets: crisp, fuzzy, and multi-value sets. Table 2.1 illustrates a non-exhaustive range of possible ways of calibrating the 'good student' as a crisp set or as a fuzzy set.[2]

Crisp sets are binary, that is, they only distinguish between members and non-members, and take on the value 0 (non-membership) or 1 (membership). For example, we could simply separate 'good students' from other students with not-good performance. This would mean that we are only interested in the qualitative *difference in kind* that separates members from non-members of the set. As such, crisp sets correspond most clearly to the basic idea of concepts as boxes into which we sort cases. For example, in the British context we could say that students with a 2:1 or higher ratio are members of the crisp set of 'good students'. We would give students with a mark of 60 or higher a set membership value of 1, and students with 59 or lower a set membership score of 0. Some phenomena lend themselves naturally to being captured in crisp sets. For instance, in the European Union, there is a set of countries that have formally adopted the Euro as a common currency. Countries are either members or non-members of this set; there are no degrees of membership in this set.[3]

However, in social science research sometimes we also want to consider different degrees of set membership in order to answer our research questions. For example, while we can distinguish good students from other, not-good

---

[2] We discuss the rarely used so-called indirect calibration method in the online appendix (https://doi.org/10.7910/DVN/S9QPM5).

[3] This clear-cut classification disappears if we are interested in the set of cases that have *informally* adopted the Euro, for there are countries that have not formally adopted the Euro but in which the Euro is used as an official currency.

Table 2.1 The 'good student': calibration techniques, anchors, and verbal interpretation

Crisp set		Fuzzy set			
		Recoding/theoretical method		Direct method	
Dichotomoous	*Anchors & interpretation*	Four-value fuzzy set	*Anchors & interpretation*	'Continuous'	*Anchors & interpretation*
I In	≥60 *Good student*	I Fully in	≥70 *Good student*	0.95 Fully in	≥70 *Good student* <70 & ≥60
		0.67 More in than	<70 & ≥60 *Quite a good student*	Degrees of being more in than out	*Different degrees of being a rather good student*
				0.5 Crossover point; neither in nor out	59.5 *Neither a good student nor not a good student*
		0.33 More out than in	<60 & ≥40 *Not-so-good student*	Degrees of being more out than in	≤59 & ≥40 *Different degrees of rather not being a good student*
0 Out	<60 *Not a good student*	0 Fully out	<40 *Not a good student (Fail)*	0.05 Fully out	<40 *Not a good student*

Source: Own illustration inspired by Ragin (2008c, table 2.1).

students, some students are still better than others. In QCA, *fuzzy sets* enable us to capture both *differences in kind* and *differences in degree* between cases of the same 'kind'. Naturally, we can only use fuzzy sets if empirical information on more fine-grained, conceptually meaningful variation between the cases is available. Fuzzy sets always range from 0 (full non-membership) to 1 (full membership). The so-called crossover point expresses the qualitative difference in kind. For fuzzy sets, the crossover point is at a set membership value of 0.5. In between, cases can be more or less in (membership scores of higher than 0.5) or more or less out (membership scores of lower than 0.5) of the set.

Table 2.1 illustrates some of the possible ways of calibrating fuzzy sets by either recoding raw data or via the 'direct' calibration method – we will return to these calibration methods below. What they all have in common is that cases with a set membership higher than 0.5 are more in than out of the set. For instance, students with a mark of 60 or higher are always rather good students, but they are good to different degrees. Similarly, students with a mark below 60 are out of the set of good students, but again, some are closer to being fully out of it than others.

Fuzzy sets give us two pieces of information at once when comparing cases. For example, two people can have fuzzy set-membership scores of 0.6 and 0.8 in the set of 'tall people'. First, this indicates that they are both qualitatively considered tall people (above the 0.5 anchor). Second, it also indicates that one is taller than the other, and thus comes closer to the ideal type of a tall person. Although fuzzy sets allow us to capture differences in degree, the choice of the crossover point of 0.5 is still absolutely crucial: it allows us to preserve the distinction in kind between different types of cases.[4]

Finally, in QCA we can work with so-called multi-value sets. Multi-value sets capture qualitative differences of more than one kind. For example, there could be different types of good students: the academically high-performing student, the engaged student, and the helpful student. None of them is 'better' than the others: they differ qualitatively, but not in degree. We can think of multi-value sets as multiple crisp sets stacked into one set.[5] Multi-value sets are less commonly used in applied QCA, and their calibration is not fundamentally different from the calibration of crisp and fuzzy sets. Therefore, we do not treat them in more depth in this chapter (but see Cronqvist and Berg-Schlosser, 2009; Haesebrouck, 2016; Dusa, 2018).

With R, we can combine all three types of sets in one QCA (see Thiem, 2014c; Dusa, 2018). The main questions we need to ask ourselves for each of the sets we use are: Are we interested in differences in degree (fuzzy sets)? Is there more than one difference in kind that matters (multi-value sets)? If the answer to both questions is no, then we can choose crisp sets. When working with fuzzy sets, we will ask ourselves whether the differences in degree capture meaningful variation in view of the meaning of the underlying concept. As a rule, we do not want to lose information about differences in degree during calibration, unless these differences are unimportant for the concept that the set represents. For example, if we are interested in the set of people who are tall enough to play basketball, we need to know how close they come to a height of two meters. However, if they are taller than, say, 220 centimeters, this is no longer important: they are already more than tall enough to play basketball. Therefore, some of the variation in the raw variable may actually not be of interest to us when calibrating sets.

---

[4] In fact, we can think of crisp sets as a special case of a fuzzy set with no empirical values in between 0 and 1. In most respects, we treat crisp and fuzzy sets the same way in QCA. We will learn about an important exception – the so-called rule of the excluded middle – in Section 2.4.1 of this chapter.

[5] To give another example, the set of 'ice cream taste' could have different categories: chocolate, vanilla, ginger, and so on. These categories are usually crisp, but they could also be fuzzy. For example, vanilla-ginger ice cream has both partial membership in the set of vanilla taste, and partial membership in the set of of ginger taste; but it is not a full member of either (see Thiem, 2014c).

Sets Are Not Variables

Remember that all types of sets preserve the qualitative difference in kind that makes the difference for a case being more in or more out of the set (the crossover point). As such, sets convey a meaning that is often socially constructed. In this sense, *sets are fundamentally different from 'variables'*. For example, the variable 'final mark' does not in itself conclusively tell us whether a given mark is actually a good mark. While marks in the United Kingdom range from 0 to 100, a mark of 59 is in fact still not a good mark in many people's eyes. However, if we are not familiar with the British education context, there is no way for us to know what the scores actually mean. Conversely, a set such as the set of 'good students' always contains precise information for each case, about the extent to which the case displays a property such as whether or not a student is a 'good student'. By being above the crossover point of 0.5, a fuzzy set membership score of 0.59 in the set of good students means that the student is more in than out of the set of good students. This qualitative difference will be crucial during the analysis of relations between sets (Chapters 3 and 4). But first, we need to implement these calibration procedures in R.

2.2.2   Recoding Method: Crisp and Fuzzy Sets

Within the R environment, we always calibrate sets based on the 'raw data', which are usually numerically measured variables, such as marks, or height in centimeters, or other, simpler scores. In what follows, we use a fake raw dataset of the marks of 17 students in Britain on a scale from 0 to 100 to illustrate the calibration techniques in Table 2.1. The raw dataset is stored within the SetMethods package and called STUR; see Table 2.2.[6]

The calibration techniques we now present require the presence of numbers. This does not mean that we cannot use more complex qualitative information for getting to these numbers and enhance our confidence in the validity of the resulting set scores. For example, we could perform participant observation in different classes. Based on our comprehensive qualitative picture of different aspects of the student performance, we could attribute each student a score of low, intermediate, or high for each aspect in an Excel sheet, and then aggregate these into a nuanced overall score of performance. Before using these scores for our QCA, we could cross-validate them by talking to different students' teachers. Accordingly, our raw dataset in Table 2.2 also contains more qualitative information about two variables: 'PARTICIPATION' refers to the

---

[6] Remember that when using your own data in csv format, you can load it using the read.csv() function and place it in an object of your choice. For example MYDATA <- read.csv("mydata.csv").

Table 2.2 Student performance, raw dataset

Name	MARK	PARTICIPATION	PEERS
Joanna	43	1	1
Hector	75	3	1
Ana	66	3	3
Alrik	56	3	1
Kyu	59	1	2
Mandakini	55	1	3
Urs	70	3	2
Zion	68	2	3
Leo	57	1	1
Kaylee	67	1	3
Malik	64	2	2
Laila	62	2	1
Zoe	68	3	2
Tama	38	1	1
Yanan	72	3	3
Bill	58	1	1
Johanna	53	1	2

Note: hypothetical dataset; 1 = low, 2 = intermediate, 3 = high.

quality and correctness of the student's comments in class, and 'PEERS' refers to the extent to which the student engages with and helps peers during interactive in-class teaching exercises. For both of these factors, we attributed each student a score of 1 (low), 2 (intermediate), or 3 (high). We briefly discuss the calibration of qualitative data in the section on good practices and refer the reader to further literature. In practice, we will implement the final stage of calibrating qualitative data in R with some variant of the recoding method to which we now turn.

In what follows, we discuss different ways of calibrating the set of good students 'GOOD'. We number the different versions of the set.

Crisp Sets

We start by calibrating crisp sets. In the case of 'naturally dichotomous' sets, such as countries that officially adopted the Euro as their currency, there is no need to additionally calibrate them. We simply attribute each member of the Eurozone a set membership score of 1, and all other countries a set membership score of 0. However, sometimes we calibrate crisp sets by recoding one or several empirical indicators. For example, we could calibrate the crisp set on the left-hand side of Table 2.1. We set an anchor such that a mark of 60 or higher, indicating at least a 2:1 ratio, attributes a student to the set of 'good students'.

R offers various ways of calibrating crisp sets. We can simply create a new variable (the set) labeled GOOD1, tie it to the dataset STUR using the dollar sign, and assign it values depending on the students' mark (variable MARK). Using the `ifelse()` function, we can then tell R to assign GOOD1 a certain value, depending on what value the variable mark takes. For instance, in the following example we tell R to assign GOOD1 a value of 0 if the mark is smaller than or equals 59, otherwise to assign it a 1.

C 2.1

```
# Calibrating crisp sets with ifelse():

STUR$GOOD1 <- ifelse(STUR$MARK <= 59, 0, 1)

#Calibrating crisp sets with calibrate():

STUR$GOOD2 <- calibrate(STUR$MARK,
                        type = "crisp",
                        thresholds = c(60))

# Look up the calibrated set:

STUR$GOOD1

# Look up the raw values:

STUR$MARK

# Compare raw and calibrated scores:

STUR[c("MARK", "GOOD1", "GOOD2")]
```

O 2.1

	MARK	GOOD1	GOOD2
Joanna	43	0	0
Hector	75	1	1
Ana	66	1	1
Alrik	56	0	0
Kyu	59	0	0
Mandakini	55	0	0
Urs	70	1	1
Zion	68	1	1
Leo	57	0	0
Kaylee	67	1	1
Malik	64	1	1
Laila	62	1	1
Zoe	68	1	1

Tama	38	0	0
Yanan	72	1	1
Bill	51	0	0
Johanna	48	0	0

We can equally calibrate crisp sets with the package QCA, which has a `calibrate()` function. We can simply indicate the threshold of 60 for calibrating the mark into GOOD2, and specify the argument `type = crisp` for the crisp set. This includes values of 60 in the set, and excludes values of 59. Both functions – `ifelse()` and `calibrate()` – will give us the same crisp set. We can check how the set looks by simply typing its name and specifying that it is contained in the student dataset. We can then compare the raw and calibrated values for each case by using square brackets to access these subsets of the dataset. As we can see in Output 2.1, the calibration worked correctly, and both calibration functions delivered the same result.

Fuzzy Sets

Let us now move to fuzzy sets. Table 2.1 illustrates that we can construct fuzzy sets in different ways. Sometimes we are mainly interested in the order of differences. For example, with the four-value fuzzy set in Table 2.1, we are mainly saying that some students are better than others, but we do not emphasize 'how much better' they are. In such situations, we can equally use the recoding method to calibrate these sets.[7] For this, we need to 'theorize' which values in the raw dataset translate into which set membership scores of cases. Accordingly, we could also call this 'theory-guided calibration' (Schneider and Wagemann, 2012, chapter 1).[8]

For theory-guided calibration, we recode values of the raw variable(s) by grouping them into qualitatively defined categories of fuzzy set membership. In Table 2.1 we have four categories: the good student, quite a good student, not-so-good student, and not a good student. We classify students with a 2:1 ratio (60–69) as being quite good students, with a fuzzy score of 0.67. However, to be a full member of the set of good students (score 1), they must have a 70

---

[7] A good area of applying the recoding method to calibrating fuzzy sets is when comparing survey responses on Likert scales. Such responses could range from 'agree' or 'rather agree' to 'rather disagree' or 'disagree', but beyond ranking, the distance between them does not have a numerical meaning. See also Emmenegger et al. (2014).

[8] Dusa (2018, chapter 4.2) calls it 'direct assignment'.

or higher, which translates into a first in the British grading system. Students that did not reach a 2:1 ratio, but did not fail (marks between 40 and 59) are coded as not-so-good students, with a fuzzy score of 0.33. Finally, students with a fail are fully out of the set of good students: we attribute marks below 40 a set membership score of 0. Note that, depending on the concept and the data at hand, we could have six or any other number of fuzzy categories.

In R, we first could create a new set 'GOOD3' in the student dataset, and assign it a value of NA. We then use logical operators to define the ranges of the raw values in 'MARK' that represent the qualitative groupings, and assign them the respective fuzzy membership score in the newly created set GOOD3 in our dataset.[9] We provide an introduction to using logical operators in R code in the online appendix.[10]

C 2.2

```
# Recoding method with a single raw variable:

STUR$GOOD3 <- NA #empty variable
STUR$GOOD3[STUR$MARK >=70] <-1
STUR$GOOD3[STUR$MARK <70 & STUR$MARK>=60]<-0.67
STUR$GOOD3[STUR$MARK <60 & STUR$MARK>=40]<-0.33
STUR$GOOD3[STUR$MARK <40]<-0
STUR$GOOD3
```

Naturally, we could construct a fuzzy set with theoretical calibration by including the more qualitative information in our raw dataset. For instance, we could say that a really good student not only needs to have a first, but also needs to show at least intermediate levels of participation and peer support. Clearly, these are skills that will make them more competitive than their peers with equally strong academic skills. Moreover, we also consider as clearly not good students those with a third (a mark between 40 and 49) but low levels of both participation and peer support. We could again use the dollar sign and operators to implement this in R, with a new fuzzy set GOOD4. For a set membership of 1, we add the requirement that the score for participation and peers has to be higher than 1. Additionally, we attribute cases with a mark of 70 or higher, but low values in either participation or peers, a set membership score of 0.67. Similarly, we code cases with marks between 40 and 49, but a value of 1 in both qualitative indicators as fully out of the set.

---

[9] The calibrate() function also offers a subset of the possibilities described here if the option is type = 'crisp'; see the QCA package manual.
[10] https://doi.org/10.7910/DVN/S9QPM5.

C 2.3

```
# Recoding method with several raw variables:

STUR$GOOD4 <- NA #empty variable
STUR$GOOD4[STUR$MARK >=70 & STUR$PARTICIPATION> 1 & STUR$PEERS >
    1] <-1
STUR$GOOD4[STUR$MARK >=70 & (STUR$PARTICIPATION == 1 | STUR$
    PEERS == 1)] <-0.67
STUR$GOOD4[STUR$MARK <70 & STUR$MARK>=60]<-0.67
STUR$GOOD4[STUR$MARK <60 & STUR$MARK>=40]<-0.33
STUR$GOOD4[STUR$MARK <50 & STUR$MARK>=40 & STUR$PARTICIPATION ==
    1 & STUR$PEERS == 1]<-0
STUR$GOOD4[STUR$MARK <40]<-0
STUR$GOOD4
```

C 2.4

```
# Visualize with histogram — combine 2 graphs:

par(mfrow=c(1, 2)) # rule to put 2 graphs in 1 row
hist(STUR$GOOD3,
    main = "GOOD3",
    xlab = "Set Membership")
hist(STUR$GOOD4,
    main = "GOOD4",
    xlab = "Set Membership")
par(mfrow=c(1, 1)) # undo rule
```

We can visualize how the cases cluster in the two four-value fuzzy sets with a histogram. When visualizing calibration, with R we can combine several plots in one graph. We just have to specify the rules before typing the command for the first plot. For example, as shown in Code 2.4, we can specify that we want to have one row of graphs, each row displaying two graphs, and then we simply list the commands for both plots below that.[11] Note that R will keep applying this rule until we undo it. From Figure 2.2, we can see that the cases differ in their membership in the two sets: when considering the qualitative information, we have fewer fully good students.[12]

We could construct another fuzzy set of students who perform highly in class, rather than in written assignments, in terms of both in-class participation

---

[11] Note that in the hist() function, we use the option main for assigning a title to the plot and the option xlab for adding a label to the x-axis.

[12] The advantage of R is that we can directly export the graphs. Above the graph (which is displayed in the lower-right window of the R Studio interface), we click the option export -> save as image…and then we can specify the size of the graph as well as its format (JPEG, TIFF, etc.).

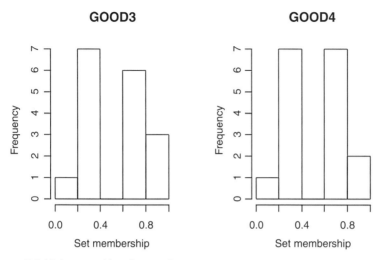

Figure 2.2 Histogram of two fuzzy sets

and peer support. To measure this set, we could add up the students' scores on the two qualitatively measured variables in Table 2.2. The resulting index of in-class performance 'inclass' ranges from 2 to 6. We can recode this index into a fuzzy set which we call CLASS, for example as follows:

6 = fully in (1)
5 = almost but not fully in (0.9)
4 = more in than out (0.67)
3 = more out than in (0.33)
2 = fully out (0)

The resulting fuzzy set of students with good in-class performance makes sense: students need to perform well on both aspects in order to be fully in. We could again use operators to implement this in R, with a new fuzzy set CLASS. Later in this chapter, we discuss how to combine several sets – such as good student (GOOD) and good in-class performance (CLASS) – in order to capture overall performance.

C 2.5

```
# Recoding method with index of two raw variables:

# Create additive index:

STUR$INCLASS <- STUR$PARTICIPATION + STUR$PEERS
STUR$INCLASS
```

```
# Calibrate 5-value fuzzy set:

STUR$CLASS <- NA #empty variable
STUR$CLASS[STUR$INCLASS ==2] <-0
STUR$CLASS[STUR$INCLASS ==3] <-0.33
STUR$CLASS[STUR$INCLASS ==4] <-0.67
STUR$CLASS[STUR$INCLASS ==5] <-0.9
STUR$CLASS[STUR$INCLASS ==6] <-1
STUR$CLASS
```

2.2.3   The Direct Calibration Method for Fuzzy Sets

Sometimes we want fuzzy sets to reflect very fine-grained, continuous differences in degree – such as the set of 'tall persons', measured in centimeters (Ragin, 2008a). To this end, Ragin (2000, 2008a, 2008c) also describes two less qualitative calibration techniques for fuzzy sets: the direct and the indirect calibration method (for an overview, see Schneider and Wagemann, 2012, chapter 1; recent discussion in Dusa, 2018, pp. 61–98). These calibration methods are more formalized and rely on statistical models. As with any other calibration technique, we should base the choice of anchors as much as possible on existing theoretical and substantive knowledge. Since the indirect method is only rarely applied, we do not cover it here, but refer the interested reader to the online appendix.[13]

The *direct calibration* method requires raw data in the form of fine-grained numerical scores. For example, we can calibrate the set of 'good students' based on their marks measured on a scale from 0 to 100 (see the 'MARK' column in Table 2.2). The basic idea of the direct calibration method is to use criteria external to the data at hand, such as conceptual or case knowledge, to specify three relevant set membership anchors: the threshold for full set membership (1), the threshold for full non-membership in the set (0), and, crucially, the point of indifference or crossover point (0.5). Recall that the crossover point establishes the qualitative difference in kind above which cases are more in than out of the set, and below which cases are more out than in the set. If possible, we choose the crossover point such that no empirical cases in the dataset end up having a set value of exactly 0.5. Assigning a membership of exactly 0.5 to a case equates to saying that we do not know whether the case is a member or not of a set. It basically amounts to admitting that we have no conclusive knowledge of that case regarding the concept to be calibrated. As we will see,

---

[13] https://doi.org/10.7910/DVN/S9QPM5.

later in QCA, this poses problems for the analysis. For example, cases with exactly 0.5 set membership cannot conclusively be attributed to a truth table row (see Section 4.3.1).

Applied to our example, those students are full members (score 1) of the set of good students GOOD5 who have a first, that is, a mark of 70 or higher. We can clearly attribute students with a fail (mark below 40) to be full non-members of the set of 'good students' (score 0). And using our field knowledge about the British job market, we have determined that students should have a mark of at least 60, indicating a 2:1 ratio or higher, to be included in this set (crossover point of 0.5). In order to avoid a membership score of 0.5, we set the crossover point at 59.5, which as a mark is never given. The direct method then usually uses a logistic function to fit the raw data in between these three anchors; see Table 2.1.

It is very easy to implement direct calibration with the `calibrate()` function of the QCA package. In the following example, we use the raw variable MARK from the student dataset STUR and create a new set called GOOD5. By default, if we do not specify the `type` argument, the `calibrate()` function produces fuzzy sets. We can then simply enter the thresholds for full non-membership (here: 40), the crossover point (here: 59.5), and full membership (here: 70).

C 2.6

```
# Direct method of calibration:

STUR$GOOD5 <- calibrate (STUR$MARK,
                         type = "fuzzy",
                         thresholds = e = 40, c = 59.5, i = 70,
                         logistic = TRUE)
STUR$GOOD 5

# Visualize with plot:

plot (STUR$MARK,
     STUR$GOOD5,
     main = "Calibration of GOOD5",
     xlab = "Raw score",
     ylab = "Calibrated score")
     abline(h = 0.5,
     v = 59.5)
```

We can then plot the scores of the raw variable against the calibrated scores, using the `plot()` function. Within the brackets, we first indicate the raw variable in the student dataset, then the calibrated set. With argument `main`, we can set a title for the plot. The arguments `xlab` and `ylab` enable us to label the x-axis and the y-axis. With the abline option, we can set a horizontal black

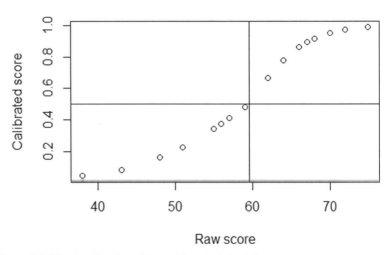

Figure 2.3 Direct calibration of the set 'good students'

line for the crossover point (h = 0.5), and a vertical black line for the raw score at which the crossover point was set (v = 59.5). Figure 2.3 shows how direct calibration results in an s-shaped distribution of set membership scores. The horizontal x-axis represents the raw scores and the vertical y-axis represents the calibrated scores. The scatterplot also illustrates that when using the logistic function, the calibrated values might never reach the actual minimum and maximum value, and the actual anchors are 0.95 for full membership, 0.5 for the crossover point, and 0.05 for full non-membership[14] (see also Schneider and Wagemann, 2012, p. 37; Thiem, 2014a; Dusa, 2018, pp. 61–98, figure 4.9).[15]

Box 2.3 Core Points – Sets and Set Calibration

- The calibration of sets is a conceptual exercise involving several steps: the definition of a concept, the choice of raw data for measuring the concept, and the attribution

---

[14] This is due to the asymptotic nature of the logistic function, that is, a curve that approaches the limits but never touches them. With argument idm in the calibrate function, we can change the value at which the fuzzy set membership scores level out. For instance, idm = 0.99 means that the maximum membership score will be 0.99 and the minimum score 0.01.

[15] The direct calibration method can result in set scores with numerous decimals. If we want to reduce decimals, we can round calibrated sets using the round() function and indicate the desired number of digits after the comma. There is no inherent advantage or disadvantage to rounding sets.

Box 2.3 (Cont.)

of cases to the set by using qualitative anchors of inclusion/exclusion on the raw data.

- Crisp sets are restricted only to membership values of 0 (full non-membership) and 1 (full membership). Crisp sets allow us to capture only differences in kind between cases and require a single calibration anchor of inclusion/exclusion.

- Fuzzy sets allow for cases to have varying degrees of membership in the sets and, therefore, capture both differences in kind and differences in degree between cases. The calibration of fuzzy sets requires at least three qualitative anchors: 0 (full non-membership), 0.5 (cross-over), and 1 (full membership). The anchor at 0.5 establishes the difference in kind.

- There are several methods through which sets can be calibrated and, depending on the method, both qualitative and quantitative data can be used for calibration.

- The recoding method (also called theory-guided calibration) can be used for calibrating both crisp and fuzzy sets. This method involves the recoding of values of the raw variable(s) by grouping them into qualitatively defined categories of crisp or fuzzy set membership.

- The direct method of calibration is used for calibrating fuzzy sets to reflect very fine-grained, continuous differences in degree. This method requires raw data in the form of fine-grained numerical scores which are fitted between three qualitative anchors (0, 0.5, 1) chosen based on conceptual knowledge, case knowledge, or both.

2.2.4 Saving Calibrated Data

After having calibrated all sets based on the raw data, we can save the calibrated sets in a new dataset that we will then use for performing the QCA. To do so, we first want to select only the calibrated sets from the raw dataset. We can use square brackets to access objects within the dataset, then specify which variables we want to include. In the example, we create a new dataset named 'STUC' containing only the five calibrated sets 'GOOD1', 'GOOD3', 'GOOD4', 'CLASS', and 'GOOD5' using the function `write.csv()`.[16] The file 'STUC.csv' is now saved on our hard drive in the folder that we specified in R as our working directory.[17]

---

[16] For hints when running into trouble with the .csv format, see the online appendix (https://doi .org/10.7910/DVN/S9QPM5).

[17] For details on how to set up R sessions, see the online appendix (https://doi.org/10.7910/DVN/ S9QPM5).

C 2.7

```
# Select the relevant sets:

STUC <- STUR[,c("GOOD1", "GOOD3", "GOOD4", "CLASS", "GOOD5")]

# Save:

write.csv(STUC, "STUC.csv")
```

2.2.5 Calibrating Qualitative Data

It is relatively straightforward to perform and present calibration based on standardized off-the-shelf data with the direct method. Set calibration based on qualitative data, for example interview transcripts, document analysis, archival data, in-depth case knowledge or visual material, is more demanding. However, we have already shown that we could of course use such data and combine different sources for calibrating sets. The sheer amount and interpretative nature of qualitative data can pose challenges. Still, adhering to appropriate, principled criteria and procedures is just as important for ensuring the validity and transparency of qualitative calibration (Wagemann and Schneider, 2015). Different techniques to systematically calibrate sets based on qualitative data exist (see, for instance, Basurto and Speer, 2012; Legewie, 2017; Toth et al., 2017). De Block and Vis (2019) discuss how researchers can determine set membership thresholds of inclusion and exclusion, degrees of set memberships, and the meaning of 'zero' based on qualitative data. They also propose ways of presenting the calibration decisions and data, and of performing sensitivity tests (see Section 5.2).

Box 2.4 Good Practice – Calibration

Transparency
- Discuss and justify the choice of calibration anchors in detail, especially of the crossover point.
- Make the data available (raw and calibrated), together with the code that transforms raw into calibrated data.

Calibration anchors criteria

- Calibration anchors should be motivated by criteria that are external to the distribution of the data at hand.
- Theoretical, not empirical, arguments are needed in order to determine which empirical evidence qualifies for set membership scores above and/or below these anchors.

Box 2.4 (Cont.)

- The exclusive use of empirical features of the data (e.g., the mean) is almost always wrong when calibrating sets.
- Some empirical features can be important for determining calibration thresholds (skewness and cases on the crossover point).

Calibrate with care

- Calibration is one of the most demanding analytic phases of a QCA.
- Dedicate sufficient time to calibration.
- Consider different possibilities of setting calibration anchors and especially the crossover point, if applicable.
- Test the robustness of the analysis against several equally plausible options for setting calibration anchors.

Labeling sets

- Sets are not variables.
- Sets establish qualitative differences between cases.
- The labels that we choose for the condition and outcome sets should explicitly express the property that members of these sets represent.
- Very often, we indicate this qualitative state with an adjective.
- Use short and intuitive labels in uppercase notation for sets.

2.3   Calibration Diagnostics

During and after calibration, we might inadvertently run into pitfalls: one or more of our sets might display skewed set membership scores, or there may be cases with exactly 0.5 membership. We now introduce functions for detecting both of these problems. These tools are particularly useful with larger case numbers and when we rely on the direct method of calibration. In addition to these tools, it is always a good idea to visualize calibration using histograms and scatterplots, as we have shown earlier.

2.3.1   Skewness

To make meaningful comparisons, our condition and outcome sets should reflect the diversity and heterogeneity of the cases chosen for analysis (Berg-Schlosser et al., 2008). At later stages of the QCA, it poses numerous analytic problems when the overwhelming majority of the cases have similar membership in a set (Schneider and Wagemann, 2012, pp. 232–250; Cooper and Glaesser, 2016b; Braumoeller, 2017; Thomann and Maggetti, 2020). One obvious and effective way to avoid these problems consists in calibrating sets such that they are not overly skewed. Short of this, we need at least to be aware if and when one or more of our sets are skewed. We discuss pitfalls arising from skewness and further remedies in more detail in Chapters 3 and 4.

There is no established, fixed threshold for what constitutes problematic skewness. However, as a rule of thumb, we neither want less than 20 per cent of our cases to be more in than out of the set, nor do we want less than 20 per cent of the cases to be more out than in the set. The skew.check() function of the SetMethods package gives us the number and percentage of cases with higher than 0.5 set values in a given set. In the following example, we check for the skewness of the set GOOD5, which we calibrated earlier. The function can also return a histogram of the calibrated set if option hist is set to TRUE.[18] We could also do this for the entire dataset by simply entering the name of the dataset in the brackets, or for selected sets (columns) only such as GOOD5 and CLASS. The share of members in set GOOD5 is 52.4 per cent, while this share is 58.8 per cent with the set CLASS. Finally, if we combine the rownames() function with the subset() function, we can also identify which cases have membership or non-membership in the set. In the code, we get the names of the 10 students who are performing highly in class (membership > 0.5 in CLASS). We could simply reverse > to < in order to get the names of those students who do not perform highly in class.

C 2.8

```
# Skewness checks:

skew.check(STUC$GOOD5)

skew.check(STUC$GOOD5, hist = TRUE)

skew.check(STUC)

skew.check(STUC[,c("GOOD5","CLASS")])
```

O 2.2

```
"Set GOOD5 - Cases > 0.5 / Total number of cases: 9 / 17 = 52.94
    %"
"Set CLASS - Cases > 0.5 / Total number of cases: 10 / 17 =
    58.82 %"
```

---

[18] We do not show here the resulting histogram due to space limitations.

C 2.9

```
# Case names in and out of set:

rownames(subset(STUC, CLASS > 0.5))
```

O 2.3

```
"Hector"   "Ana"      "Alrik"   "Mandakini" "Urs"
"Zion"     "Kaylee"   "Malik"   "Zoe"        "Yanan"
```

Even if a given crossover point makes much sense theoretically, we may need to make compromises in order to avoid overly skewed sets (Thomann, 2019). For instance, we can restructure the set so that it becomes easier (or more difficult) for a case to be a member of the set. Changing the calibration might require the relabeling of the set. For instance, the set of 'good students' might need to be relabeled as the set of 'very good students'. We discuss this possibility in the following subsection.

2.3.2   Cases on Crossover Point

The crossover point is sometimes also called the point of maximum ambiguity: a set membership score of exactly 0.5 essentially means that for this specific case we are not able to establish whether it is more in or more out of the set. However, for the truth table analysis, we need to know whether a case belongs to a given set in order to tell whether the case supports or refutes a given subset relation (see Section 4.3.1). During calibration, we hence want to check whether there are empirical cases on the crossover point. The function `ambig.cases()` of the `SetMethods` package will tell us the row number in the dataset where set membership is 0.5. As with the `skew.check()` function, we can do this for a specific set, a list of sets, or all sets in the dataset. The function will give an error if used on uncalibrated data; thus, we only include the calibrated subsets of the dataset. In the following example, we check for cases on the crossover point for the set GOOD5 – there are none, because we have set the crossover point at a value (59.5) that no case in our data displays. Additionally, we could also identify ambiguous cases by name, using the `subset()` function.

C 2.10

```
# Cases on crossover point:

ambig.cases(STUC$GOOD5)

rownames(subset(STUC, GOOD5 == 0.5))
```

O 2.4

"There are no cases with fuzzy-set scores of 0.5."

In practice, we want to avoid setting the crossover point on a value that is populated by one or more empirical cases. If this appears difficult, it can help to remember what the conceptual meaning of the set is (Mahoney, 2010). For example, the absence of 'high satisfaction with democracy' is everything that is not high satisfaction, which includes 'neither satisfied nor dissatisfied' (Emmenegger et al., 2014). Similarly, the negation of the set of good students is the set of all other students – not necessarily just the 'bad' students. Note that cases that are very close to, but not exactly on, the point of indifference do not pose technical problems. They are still difficult to interpret substantively because they are very close to the point of maximum conceptual ambiguity.

Box 2.5 Core Points – Calibration Diagnostics

- Two issues that could arise during calibration are skewed set membership scores, and cases on the crossover point (0.5 membership). These two issues should be diagnosed early on as they can pose several problems at later stages in the analytic moment.
- While there is no fixed threshold for what constitutes problematic skewness, as a rule of thumb, we would not want less than 20 per cent of the cases to be more in than out (or more out than in) of the calibrated set.
- Assigning a 0.5 membership to a case in a set indicates that we cannot establish whether the case is more in or more out of the set. This non-information influences the analyses necessity (Chapter 3) and sufficiency (Chapter 4) of this set.

2.4   Combining Sets

Once we have attributed cases to sets, we can start looking at various forms of combining sets. It is only when we start combining different sets that we tap into patterns of complexity that lie at the heart of QCA and set-theoretic methods more widely, as mapped in Section 1.2.1. Indeed, we will now see that using the logical operators AND, OR, and NOT leads us to detect conjunctions of conditions, equifinality (that is, disjunctions), and asymmetry. In this chapter, we look at *descriptive* complexity, by diving into complex set-theoretic structures of concepts. In the following Chapters 3 and 4, we then apply the same operations to uncover *causal* complexity when analyzing set relations.

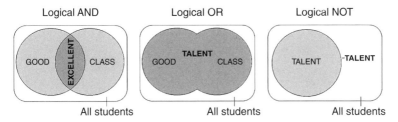

Figure 2.4 Logical operations

2.4.1   Logical Operations

In QCA, we use three logical operators to combine sets: the logical AND, the logical OR, and the logical NOT (see Figure 2.4 and Schneider and Wagemann, 2012, pp. 42–55). To illustrate this, we will rely on the two sets of academically well-performing, 'good students' (GOOD) and 'good in-class performance' (CLASS) that we calibrated in the previous section.

For example, we might be interested in the set of excellent students EXCELLENT who perform well both academically AND in class. On the left-hand side of Figure 2.4, this is the gray shaded area where the sets GOOD and CLASS overlap. In Boolean and fuzzy algebra, this operation is known as Boolean or fuzzy multiplication, thus we use the multiplication sign '*' for the logical AND. In set theory, we call the resulting combination a conjunction or intersection of different sets:

EXCELLENT = GOOD * CLASS

Naturally, we now want to know the membership of the students in the set of 'excellent students'. For the logical AND, the membership of a case in the combined sets equals its smallest membership in the component sets. We call this rule the *minimum rule* (or cumulation assumption; see Braumoeller, 2017). In the following example, we calculate the membership of the cases in the intersection EXCELLENT, using the `fuzzyand()` function of the QCA package and the STUC dataset. To simplify things, we first rename the fuzzy set GOOD5 as GOOD.

C 2.11

```
# Rename set GOOD5 into GOOD:

STUC$GOOD <- STUC$GOOD5

# Logical AND:
```

```
STUC$EXCELLENT <- fuzzyand (STUC$GOOD, STUC$CLASS)

# Logical OR:

STUC$TALENT <- fuzzyor (STUC$GOOD, STUC$CLASS)

# Logical NOT:

STUC$NOTALENT <- 1- STUC$TALENT

# Compare the set membership scores:

STUC[c("GOOD", "CLASS", "EXCELLENT", "TALENT", "NOTALENT")]
```

We could also be interested in the set of 'in some way talented students', TALENT, who are either good students OR perform well in class. In the center of Figure 2.4, this is the grey shaded area, that is, the full area covered by sets GOOD and CLASS. This operation is called Boolean or fuzzy addition and we denote it with a '+'. The OR combination is the *disjunction* or *union* of the different component sets:

TALENT = GOOD + CLASS

Again, we could easily find out the membership of our students in the set of talented students. The so-called maximum rule (Ragin, 2008c) helps us calculate the membership of cases in such OR combinations. That is, the membership of a case in a disjunction of sets always equals its biggest membership score in the component sets. In R, we use the `fuzzor()` function (package: QCA) for this. We can calculate the cases' membership in the set TALENT.

Finally, let us identify the set of students who are NOT talented according to this definition and call it NOTALENT. As we can see in the right-hand side of Figure 2.4, the set NOTALENT covers all cases that are not members of the set TALENT. The logical NOT is also called *set negation*. There are two ways of denoting it formally, either by using a tilde sign, $\sim$, as we do in this book, or by using lowercase notation:

NOTALENT = $\sim$TALENT

Figure 2.4 also tells us that every student is either a member of the set of talented students or a non-member of it. A way of saying this more formally is that the union of a set with its complement always yields the universal set:

$X + \sim X = U.$

As a rule, the membership of cases in the negated set is always 1 minus their membership in the set. Cases that are members of a crisp set are always full non-members of the negated set. From this, we can derive the so-called rule of the excluded middle: there is no single element that a set and its complement have in common. For example, a country has either adopted the Euro as a currency or not adopted it, but not both at the same time. Yet, the rule of the excluded middle does not hold for fuzzy sets, where we allow for degrees of set membership. Take Kaylee, for instance: her membership in the set of talented students is 0.89 (see Output 2.5). Her membership in the set of not talented students $\sim$TALENT is $1 - 0.89 = 0.11$. When cases have partial membership scores in a fuzzy set, they also have partial membership in the negated set. It follows that the intersection $TALENT * \sim TALENT$ is not empty: when applying the minimum rule, Kaylee's membership in this intersection is still 0.11. It can never be higher than 0.5 though, because it cannot be higher than the smaller of the two values, one of which will indicate qualitative non-membership in the set. This means that with fuzzy sets, a case can be attributed qualitatively to either a set or its negation. The only exception is when a case holds a fuzzy set membership score of exactly 0.5 (Schneider and Wagemann, 2012, sections 3.2 and 9.2).

O 2.5

	GOOD	CLASS	EXCELLENT	TALENT	NOTALENT
Joanna	0.08549584	0.33	0.08549584	0.33000000	0.67000000
Hector	0.98721421	0.67	0.67000000	0.98721421	0.01278579
Ana	0.86089553	1.00	0.86089553	1.00000000	0.00000000
Alrik	0.37690423	0.67	0.37690423	0.67000000	0.33000000
Kyu	0.48205382	0.33	0.33000000	0.48205382	0.51794618
Mandakini	0.34381472	0.67	0.34381472	0.67000000	0.33000000
Urs	0.95000000	0.90	0.90000000	0.95000000	0.05000000
Zion	0.91556764	0.90	0.90000000	0.91556764	0.08443236
Leo	0.41118279	0.00	0.00000000	0.41118279	0.58881721
Kaylee	0.89121097	0.67	0.67000000	0.89121097	0.10878903
Malik	0.77935342	0.67	0.67000000	0.77935342	0.22064658
Laila	0.66842206	0.33	0.33000000	0.66842206	0.33157794
Zoe	0.91556764	0.90	0.90000000	0.91556764	0.08443236
Tama	0.04360204	0.00	0.00000000	0.04360204	0.95639796
Yanan	0.97083776	1.00	0.97083776	1.00000000	0.00000000
Bill	0.22778427	0.00	0.00000000	0.22778427	0.77221573
Johanna	0.16087143	0.33	0.16087143	0.33000000	0.67000000

We can then compare the set membership values of the cases, using the square brackets. We see that, indeed, the cases' value on EXCELLENT is always equal to their smaller membership value in GOOD or CLASS; their membership in the set TALENT is always equal to their greater membership score in these sets; and membership in NOTALENT always equals 1 minus membership in TALENT.

2.4.2 Set-Theoretic Concept Structures

Let us now return to our initial question: what is a high-performing student? Going back to Table 2.2, the raw dataset, we could argue that good academic performance, active participation in class, and helping peers are all defining elements of a high-performing student. We could calibrate them all into three separate sets. We have already calibrated academic performance as GOOD. We could also calibrate a three-value fuzzy set of students participating actively in class and call it PART.[19] Similarly, the set PEER could capture those students who support their peers in class. Based on the students' scores in 'PARTICIPATION' and 'PEERS' in Table 2.2, the raw dataset, a value of 1 is calibrated as being fully out (0), a value of 2 being partly but not fully in (0.67), and 3 indicates full set membership (1). We save the sets GOOD, PART, and PEER in an object called perfdata.

Now we can use the three logical operators to combine the secondary-level sets GOOD, PART, and PEER into one combined, basic-level set of overall high-performing students PERF (Adcock and Collier, 2001; Goertz and Mahoney, 2005; Goertz, 2006). The question is: how do the academically well-performing, good student GOOD, vivid in-class participation PART, and strong peer support PEER combine into high overall student performance?

With the first, 'classical' approach to concept formation, all secondary-level conditions need to be present simultaneously. This means that the three component sets combine with the logical AND. For instance, we could say that high-performing students are students who perform well academically, participate strongly in class, and help their peers. This approach is depicted on the left-hand side of Figure 2.5. A second approach to structuring the concept would be based

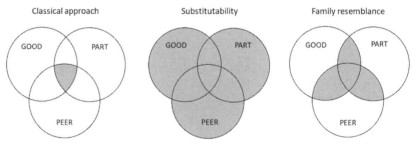

Figure 2.5 Concept structures

Source: own illustration based on Mahoney and Vanderpoel (2015).

---

[19] Note that active in-class participation (PART) is different from the set high in-class performance (CLASS) that we used earlier. The latter entailed both participation and peer support.

on the idea of 'substitutability', using the logical OR: a high-performing student is one who either performs well academically, participates in class, or helps students. The idea here is that one element can effectively compensate for the other: the component sets are functionally equivalent for high student performance. This approach is depicted in the center of Figure 2.5). Finally, we could use a so-called family resemblance structure that combines the logical AND and OR (see Barrenechea et al., 2019). We could think of the high-performing students as the family of students who are sufficiently similar because they have enough of the three criteria GOOD, PART, and PEER. Formally, this can mean that for the basic-level concept to be present, at least M out of N secondary-level criteria must be present. In our example, we could say that a student should have two of the three defining criteria for high student performance:

PERF = GOOD * PART + GOOD * PEER + PART * PEER

The right-hand side of Figure 2.5 illustrates the flower-like structure of family resemblance concepts.

When comparing the three diagrams in Figure 2.5, a basic rule becomes evident: using the logical AND, a basic-level concept covers fewer cases as more component sets are added. In other words, there is a trade-off between the extension (breadth) and the intension (depth) of the concept (Sartori, 1970; Goertz, 2006). However, the opposite is the case for the logical OR: the extension of the basic-level concept increases as intension, that is, the number of component sets, increases. The extension of the family resemblance structure is somewhere in between the classic and the substitutability approach.

When attributing cases to these concept structures in R, we could simply use the compute() function, which allows us to flexibly calculate the membership of cases in any Boolean combination. We enter the expression within quotation marks, and specify the dataset we use (see Code 2.12). The compute() function does not work if there are uncalibrated sets in your dataset. In R, when checking the membership of the cases in the sets with skew.check(), we can indeed see the different extensions of the concepts: more cases are qualitative members of PERF2 than of PERF1, and PERF3 is in between the two.

C 2.12

```
# Classic approach:

PERFDT$PERF1 <- compute("GOODFS*PARTFS*PEERFS", data=PERFDT)

# Substitutability:

PERFDT$PERF2 <- compute("GOODFS + PARTFS + PEERFS", data=PERFDT)
```

```
# Family resemblance:

PERFDT$PERF3 <- compute("GOODFS*PARTFS + GOODFS*PEERFS + PARTFS*
    PEERFS", data=PERFDT)

# Compare concept extension:

skew.check(PERFDT[,c("PERF1","PERF2", "PERF3")])
```

O 2.6

```
"Set PERF1 - Cases > 0.5 / Total number of cases: 6 / 17 =
35.29 %"
"Set PERF2 - Cases > 0.5 / Total number of cases: 14 / 17 =
82.35 %"
"Set PERF3 - Cases > 0.5 / Total number of cases: 9 / 17 =
52.94 %"
```

2.4.3   Rules for Combining Logical Operations

There are some basic rules that apply when we perform logical operations on more complex sets (Schneider and Wagemann, 2012, pp. 47–55). R offers some very helpful functions to implement these rules.

Sometimes we want to negate complex Boolean statements. For instance, recall that earlier we defined the set of excellent students EXCELLENT as the set of students who are both good students in terms of academic performance (GOOD) and perform well in class (CLASS). The set of not excellent students ~EXCELLENT is then essentially the set ~(GOOD * CLASS). *De Morgan's law* tells us that to calculate the negation of combined sets, we simply need to reverse all operators. Thus, AND becomes OR, OR becomes AND, and present sets are negated, and negated sets become present:

$$\sim(\text{GOOD} * \text{CLASS}) = \sim\text{GOOD} + \sim\text{CLASS}.$$

We can tell R to apply this rule using the **negate()** function. We enter the expression we wish to negate within the quotation marks, then specify the set names using the option **snames**.

C 2.13

```
# Negating complex sets:

negate(input = "GOOD*CLASS",
       snames = "GOOD, CLASS",
       use.tilde = TRUE)
```

O 2.7

Sometimes we want to combine different complex sets. Recall that we earlier defined the set of talented students TALENT as those students who either are good students GOOD, or perform well in class CLASS. For instance, now, say, we want to identify the set of not excellent, but talented students ~EXCELLENT * TALENT. Having just negated the set of excellent students using De Morgan's law, we now know this amounts to the following intersection:

(~GOOD + ~CLASS) * (GOOD + CLASS)

We could write out all the different intersections between the sets in the brackets:

~GOOD * GOOD + ~GOOD * CLASS + ~CLASS * GOOD + ~CLASS * CLASS

When dealing with this kind of Boolean formula, three rules apply (Schneider and Wagemann, 2012, section 2.4). First, *commutativity* means that the order in which elements appear in a conjunction or disjunction is unimportant. Also, the rule of *associativity* tells us that if we perform the same operation on several sets, the sequence of these operations is not important. Finally, the rule of *distributivity* tells us that when both AND and OR operators are used in the same logical expression, we can factor out elements shared by the various conjunctions.

The preceding expression is still unnecessarily complex. For instance, the rule of the excluded middle tells us that the intersection ~GOOD * GOOD is empty, so we could simply skip it. The `simplify()` function (package: `admisc`, automatically installed with `QCA`) helps us to minimize any logical expression into its simplest equivalent logical expression, using the different logical rules we have just discussed. The function works like the `negate()` function. The argument `use.tilde`, if set to false, allows for using lowercase notation to negate sets. When using this function in the following example, we get a much simpler formula.

~GOOD * CLASS + GOOD * ~CLASS

C 2.14

```
# Simplifying complex combined sets:

simplify(expression = "~GOOD*GOOD + ~GOOD*CLASS +
         ~CLASS *GOOD + ~CLASS*CLASS",
         snames = "GOOD, CLASS",
         use.tilde = TRUE)
```

O 2.8

```
S1:  ~GOOD*CLASS  +  GOOD*~CLASS
```

C 2.15

```
# Intersecting complex sets:

intersection("~GOOD + ~CLASS", "GOOD + CLASS",
             snames = "GOOD, CLASS")
```

O 2.9

```
E1:  (~GOOD + ~CLASS)(GOOD + CLASS)
  I1:  ~GOOD*CLASS  +  GOOD*~CLASS
```

C 2.16

```
# Factoring out:

factorize(input = "GOOD*PART + GOOD*PEER + PART*PEER",
          snames = "GOOD, PART, PEER")
```

O 2.10

```
F1:  GOOD*(PART + PEER)  +  PART*PEER
F2:  GOOD*PEER  +  PART*(GOOD + PEER)
F3:  GOOD*PART  +  PEER*(GOOD + PART)
```

In fact, instead of calculating the intersection ourselves, the intersection() function of the QCA package can do this for us. It works the same way as the other two functions. With just one command, we get exactly the same result. Intersecting complex sets can be used when comparing various QCA solutions (for example, in robustness tests; see Section 5.2), or when comparing theories specified in Boolean terms with our QCA solution (see Section 6.2 on theory evaluation). Finally, the factorize() function allows us to identify all the possible ways in which elements of a complex Boolean expression can be factored out (package: QCA). The function helps us identify three ways of factoring out the family resemblance structure for PERF, which we discussed earlier. We could use this function also on QCA solution formulas, especially complex solutions obtained in the analysis of sufficiency (see Chapter 4). The intersection() and factorize() functions automatically simplify the expressions that are entered. For any complex combination of sets, the compute() function, which we introduced earlier, will then determine the membership of the cases in it.

Box 2.6 Core Points – Set Operations

- The logical AND operator (also called Boolean multiplication, intersection, conjunction) takes the minimum value across sets and is denoted by the sign '*'.
- The logical OR (also called Boolean addition, union, disjunction) takes the maximum value across sets and is denoted by the sign '+'.
- Negation (logical NOT) is denoted with a '$\sim$' sign placed in front of the set. Membership in the set non-X ($\sim X$) is calculated as 1-X.
- The three main logical operators are not only applied to single sets, but also to more complex logical expressions.
- Set operations are commutative, associative, and distributive.
- The rule of the excluded middle states that there is no element that can simultaneously be a member of both a set and its negation. This rule applies to crisp sets only, as with fuzzy sets cases have partial membership in both a set and its negation.
- De Morgan's law is used for the negation of combined sets by simply reversing all operators and negating all sets (e.g., $\sim(X+Y) = \sim X * \sim Y$).

2.5 Summary

As QCA is a set-theoretic method, we attribute cases to sets in three interrelated steps: conceptualization, measurement, and calibration. Sets can be crisp, fuzzy, or multi-value, depending on whether and how they capture differences in kind or also differences in degree. We can calibrate them using a variety of techniques, and both quantitative and/or qualitative raw data. The most decisive calibration decision is the one that establishes the difference in kind between qualitative membership and non-membership in a set. A number of good practices and diagnostic tools help us ensure our measurement and calibration decisions are transparent and adequately represent the meaning of the concept that underlies the set.

We use three basic operations to combine calibrated sets: AND, OR, and NOT. With calibrated data, we can equally attribute cases to combined and negated sets. Based on these operations, we can structure social science concepts in different ways that affect the set of cases captured by the concept. We have also learned about a number of rules for logical operations on complex sets. Having linked our cases with the concepts that inform our set-theoretic analysis, we are now equipped with all the necessary knowledge to analyze relations between sets.

Part III

During the Analytic Moment

3 Necessary Conditions

3.1 Introduction and Learning Goals

We have seen that we can think of cases as members in different sets. The core goal of set-theoretic methods is to investigate relations between such sets. For example, we can observe that all countries that have officially adopted the Euro are members of the European Union (EU). On the one hand, there are no countries that use the Euro as their only official currency but are not part of the EU. On the other hand, there are countries that are members of the EU but do not have the Euro as their national currency (for example, Denmark or Sweden). We can say that being a member state of the European Union is necessary for having the Euro as the official currency. This example illustrates that we can think of necessary conditions (and sufficient conditions for that matter, as we explain in Chapter 4) in terms of set relations. The set of EU member states comprises the set of countries that have the Euro as their national currency. In other words, the set of EU member states is a superset of the set of countries with the Euro as a national currency, as there is no country that has adopted the Euro and is not part of the EU.

This example illustrates that, generally, if a condition X is necessary for an outcome Y, then X is a superset of Y. In this chapter, we introduce the notion of necessity and discuss the analysis of necessary conditions in R. We explain what necessity is, how to analyze and visualize necessary conditions, how to interpret the results, and how to avoid common pitfalls. To this end, the chapter first introduces the logic of necessary conditions, explains how to spot a pattern of necessity in crisp and fuzzy sets, and introduces parameters of fit for empirically evaluating claims of necessity. We then outline the basic protocol for the analysis of necessity in R, both for the analysis of individual necessary conditions and for conditions combined with a logical OR, that is, necessary disjunctions composed of so-called SUIN conditions (Mahoney et al., 2009). Subsequently, we discuss the possible pitfall of trivialness and how to diagnose it when interpreting necessary conditions. Finally, we present approaches to visualizing necessary conditions. The logic of necessary condition analysis is discussed in further detail in, among others, Goertz and Starr (2003), Ragin (2008b, chapters 1 and 3), and Schneider and Wagemann (2012, sections 3.2 and 9.1).

Box 3.1 Learning Goals – Necessity

- Understanding of the basic logic of necessity.
- Familiarity with different approaches to analyzing necessity in QCA and the protocol for the analysis of necessity.
- Basic understanding of possible analytic pitfalls when analyzing necessity and ways of avoiding them.
- Ability to implement an analysis of necessity in R and visualize the results.

3.2 Analysis of Necessary Conditions

Figure 3.1 illustrates the three basic steps involved in an analysis of necessity: determining empirical consistency, empirical relevance, and conceptual meaningfulness (Schneider, 2018). In the current section, we discuss each of these three steps. After defining necessity and introducing ways of visualizing it, we

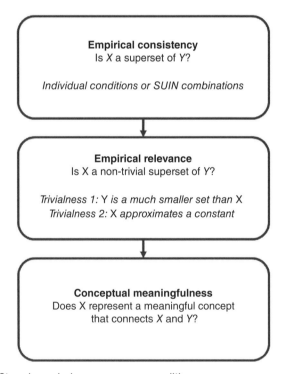

Figure 3.1 Steps in analyzing a necessary condition

present the 'consistency necessity' parameter of fit used for evaluating whether a condition is a superset of the outcome. In terms of empirical relevance, we discuss two possible sources of trivialness of conditions that are found to be supersets of the outcome, and introduce two parameters of fit for assessing them. Finally, throughout the chapter we stress the need for a theoretically meaningful interpretation of any potential necessary condition.

3.2.1 What Are Necessary Conditions?

A condition X is necessary for an outcome Y if, whenever we see the outcome Y present, condition X is also present. When a condition is necessary, there are no cases that display the outcome without the necessary condition being present too. Still, there might be cases that are members of set X but not of Y. We write this as $X \leftarrow Y$, where X is necessary for Y. Following the direction of the arrow, we can also read this as 'whenever there is Y, there is also X', or 'Y implies X'.

Importantly, using the preceding example, we can see that just knowing that a country is an EU member does not tell us whether that country has adopted the Euro as the national currency. Generally, that a case is a member of the necessary condition set does not tell us yet whether the case is also a member of the outcome set. A statement of necessity only gives us an expectation about what happens when the outcome is present: the necessary condition must also be present. Conversely, it does not tell us whether the condition is present when the outcome is absent. Therefore, a statement of necessity is only an expectation about the cases that have the outcome Y, as those must exhibit the necessary condition X. For cases that do not have the outcome ($\sim Y$), we do not know about their membership in the necessary condition. This illustrates the asymmetrical nature of set relations.

3.2.2 How to Visualize Necessity for Crisp and Fuzzy Sets

With crisp sets, the subset–superset nature of necessity relations is easy to grasp. All the cases that have officially adopted the Euro are members of the EU. In other words, in all (or most) cases in which the outcome is present, the condition must also be present. All (or most) cases with a membership score of 1 in the outcome must also have a membership score of 1 in the condition. One of the most common tools for visualizing set relations between crisp sets is the Euler diagram. By displaying multiple sets at once, an Euler diagram allows us to see how many cases are situated in each overlapping area between them and, therefore, whether there are any subset relationships (as seen in Section 1.2).

Box 3.2 Mock Example – Adopting the Euro as Currency

- *Research question*: Why do countries adopt the Euro as national currency?
- *Outcome*: Adoption of Euro as official national currency (EURO)
- *Cases*: Countries
- *Conditions*: Being a member state of the European Union (EU); Being a democracy (DEM)
- *Sets*: Crisp

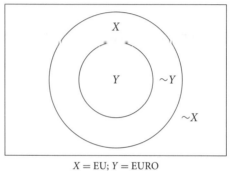

$X = \text{EU}; Y = \text{EURO}$

Figure 3.2 Euler diagram of a necessity relation

Using the preceding example, we can draw the necessity relation between condition X denoting countries that are EU members and outcome Y denoting countries that have the Euro; see Figure 3.2. All cases belonging to circle Y also belong to circle X. At the same time, we do have cases in circle X that are outside circle Y, that is, EU members without the Euro. This Euler diagram tells us that the set of EU member countries is a superset of the set of countries with the Euro. This can be interpreted as a necessity relation between condition X, EU membership, and outcome Y, officially using the Euro.

We can also visualize necessity relations for crisp sets with a two-by-two table. Table 3.1 illustrates where cases should (not) cluster in two-by-two tables for necessity. For a condition to be necessary, we should see cases in the upper-right corner, where both condition X and outcome Y are present. What we do not want to see are cases in the upper-left corner, as these cases display the outcome, but without the necessary condition. Cases that are not members of the outcome ($Y = 0$) are not directly relevant (n.d.r.) for establishing whether X is a superset of Y. They will play a role, though, when evaluating whether a subset relation is empirically trivial, as we explain in more detail in Section 3.2.3.

With fuzzy sets, too, a necessary condition X must be a superset of outcome Y. However, since cases have partial membership in the two sets, what we want

Table 3.1 Two-by-two table for necessity

	1	NO CASES	CASES
Outcome Y	**0**	n.d.r.	n.d.r.
		0	**1**
		Condition X	

Note: n.d.r. = not directly relevant.

Table 3.2 Hypothetical fuzzy-set data matrix for necessity

Cases	**HS**	**HM**
Amanda	0.7	0.6
Bob	0.6	0.6
Carl	0.9	0.8
Cecilia	0.45	0.1
Ana	1	0.9
Alex	0.92	0.7
Olivia	0.8	0.3

to see in this situation are membership values in the condition X that are higher or equal to membership values in the outcome Y across all (or most) cases. For example, let us assume that having a high salary (HS) is necessary for an employee to have high workplace motivation (HM). The set HS is a superset of HM if each employee's membership in *HS* is higher than or equal to their membership in HM. Table 3.2 presents a hypothetical data matrix with seven cases – seven employees – and their fuzzy-set membership scores in condition HS and outcome HM. When comparing the scores case by case, we notice that $HS_i \geq HM_i$ across all cases i, meaning that having a high salary is a superset and, hence, potentially necessary for being highly motivated.

Box 3.3 Fake Example – Conditions for Workplace Motivation

- *Research question*: What are the conditions for high workplace motivation?
- *Outcome*: High workplace motivation (HM)
- *Cases*: Employees
- *Conditions*: High salary (HS); flexible schedule (FS); lenient supervisor (LS); low job security (LJS); high promotion potential (PP)
- *Sets*: Fuzzy

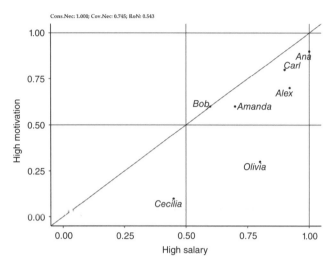

Figure 3.3 XY plot for necessity

With fuzzy sets, we use XY plots for visualizing set relations of necessity (and sufficiency for that matter; see Chapter 4). XY plots allow us to visualize the relationship between a condition X (or a combination of conditions) and an outcome Y in a two-dimensional space. We place the condition, in our case 'High Salary', on the horizontal x-axis and the outcome, 'High Motivation', on the vertical y-axis (see Figure 3.3). Cases appear as dots in this plot, and they are placed depending on their set-membership values in the condition set and the outcome set. While basic scatter plots allow us to visualize relationships between any kind of variables, XY plots designed specifically for QCA allow us to plot set-membership scores and set relations. XY plots in QCA usually contain three guiding lines for better visualizing set relations: (1) a diagonal line where values in X and Y coincide ($X = Y$); (2) a horizontal line at $Y = 0.5$ to identify differences in kind, that is, cases where the outcome is more present than absent; and (3) a vertical line at $X = 0.5$ for identifying differences in kind between cases in the condition set X. The result is a so-called enhanced XY plot (Schneider and Rohlfing, 2013). Cases below the diagonal are in line with the statement of necessity $X \leftarrow Y$, as they hold memberships $X \geq Y$. Cases below the diagonal, and more specifically in the triangle with $X > 0.5$ and $Y > 0.5$ (that is, the upper-right quadrant), are considered typical for necessity as they do not only have a membership in $X \geq Y$, but they are also more in than out of both the outcome and the condition sets.

3.2.3   Parameters of Fit for Necessity

In applied QCA, set relations can be less clear-cut than the example we have just discussed. When dealing with 'real-world' data, subset relations are usually less than perfect. For instance, we might find a few employees who are highly motivated at work (HM, the outcome) without, however, receiving a high salary (~HS, our necessary condition). Do these cases make us conclude that HS is not actually necessary for HM, or can we allow slight deviations from the pattern of necessity?

In applied QCA, we usually allow necessary and sufficient relations to deviate by a small margin from a perfect set-relational pattern. Parameters of fit indicate the degree of such deviations and allow us to assess the goodness and strength of set relations. The main parameters of fit used for assessing necessity relations (and sufficiency relations, see Chapter 4) are consistency and coverage, or, relevance (Ragin, 2008b, chapter 3; Schneider and Wagemann, 2012, chapter 5 and section 9.2).

Consistency

The consistency measure is a numerical expression of the extent to which empirical evidence is in line with a set relation – here, necessity. For example, Figure 3.4a shows a perfect pattern of necessity, such as the ones discussed in the beginning of this chapter. Figure 3.4b, in contrast, presents a pattern that deviates from a perfect superset relationship, if only just slightly.

The consistency measures allow us to quantify such deviations. In other words, consistency necessity expresses how much a set relation departs from a perfect necessity pattern. Formula 3.1 shows how consistency for necessity is calculated. This parameter varies from 0 to 1, with higher values representing more consistent necessity relations. As a rule of thumb, the consistency threshold above which a condition could be considered necessary should not be smaller than 0.9. However, note that with crisp sets, the deviation of consistency from 1 indicates the presence of cases that do display the outcome, despite not displaying the alleged necessary condition. This is why it is sometimes recommended to apply a consistency necessity threshold of 1 with crisp sets.

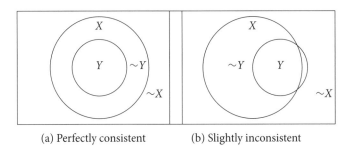

(a) Perfectly consistent   (b) Slightly inconsistent

Figure 3.4 Consistency necessity

With fuzzy sets, a consistency value smaller than 1 could either indicate the presence of such cases or simply that membership in the condition set is not always greater than membership in the outcome set. This issue, specific to fuzzy sets, of so-called deviant cases consistency in kind vs. in degree deserves further attention in the next section.

$$Cons_{nec} = \frac{\sum min(X_i, Y_i)}{\sum Y_i} \tag{3.1}$$

Deviant Cases Consistency in Kind

While the consistency measure indicates how much the empirical evidence deviates from a perfect superset pattern, it should not be the only source of information used for assessing whether there is a superset relation. The presence of cases which qualitatively contradict the necessity relation should also be taken into account. In the case of crisp sets, it turns out that all inconsistent cases are of similar methodological importance.[1] All cases that display the outcome but not the condition (upper-left cell in Table 3.1) lower the consistency score to the same extent. These cases are inconsistent with necessity as they logically contradict such a statement: they have the outcome without the necessary condition.

With fuzzy sets, on the other hand, not all inconsistent cases are of similar methodological importance. This happens because fuzzy sets establish both differences in kind and differences in degree. To illustrate, imagine we were to obtain data on three new employees, Dee, Fiona, and Mark. In Figure 3.5, we can see that all three cases are inconsistent with the statement of necessity: their workplace motivation is higher than their salary, so they are situated above the diagonal line. In Table 3.3, we calculate the consistency necessity score using formula 3.1. We first obtain the minimum score across the condition HS and the outcome HM and sum it up for all cases (5.2). We then divide this by the sum of membership scores of all cases in the outcome HM (5.8), and obtain a consistency necessity score of 0.897.

Looking at the three inconsistent cases (Mark, Fiona, and Dee) it just so happens that for all three cases the membership in the outcome exceeds that in the condition by the same amount (0.2) – that is, they all show the same distance to the diagonal (see Figure 3.5). They, therefore, all contribute equally to the inconsistency of the set relation. However, these cases are not equally problematic for evaluating whether there is a set relation. Dee suggests more

---

[1] Cases might differ in their substantive importance, for example when a very prominent case is inconsistent.

Table 3.3 Hypothetical fuzzy-set data for
necessity with inconsistencies

Cases	HS	HM	min(HS, HM)
Amanda	0.7	0.6	0.6
Bob	0.6	0.6	0.6
Carl	0.9	0.8	0.8
Cecilia	0.3	0.1	0.1
Ana	1	0.9	0.9
Alex	0.92	0.7	0.7
Olivia	0.8	0.3	0.3
Mark	0.6	0.8	0.6
Dee	0.4	0.6	0.4
Fiona	0.2	0.4	0.2
Sum	–	5.8	5.2
Cons. Nec.		5.2/5.8 = 0.897	

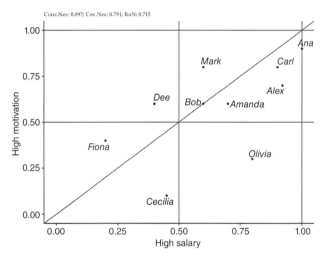

Figure 3.5 Inconsistent DCD and DCK cases for necessity

strongly than Fiona or Mark that HS should not be interpreted as a necessary
condition for HM. Why? Dee, unlike the other two, holds *qualitatively* different
membership in the condition (below 0.5 – more out than in) and in the outcome
(above 0.5 – more in than out). Mark and Fiona, instead, both fall on the same
side of the qualitative anchors of X and Y, respectively. In other words, Mark is
a member of both X and Y and Fiona is not a member of either X or Y. As such,

they contradict the notion that high salary is needed for high motivation much less than Dee. Cases like Dee are called 'deviant consistency in kind' (DCK) cases (Schneider and Rohlfing, 2013)[2], whereas cases like Fiona and Mark are 'deviant consistency in degree' cases (DCD).

The horizontal and vertical lines in an XY plot allow us to observe such differences in kind. Therefore, in addition to the consistency value, we should check how many and which cases are DCK when assessing a set relation. For instance, we may want to perform a follow-up interview with Dee in order to find out more about the mechanisms that lead Dee to be highly motivated despite having a rather low salary.[3] Based on this in-depth engagement with the deviant case, we need to decide whether the deviant case 'falsifies' the set relation or whether it is an idiosyncrasy that does not in principle invalidate the statement of necessity. The best scenario, of course, is when no DCKs exist.

Empirical Relevance

Once we have identified conditions that are consistently necessary for our outcome – using the consistency measure together with identifying and engaging with DCK cases – we need to turn to the question of how empirically important or trivial this alleged necessary condition is. For this, we have two parameters at our disposal: coverage necessity (Ragin, 2008b, chapter 3) and Relevance of Necessity (RoN) (Schneider and Wagemann, 2012, section 9.2).

A necessity claim becomes trivial if there is a big difference in size between the outcome set and the condition set, either because the outcome is very small (only very few cases are members) or because the condition set is very big (almost all cases are members). For example, we could ask whether being a democracy is necessary for having the Euro as their currency. Indeed, all Eurozone countries are democracies. However, it seems trivial to state this as there are many more democracies in the world that do not use the Euro. The coverage formula (3.2) captures this first source of trivialness: when the condition set is much bigger than the outcome set (see Figure 3.6a). The coverage value also ranges from 0 to 1 and the lower the coverage value, the more X could be interpreted as trivial for Y.

$$Cov_{nec} = \frac{\sum min(X_i, Y_i)}{\sum X_i} \tag{3.2}$$

---

[2] They have sometimes also beem called 'true logical contradictory' cases (Schneider and Wagemann, 2012).

[3] See Section 6.3 on case selection based on QCA results in the framework of set-theoretic multi-method research (SMMR).

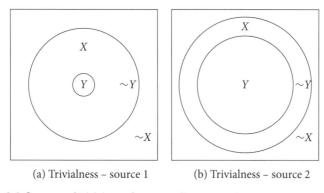

(a) Trivialness – source 1   (b) Trivialness – source 2

Figure 3.6 Sources of trivialness for necessity

The coverage parameter only expresses the difference in size between the condition and outcome sets. If both sets are very large, as illustrated in Figure 3.6b, then the coverage score will be high. This can be a problem because a very large X set is nothing but an almost constant condition. Take, for instance, the example of democracy (X) as a necessary condition for adopting the Euro (Y). If we analyze only European countries, then X is a quasi-constant because (almost) all European countries are considered democracies; there are no (or only a few) non-democracies ($\sim X$). So, looking only at European countries and then finding that being a democracy is necessary for adopting the Euro is very unsurprising, or, trivial. There are hardly any cases (undemocratic European countries) that could make us conclude otherwise. Virtually all (or most) cases are members of X, and hardly any cases are members of $\sim X$. Stating that a near-constant X ought to be considered necessary for a given outcome Y amounts to a trivial statement, because that very same near-constant X is, by pure empirical force, a superset of any other set. If X is near-constant, it could happen with fuzzy sets that X becomes a consistent enough superset not only of outcome Y, but also of the *negation* of the outcome Y. This certainly amounts to a trivial statement.

This is why Schneider and Wagemann (2012, p. 235 ff.) propose the parameter of Relevance of Necessity (RoN). This is calculated based on formula 3.3 and takes into account both sources of trivialness: a big difference in size between X and Y and between X and $\sim X$. In applied QCA, it is best to calculate both parameters. Generally, RoN is the more conservative measure, which means its values tend to be lower than those for the coverage parameter.

$$RoN = \frac{\sum(1 - X_i)}{\sum(1 - min(X_i, Y_i))} \tag{3.3}$$

It is good to keep in mind the following when interpreting parameters of fit. First, it is meaningless to interpret the coverage and RoN of a condition that has not passed our consistency check. Thus, we always check consistency first when assessing set relations. In this respect, we usually use a rule-of-thumb threshold for consistency necessity (≥ 0.9). For coverage and RoN, no such strict thresholds exist (yet). Research practice indicates that a RoN close to 0.5 could be reason for concern. One should then resort to our caveat: parameters of fit should not substitute the focus on cases. Part of assessing consistency is to identify and engage with DCK cases. Similarly, part of assessing empirical trivialness (coverage/RoN) is to visually inspect the empirical pattern using an XY plot, histograms for X and Y, and dedicated functions introduced in the remainder of this chapter. Whenever the cases cluster very unevenly in either the condition set and/or the outcome set, that is, whenever X or Y or both are skewed, this can indicate that the necessity relation is trivial.

3.2.4 Conceptual Meaningfulness

Finally, before showing how to perform analyses of necessity in R, we must stress that any potential necessary condition must also be conceptually meaningful (Schneider, 2018). That is, even if a condition displays a very high consistency necessity value and is non-trivial (indicated by high values of coverage and RoN), we still have to engage in a theoretical interpretation of the necessity relation between X and Y. For example, we would need to be able to show that there is a theoretically plausible mechanism that makes it impossible (or very hard) for employees to be highly motivated in the absence of a high salary. While all necessary conditions should be conceptually meaningful supersets of the outcome, we will see that the need for theoretical interpretation of the superset relation becomes particularly important when identifying combinations of conditions that are necessary (so-called necessary disjunctions of SUIN conditions). We discuss the analysis and interpretation of such necessary combinations of conditions in more depth in Section 3.3.2.

Box 3.4 Core Points – Necessity

- A condition X is necessary for an outcome Y if, whenever we see the outcome Y present, condition X is also present. In other words, a necessary condition X is a superset of the outcome Y.
- With crisp sets, set relations are visualized using Euler diagrams of the condition(s) and the outcome, or using two-by-two tables.

Box 3.4 (Cont.)

- With fuzzy sets, set relations are visualized using XY plots with the condition (or combination of conditions) on the horizontal x-axis and the outcome on the vertical y-axis.
- Parameters of fit measure deviations from perfect set relations and are used to assess the goodness and strength of a set relation.
- The consistency necessity parameter of fit measures the extent to which the empirical evidence indicates the presence of a necessity relation.
- Consistency takes values between 0 and 1, with higher values indicating more consistent relations. As a rule of thumb, the consistency threshold above which a condition could be considered necessary should not be smaller than 0.9.
- The coverage and Relevance of Necessity (RoN) parameters of fit indicate two potential sources of trivialness in necessary conditions: when the condition and outcome set differ a lot in size, and when both the condition and the outcome sets are very large.
- Coverage and RoN take values between 0 and 1 with higher values indicating less trivial relations.

3.3 Necessary Conditions in Practice

In this section, we show how to perform analyses of necessity in R using functions from the SetMethods and QCA packages. First, we illustrate how one can obtain consistency, coverage, and RoN parameters of fit for evaluating single necessary conditions, but also how to visualize such necessary conditions for the identification of DCK cases. Second, we turn to the issue of causal complexity in necessity and discuss the analysis of necessary combinations of conditions (so-called SUIN conditions) in practice.

3.3.1 Single Necessary Conditions

To show the implementation and interpretation of necessity, we turn to the example of job motivation used previously. Imagine that the owner of a company collected data on 51 employees, trying to find out what lies behind their high motivation (HM) in doing their work. For this purpose, she calibrates the fuzzy membership scores of the employees in five condition sets: high salary (HS), flexible schedule (FS), lenient supervisor (LS), low job security (LJS), and

high promotion potential (PP). We can load these data called 'JOBF' from the
SetMethods package using the data() function.[4]

C 3.1

```
# Load data set:

data("JOBF")
```

To check parameters of fit for the necessity of individual conditions, but also
for all conditions in a dataset, we use the QCAfit() function. In its most basic
form, this function takes as the first argument the condition(s) that we want
to evaluate, and as the second argument the outcome that we want to evaluate
it against. For example, let us say we want to evaluate whether having a high
salary (HS) is necessary for being highly motivated (HM) at work. We use
the QCAfit() function and first specify the condition HS from our dataset
JOBF[5] using the $ operator. We then specify the outcome HM from the same
dataset. Finally, we can add an optional argument to make the output more
appealing, in which we can specify the label that we want printed for this
condition (cond.lab = "High Salary").

C 3.2

```
# Obtain parameters of fit:

QCAfit(JOBF$HS,
       JOBF$HM,
       cond.lab = "High Salary")
```

The output gives us three parameters of fit for evaluating this relationship.
All three vary from 0 to 1, and higher values indicate a better fit. Cons.Nec.
indicates how much a set relation approaches a perfect superset pattern. In
this example, consistency is quite high at 0.91. This value is above the usual
threshold for consistency necessity (around 0.9), which means we can also
investigate the other parameters of fit. Cov.Nec is the coverage parameter
(value 0.754) and RoN the Relevance of Necessity parameter (value 0.781). These
values indicate that a high salary, HS, is not a trivial condition for HM. We can,
therefore, proceed to visually inspecting the relation between the two sets and
further check whether we have any DCK cases.

---

[4] Remember that when using your own data in csv format, you can load it using the read.csv()
function and place it in an object of your choice. For example, MYDATA <-
read.csv("mydata.csv").

[5] We are working with data that are already calibrated into fuzzy sets (see Chapter 2).

O 3.1

```
          Cons.Nec Cov.Nec    RoN
High Salary     0.91    0.754 0.781
```

Since the data we have consist of fuzzy sets, we can graphically display the empirical pattern via an XY plot using the `xy.plot()` function in which we specify the name of the condition for the *x*-axis, the name of the outcome for the *y*-axis, and the name of the data. Option `necessity = TRUE` specifies that we are investigating necessity, option `jitter = TRUE` creates non-overlapping case labels, while options `xlab` and `ylab` specify the labels of the axes. While here we do not use this option, as we are working with fuzzy sets, the `xy.plot()` function can also display two-by-two tables with parameters of fit by just specifying `crisp = TRUE` in the list of options.

By looking at the XY plot in Figure 3.7, we see that, although parameters of fit were quite good, there are two DCK cases located in the upper-left quadrant (that is, E47 and E8). Employees 47 and 8 are rather motivated, while having a not-high salary. These two cases should be investigated in more depth by the owner of the company to check whether they indeed invalidate the claim that HS is necessary for HM, or whether there is some idiosyncrasy at play in these cases (for example, maybe E47 and E8 are already very rich).

C 3.3

```
# Produce XY plot:

xy.plot(x = "HS",
        y = "HM",
        data = JOBF,
```

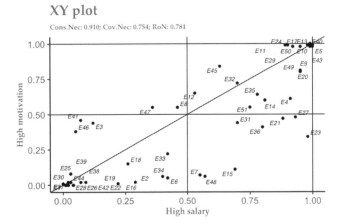

Figure 3.7 High salary as necessary for high motivation

```
necessity = TRUE,
jitter = TRUE,
xlab = "High salary",
ylab = "High motivation",
crisp = FALSE)
```

Using the same QCAfit() function, we can also evaluate whether the absence of a condition is necessary for the outcome. For example, we can investigate whether *not* having low job security (~LJS) is necessary for high job motivation (HM). The arguments follow the same pattern, but we use a 1− to obtain the negated condition. The output in this case shows that the consistency necessity of ~LJS for HM is rather low at 0.82, being below the usual rule-of-thumb threshold for consistency necessity around 0.9. Therefore, we do not need to interpret the other two parameters of fit, as it does not make sense to check whether an inconsistent necessary condition is trivial. We can also plot the absence of the condition 'low job security' using the xy.plot() function by just adding a tilde ~ in front of the condition name, as in the following example (due to space limitations, we do not show the resulting plot here).

C 3.4

```
# Obtain parameters of fit for negated condition:

QCAfit(1−JOBF$LJS ,
       JOBF$HM,
       cond.lab = "~ Low job security")
```

O 3.2

```
              Cons.Nec Cov.Nec  RoN
~ Low job security     0.82     0.522 0.48
```

C 3.5

```
# Produce  XY plot for negated condition:

xy.plot(x = "~LJS",
        y = "HM",
        data = JOBF,
        necessity = TRUE,
        jitter = TRUE,
        xlab = "~LJS",
        ylab = "HM")
```

Frequently in applied QCA, we do want to see the parameters for all conditions and their negations. Instead of writing separate lines of code for each condition, we can use the square brackets to indicate a whole range of conditions. In our example, we need to specify the names of each of the conditions we want to test using quotation marks and combining them together, using the c() function. Within the square brackets, we write the combined conditions after a comma. Alternatively, as the conditions are located in the first five columns in the dataset, we could also write the range 1:5 after a comma. Note that when analyzing multiple necessary conditions at the same time, we do not need to specify their labels or the fact that we also want the analysis performed for their negation. When denoting a range of conditions using the square brackets, the QCAfit() function automatically identifies their labels from the dataset and prints parameters of fit for both their presence and their absence. Using the same procedure, we can also investigate whether there are any necessary conditions for the negation of the outcome, that is, *not* high motivation, by just adding the option neg.out = TRUE to the QCAfit() function. By quickly checking the output, we see that apart from HS, no other condition, in either its presence or absence, passes the 0.9 threshold for necessity.

C 3.6

```
# Obtain parameters of fit for an entire dataframe:

QCAfit(x = JOBF[,c("HS", "FS", "LS", "LJS", "PP")],
       y = JOBF$HM)
```

O 3.3

	Cons.Nec	Cov.Nec	RoN
HS	0.910	0.754	0.781
FS	0.843	0.723	0.773
LS	0.850	0.537	0.481
LJS	0.360	0.519	0.825
PP	0.876	0.825	0.866
~HS	0.283	0.268	0.609
~FS	0.312	0.284	0.597
~LS	0.306	0.449	0.808
~LJS	0.820	0.522	0.480
~PP	0.332	0.276	0.549

If we analyze whether there are necessary conditions for the negated outcome, we find that no condition, in either its presence or absence, passes the consistency threshold of being necessary for not being motivated.

C 3.7

```
# Obtain parameters of fit for the negated outcome:

QCAfit(x = JOBF[,1:5],
       y = JOBF$HM) neg.out = TRUE)
```

O 3.4

	Cons.Nec	Cov.Nec	RoN
HS	0.387	0.406	0.596
FS	0.379	0.410	0.615
LS	0.703	0.562	0.495
LJS	0.406	0.741	0.897
PP	0.311	0.371	0.643
~HS	0.765	0.915	0.930
~FS	0.744	0.857	0.882
~LS	0.420	0.780	0.914
~LJS	0.736	0.593	0.520
~PP	0.853	0.897	0.895

3.3.2 Necessary Disjunctions of SUIN Conditions

In Section 1.2, we noted that one of the main features of QCA is that it assumes causal complexity. When it comes to necessity relations, one form in which causal complexity might be present is through SUIN conditions. A SUIN condition is a condition that is a '... sufficient but unnecessary part of a factor that is insufficient but necessary for an outcome' (Mahoney et al., 2009, p. 126). Combinations of SUIN conditions, therefore, represent logical OR combinations of conditions that are supersets of the outcome. Since they use the logical OR, combinations of SUIN conditions can also be called necessary disjunctions of conditions. Since the logical OR operator takes the maximum membership value across sets (see Section 2.4.1), we obtain condition sets which may or may not be necessary on their own, but which become large enough to be supersets of the outcome when combined via the logical OR. For example, neither the condition 'writing a monograph dissertation' (MD), nor the condition 'writing a paper-based dissertation' (PD) on their own are consistent supersets of the outcome 'obtaining a PhD degree' (PhD); yet, their logical OR combination, 'writing a monograph or a paper-based dissertation' is (MD + PD ← PhD).

If we combine many conditions through the logical OR operator, sooner or later we will produce a big set that is a consistent enough superset of the outcome. It might be so big, indeed, to become empirically trivial. Also, by combining many conditions into one disjunction, we need to provide conceptual arguments regarding what this disjunction stands for, that is, we need to meaningfully interpret the SUIN conditions as functional equivalents of a higher-order concept (Schneider and Wagemann, 2012; Schneider, 2018). This underlying concept, which the necessary disjunction represents, is then the actual necessary condition. In the preceding example, we can argue that both conditions are functional equivalents of the higher-order necessary condition 'writing a dissertation'.

In practice, we can easily analyze necessary disjunctions in R, using the superSubset() function in the QCA package. We simply specify the dataset we want to use, the outcome, and the conditions, and we can set a threshold for consistency (incl.cut) above which to identify such logical OR combinations. Thresholds for coverage and RoN must also be set using the options cov.cut and ron.cut. When specifying thresholds of 0.6 for both coverage and RoN, this command returns one individual condition and five SUIN combinations that are consistent and empirically nontrivial supersets of the outcome. The final step of our analysis will be to use external knowledge, such as extant theory, to see which of these conditions can be interpreted as a conceptually meaningful necessary condition. Let us now see what happens if we do not set the coverage and RoN thresholds that help us avoid trivial necessary conditions.

Applied to our job motivation example, we see that the software found five such logical OR combinations that pass the thresholds we specified (0.9 for consistency necessity, and 0.6 for coverage and RoN). However, as mentioned earlier, one should be careful in simply reporting all combinations of SUIN conditions without using a threshold a coverage and RoN. Combining conditions with the logical OR results in sets that, while consistent enough, might not be conceptually meaningful or might be empirically trivial as necessary conditions. We can also see this issue in the quite low values of the RoN parameter of fit in the second part of Output 3.5, which indicates that most of these logical OR combinations of conditions might be trivial because membership of cases in them is highly skewed.

For illustration of the issue of trivialness due to a highly skewed set, take the disjunction FS + LS (number 7 in Output 3.5. Its consistency looks good (0.944) and, conceptually, we could even argue that FS (a flexible schedule) and LS (a lenient supervisor) are functional equivalents of the higher-order necessary condition 'flexible working environment'. However, the low RoN (and coverage) values indicate that there seems to be a problem of empirical trivialness.

C 3.8

```
# Detect SUIN conditions:

SS_Y <- superSubset(data = JOBF,
                    outcome = "HM" ,
                    conditions = c("HS","FS","LS","LJS","PP"),
                    incl.cut = 0.9,
                    cov.cut = 0.6
                    ron.cut = 0.6)
# Including trivial supersets (for illustration;
not recommended)
```

```
SS_Y <- superSubset(data = JOBF,
                    outcome = "HM",
                    conditions = c("HS","FS","LS","LJS","PP"), %
                    incl.cut = 0.9)
SS_Y
```

O 3.5

		inclN	RoN	covN
1	HS	0.910	0.781	0.754
2	FS+~LS	0.913	0.602	0.629
3	FS+LJS	0.929	0.602	0.636
4	FS+PP	0.919	0.721	0.710
5	LS+PP	0.972	0.622	0.665
6	LJS+PP	0.944	0.654	0.674

		inclN	RoN	covN
1	HS	0.910	0.781	0.754
2	hs+FS	0.929	0.318	0.505
3	hs+LS	0.943	0.265	0.493
4	hs+PP	0.945	0.326	0.515
5	fs+LS	0.933	0.297	0.499
6	FS+ls	0.913	0.602	0.629
7	FS+LS	0.944	0.374	0.533
8	FS+ljs	0.927	0.358	0.519
9	FS+LJS	0.929	0.602	0.636
10	fs+PP	0.969	0.324	0.525
11	FS+pp	0.944	0.238	0.484
12	FS+PP	0.919	0.721	0.710
13	LS+ljs	0.937	0.305	0.504
14	LS+LJS	0.945	0.343	0.522
15	ls+PP	0.972	0.622	0.665
16	LS+pp	0.961	0.217	0.485
17	LS+PP	0.917	0.424	0.542
18	ljs+PP	0.954	0.401	0.548
19	LJS+PP	0.944	0.654	0.674
20	hs+fs+ljs	0.913	0.233	0.468
21	hs+ls+ljs	0.908	0.213	0.459
22	fs+ls+ljs	0.930	0.226	0.474
23	fs+ljs+pp	0.905	0.224	0.461
24	ls+ljs+pp	0.907	0.198	0.454

To investigate this further, we plot all the logical OR combinations of conditions returned by the superSubset() function using the pimplot() function in the SetMethods package. We present here only the plot for disjunction FS + LS (Figure 3.8). Despite the quite high consistency and the fact that there are no DCK cases, the problem of skewness is visible in this plot, as most cases

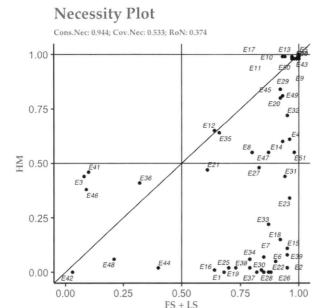

Figure 3.8 XY plot of FS or LS as necessary for HM

cluster to the right-hand side of the plot. This could also be spotted through the quite low value of the RoN parameter (0.374), indicating trivialness (source 2).

C 3.9

```
# Produce XY plots for SUIN conditions:

pimplot(data = JOBF,
        results = SS_Y,
        outcome = "HM",
        necessity = TRUE,
        jitter = TRUE,
        all_labels = TRUE)
```

To further check the problem of skewness and, therefore, of the trivialness of this combination of SUIN conditions, we can also look at the percentage of cases that are members of FS+LS with the **skew.check()** function. For this, we first create a new column in the data containing the scores of all cases in the union of FS and LS using the **fuzzyor()** function, and then apply the **skew.check()** function to this column. The results show that 86.27 per cent of cases are members of FS + LS, that is, about nine out of 10 of the employees have either flexible schedules or a lenient supervisor, making it quite a skewed set. Another

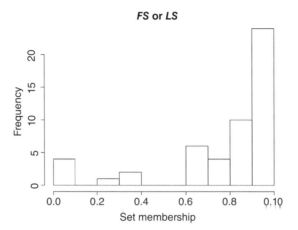

Figure 3.9 Distribution of scores in FS or LS

way of displaying the size of FS + LS and its membership distribution is through a histogram of membership score (see Figure 3.9). Function `skew.check()` prints a histogram when options `hist` is set to TRUE. Additionally, we can also add a title for the figure (`main`). The histogram obtained also shows that most employees have very high set-membership scores (that is, they are almost full members) in the union set FS + LS.

C 3.10

```
# Add SUIN conditions to data set:

JOBF$FSorLS <- fuzzyor(JOBF$FS, JOBF$LS)

# Skewness check:

skew.check(JOBF$FSorLS,
           hist = TRUE,
           main = "FS or LS")
```

O 3.6

```
"Cases > 0.5 / Total number of cases: 44 / 51 = 86.27 \%"
```

Box 3.5 Good Practice – Necessity

- When evaluating whether a relationship is necessary, the consistency measure should be complemented with identifying Deviant Consistency in Kind (DCK) cases. These are cases that qualitatively contradict the necessity relation by displaying the outcome without displaying the condition.

Box 3.5 (Cont.)

- Consistency necessity should not be lower than 0.9.
- It is meaningless to interpret the trivialness of a condition that is not consistently necessary. Consistency and DCK cases should always be interpreted before coverage and RoN.
- Coverage and RoN should be combined with plotting and skewness functions for spotting potential sources of trivialness in necessary conditions.
- Any potential necessary condition must also be conceptually meaningful.
- Disjunctions of SUIN conditions (that is, conditions combined with a logical OR) should only be considered necessary when they are non-trivial and can be meaningfully interpreted as functional equivalents of a higher-order necessary condition.

3.4 Summary

The goal of QCA as a set-theoretic method is to analyze relations between sets. One of the possible relations between sets is necessity. Generally, a condition can be considered necessary if it is a superset of the outcome of interest. In other words, a condition can be necessary if all (or most) of the cases that are members of the outcome are also members of the necessary condition.

If the general idea of necessity is having a superset relation between a condition and the outcome, finding a necessary condition in practice actually requires the application of three different steps. First, for a condition (or combination of conditions) to be necessary, it must be an empirically consistent superset of the outcome. During this step, researchers should use the consistency necessity parameter of fit, together with visualization tools for identifying DCK cases that might contradict the statement of necessity. Second, any consistent enough superset of the outcome should also be empirically relevant. During this step, researchers should use the coverage necessity and RoN parameters of fit together with skewness identification tools (plots, skewness functions, etc.) for identifying two potential sources of trivialness in necessary (combinations of) conditions. A necessary condition is trivial when the necessary condition is much bigger than the outcome set, or when both the condition and the outcome are very large. Finally, any necessary (combinations of) conditions should also be conceptually meaningful. Above and beyond simply reporting parameters of fit and identifying types of cases, we argue that researchers should always engage in the theoretical interpretation of the necessity relations obtained after the first two steps.

4 Sufficient Conditions

4.1 Introduction and Learning Goals

Soccer coach Susan is responsible for dozens of kids each week. To keep order in organizing the training sessions, it is very important to her that players arrive in time. Some of them are diligent and are ready to practice at the established time, whereas others often arrive late. She wonders what it is that explains this difference. After a closer look, she discovers that all those kids that live nearer to the training site do arrive in time. Sharing this observation with her team, some point out that they also arrive in time but do not live close by. Susan further investigates and finds that kids who come by bike rather than being brought in their parent's car arrive in time. Still, there are kids to whom this explanation does not apply, and Susan notices that those female players arrive in time who come from families in which punctuality is taught as a virtue.

Box 4.1 Mock Empirical Example – Susan, the Soccer Coach

- *Research question*: Under what conditions do soccer players arrive in time for training sessions?
- *Cases*: Children who play in the football team.
- *Outcome:* Arriving in time (Y).
- *Conditions*: Living close to the pitch (X); Coming by bike rather than by parent's car (A); Being female (B); Coming from a family with punctuality as a virtue (C); Being a seasoned player (D); Being a goalkeeper (E)

Note: To illustrate different aspects of truth table analyses, we vary the example throughout the chapter, using both crisp and fuzzy sets and various sample sizes.

What Susan has discovered is that there are different sufficient conditions for the outcome 'arriving in time' (Y): living close to the pitch (X), or coming by bike rather than by car (A); or being a female (B) from a family with punctuality (C) as a virtue ($B * C$). As discussed in Section 1.2, this is a typical QCA result in which different (combinations of) factors lead to the same outcome. We can write this typical sufficiency solution formula as follows:

$$X + A + B * C \rightarrow Y \tag{4.1}$$

None of the three sufficient conditions fits all punctual players. This means that none of these three conditions is necessary for arriving in time. Instead, each condition explains a different, probably partially overlapping, group of punctual players. Also, often it is not a single feature that explains the outcome but a combination of features, like $B * C$ in our example. Furthermore, these sufficient conditions are not mutually exclusive: some players do live close by, come by bike, and are female who see punctuality as a virtue. Such players arrive in time for more than one reason.

In this chapter, we explain how to perform an analysis of sufficiency. We introduce the basic logic of sufficiency by using a situation in which only one condition at a time is considered. Along these lines, we introduce various parameters of fit for sufficient conditions (consistency, PRI, and coverage). After that, we explain how two or more sufficient conditions for one outcome are analyzed, that is, when we allow for causal complexity in terms of conjunctural causation, equifinality, and asymmetry (see Section 1.2). This, of course, is the most common and realistic scenario in applied QCA. As will become clear, the key tool for detecting subset relations of sufficiency is the so-called truth table. We explain how to summarize and present data in the form of a table and how to then analyze that truth table via the process of logical minimization, in order to identify sufficient conditions for the outcome. The logic of sufficient condition analysis is discussed in further detail in, among others, Ragin (2008b, chapters 7–9) and Schneider and Wagemann (2012, chapters 3–9).

Box 4.2 Learning Goals – Sufficiency

- Understanding of the basic logic of sufficiency.
- Assessing deviations from perfect subset relations of sufficiency using parameters of fit.
- Understanding of how to represent data in a truth table.
- Understanding of how to analyze and logically minimize truth tables for detecting set relations.
- Familiarity with the various ways of dealing with limited diversity.
- Ability to implement all of the preceding in R for both crisp and fuzzy sets.

4.2   Single Sufficient Conditions

In a sense, sufficiency and necessity are mirror images of each other. As explained in Chapter 3, a necessary condition X is a superset of outcome Y. With sufficiency, it is the other way round.

Let X be the condition 'living close to the training site' and Y the outcome 'arriving in time'. If empirically it turns out that, indeed, all players who are members of set X are also members of set Y, then X implies Y, or X is a subset of Y. This empirical pattern provides support for interpreting X as sufficient for Y. If we know that a player lives close to the training ground, we also know that they arrive in time for practice.

Just as in Section 3.2.2 on necessity, in the following section we also visualize patterns of sufficiency with the help of two-by-two tables, Euler diagrams, and XY plots.

4.2.1   How to Spot Sufficiency for Crisp and Fuzzy Sets

The Euler diagram in Figure 4.1 displays a situation in which condition X is a perfect subset of outcome Y ($X \rightarrow Y$). All players living close to the training ground, depicted by the circle for X, are also players that arrive in time for practice, the larger circle of Y. At the same time, as Figure 4.1 shows, there are also cases of $\sim X$ contained in circle Y. These are all the other players who, despite not living close by ($\sim X$), still arrive in time (Y). One can nicely see that kids who do not live close by yet arrive in time [$\sim X$, Y] do not provide evidence against the claim that living close by is sufficient for arriving in time ($X \rightarrow Y$).

The two-by-two table shown in Table 4.1 represents the same empirical situation as Figure 4.1. Among players who live close by ($X = 1$), everyone arrives in time ($Y = 1$). There are no cases that are members of X, but are not

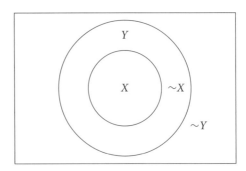

Figure 4.1 Euler diagram of a sufficiency relation

Table 4.1 Two-by-two table for sufficiency

Outcome Y	**1**	n.d.r.	CASES
	0	n.d.r.	NO CASES
		0	**1**
		Condition X	

Note: n.d.r. = not directly relevant.

Table 4.2 Hypothetical fuzzy-set data matrix for sufficiency

Cases	X	Y
Amanda	0.6	0.7
Bob	0.6	0.6
Carl	0.2	0.9
Cecilia	0.1	0.3
Ana	0.9	1
Alex	0.7	0.8
Kim	0.3	0.4
...	...	...

members of Y (i.e., $\sim Y$).[1] Table 4.1 also indicates that players not living close by ($X = 0$) are not directly relevant (n.d.r.) for the claim $X \to Y$. Such cases of $\sim X$ will play a role in Section 6.3, though, when we assess the causal properties of the sufficiency claim $X \to Y$.

So far, we have looked at patterns of sufficiency based on crisp sets. Let us now transfer what we have learned to fuzzy sets. The same holds here: if X is a subset of Y, we have empirical support for claiming that X is sufficient for Y. A subset relation is given when for each case i it holds that its membership in X is smaller than or equal to its membership in Y ($X_i \leq Y_i$). For illustration, Table 4.2 displays the fuzzy-set membership scores of some of our players in the sets of living close by (X) and arriving in time (Y). If we go line by line, we notice that the values in column X are smaller than or equal to the corresponding values in column Y. The set of players living close by (X) is a subset of the players that arrive in time (Y).

Just as for necessity, also for sufficiency XY plots are a powerful tool to visualize set relations between fuzzy sets. The XY plot shown in Figure 4.2 displays the empirical situation presented in Table 4.2. On the x-axis, each case's

[1] Note that this particular combination – $[X, \sim Y]$ – is therefore missing from Figure 4.1: the Euler diagram does not depict this area because there are no cases that fall into it.

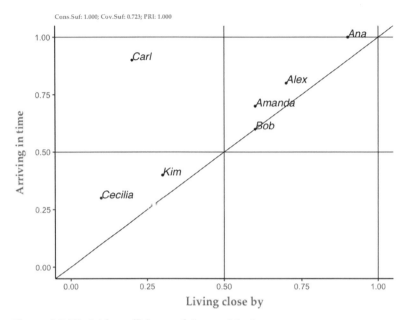

Figure 4.2 XY plot for sufficiency - fully consistent

membership in X, and on the y-axis, each case's membership in Y is plotted. In this example, all cases fall above or exactly on the main diagonal. Since the area above the diagonal is where $X_i \leq Y_i$, the empirical pattern in Figure 4.2 shows that X is a perfect subset of Y. No case contradicts this statement of sufficiency $X \rightarrow Y$.

4.2.2   Parameters of Fit for Sufficiency

In Section 3.2.3, we already explained that perfect subset relations are the exception rather than the norm in social science research. Often there are a few cases that buck the general trend. This can be because our 'theories' are too vague or our data too imprecise, or simply due to some idiosyncratic events. For instance, there might be a few who, despite living close by, tend to arrive late. This could be because for these kids we mis-measured their distance to the training site as we ignored the fact that they need to pass a railway crossing gate. Or it could be that these kids have just recently moved to the neighborhood and still need to figure out the shortest and fastest way to the pitch. Or maybe they occasionally come late because it was their mother's birthday, they had trombone lessons, or their shoe laces accidentally came undone.

For illustration, see the XY plot in Figure 4.3. It depicts the empirical situation of coach Susan's soccer team. On the x-axis, it displays each of the soccer team

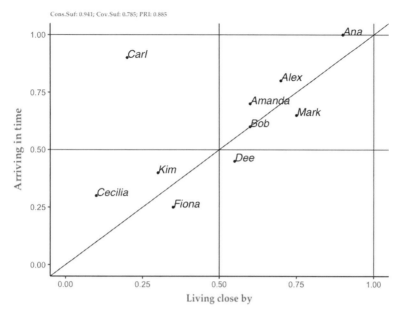

Cons.Suf: 0.941; Cov.Suf: 0.785; PRI: 0.885

Figure 4.3 XY plot for sufficiency - not fully consistent

player's membership in the set of 'players living close to the training ground' (X) and on the y-axis their membership in the set of 'players arriving in time' (Y). For most of the players, it holds that their membership in X is smaller than or equal to their membership in Y. X therefore can be considered a subset of, and potentially sufficient for, Y. However, there are a few cases that do not follow this general pattern and potentially contradict the statement of sufficiency. Mark, Dee, and Fiona are players whose membership in X exceeds that in Y. They therefore are located below the main diagonal. How are such deviations from perfect set relations handled in applied QCA?

Criterion 1: Consistency

The most prominent way of numerically expressing deviations from perfect subset relations is via the parameter of fit 'consistency', sometimes also called the inclusion score. We have already learned about consistency for necessary conditions in Section 3.2.3. Consistency sufficiency works in a similar way. In fact, its formula – shown in Equation 4.2 – is almost identical to the one for consistency necessity (see Equation 3.1). The numerator is the same. The only difference is that the denominator consists of the sum of all cases' membership scores in condition X rather than in outcome Y. Consistency can range between 0 and 1, and the higher the value, the more consistent the empirical pattern is with the statement of sufficiency. The more cases fall below the diagonal and the farther below the diagonal they are, the lower the consistency score becomes. The consistency score thus expresses how much the empirical evidence at hand is in line with the formal logical claim. The consistency formula in Equation 3.1 works for both crisp and fuzzy sets.

$$Cons_{suf} = \frac{\sum min(X_i, Y_i)}{\sum X_i} \qquad (4.2)$$

The empirical situation depicted in the XY plot in Figure 4.3 yields a consistency of 0.941 for the sufficiency statement $X \rightarrow Y$. While not fully consistent (a score of 1), 0.941 is usually considered as quite a high level. In the literature, a value of 0.8 or 0.75 has been established as a lower bound for consistency sufficiency (Ragin, 2008b; Schneider and Wagemann, 2012).

Before, however, jumping directly to the conclusion that X should be considered sufficient for Y because it passed the consistency threshold, we should further scrutinize three further aspects of the empirical pattern: (2) Are there deviant cases consistency in kind? And (3) is there a simultaneous subset relation? In addition, we want to (4) express the empirical importance of those subsets that have passed our litmus test of being considered sufficient conditions.

Criterion 2: Deviant Cases Consistency in Kind

Any case below the main diagonal in Figure 4.3 is a deviant case consistency. They come, however, in two distinct types: some cases deviate only in degree, while others also deviate in kind (Schneider and Rohlfing, 2013; see also Section 3.2.3 on this).

Take the three players below the diagonal in Figure 4.3. All three deviate to the same degree from a perfect subset relation. That is, each player's membership in X exceeds their membership in Y by the same margin (by 0.1 fuzzy-set membership). According to our formula for consistency sufficiency in Equation 4.2, each of the three cases contributes equally to the inconsistency of the sufficiency claim $X \rightarrow Y$. However, Dee in Figure 4.3 is stronger evidence against this sufficiency claim than either Mark or Fiona. Why?

Dee is a deviant case consistency in kind, whereas the other two are only deviant cases consistency in degree. Dee, in other words, contradicts our sufficiency claim more because she is one of the players who live close by ($X > 0.5$) and, at the same time, tends to *not* arrive in time ($Y < 0.5$). Fiona and Mark, in turn, do not have qualitatively different membership in X and Y. This means their membership scores in X and Y, respectively, are located on the same side of the 0.5 anchor. We therefore suggest always checking how many and which cases are behind a less-than-perfect consistency score. The more deviant cases consistency in kind there are, the less solid is the empirical ground for our sufficiency claim. Checking how many and which cases are deviant consistency in kind is therefore part of the standard protocol for assessing set relations.

Criterion 3: Simultaneous Subset Relations (PRI)

The second potential issue to be scrutinized is that of a so-called simultaneous subset relation. This issue can only occur with fuzzy sets. Crisp sets are not affected by this problem. As the name might suggest, simultaneous subset relations denote a situation in which one and the same condition X is a consistent enough subset both of outcome Y and its logical negation $\sim Y$ (Schneider and Wagemann, 2012, p. 237ff.). We therefore might be tempted to declare the same condition X as sufficient for both outcome Y and $\sim Y$ because it displays a high enough consistency score for both outcomes. This, clearly, would amount to a non-sensical claim. For illustration, Figures 4.4 and 4.5 display such a simultaneous subset relation. The condition 'living close by' is a subset of 'arriving in time' (Cons.Suf = 0.859), but also of 'not arriving in time' (Cons.Suf = 0.803).

Simultaneous subset relations can occur because, with fuzzy sets, one and the same case is allowed to have partial membership both in a set and its negation.

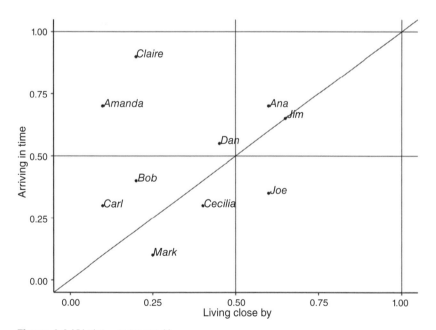

Figure 4.4 XY plot – outcome Y

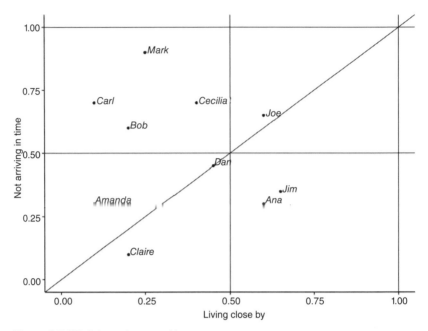

Figure 4.5 XY plot – outcome ~Y

For instance, Cecilia's membership in the set of players arriving in time (Y) is 0.3 (see Table 4.2). Her membership in the set of players *not* arriving in time (~Y) is therefore 0.7. Both scores are higher than Cecilia's membership in the condition X (0.1).[2]

If many cases show this feature similar to Cecilia's, then we have the problem of simultaneous subset relations. For illustration, let us look at a slightly modified version of our soccer team example in Figures 4.4 and 4.5. Compared to the previous version (Figure 4.3), now several players are living farther away from the training ground. This means most players have a much smaller membership in X, or, the set of X has become smaller. This is visible in the XY plot: cases tend to be located on the left-hand side, and there are only three cases with a membership in X higher than 0.5. Because X is so small and many cases cluster on the left-hand side, it comes as no surprise that most cases are also located above the main diagonal. This, in turn, means that because X is so small, it easily

---

[2] It is important to note, though, that despite partial membership in both Y and ~Y, a case can be above 0.5 in just *one* of the two sets and therefore qualitatively attributed to one set only. Cecilia is a case of ~Y because her partial membership in ~Y is above 0.5, whereas it is below 0.5 for Y. The only exception to this if we assign a membership score of exactly 0.5 to a case. Such cases cannot be qualitatively attributed to either a set or its negation.

passes the consistency test. For the empirical situation depicted in the XY plot in Figure 4.4, consistency is 0.859. We therefore might be tempted to endorse the sufficiency claim $X \rightarrow Y$.

This, in itself, is not the problem. But now have a look at the XY plot in Figure 4.5. On the x-axis, we again display each case's membership in X, but on the y-axis, we now show each case's membership in the negated outcome $\sim Y$. We see that again most cases fall above the diagonal and the relation $X \rightarrow \sim Y$ reaches a consistency of 0.803. We might therefore be tempted to endorse the sufficiency claim $X \rightarrow \sim Y$. However, we have already made the sufficiency claim $X \rightarrow Y$. Both statements cannot be true at the same time. Living close to the training ground (X) can be sufficient either for arriving in time (Y) or for not arriving in time ($\sim Y$), but not both. Claiming that it is sufficient for both is nonsensical. Such statements must be avoided. Either we declare X as sufficient for Y or $\sim Y$, or neither of the two outcomes.

Another way of graphically illustrating the issue of simultaneous subset relation is depicted in Figure 4.6. It shows the two outcomes Y and $\sim Y$. Because these are fuzzy sets, the intersection between the two is not empty. Different conditions (X_1 to X_4) can show different degrees of simultaneous subset relations with Y and $\sim Y$, respectively. X_1 is exclusively a subset of Y, whereas X_2 is exclusively a subset of $\sim Y$. For them, there is no problem of simultaneous subset relations. X_3 and X_4 are problematic, though. Both overlap to different degrees with both outcomes Y and $\sim Y$, indicating a simultaneous subset relation.

Which empirical strategies exist to first detect simultaneous subset relations and then to avoid making nonsensical statements of sufficiency? Charles Ragin has introduced the PRI parameter (proportional reduction in inconsistency) for this purpose. In essence, PRI is a numerical expression of the degree to which

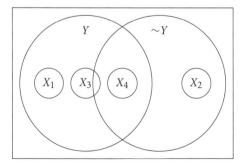

Figure 4.6 Simultaneous subset relations – Euler diagram

a given condition X is a subset of only outcome Y rather than also of outcome $\sim Y$. Equation 4.3 gives us the formula for calculating PRI.[3]

$$PRI = \frac{\sum min(X_i, Y_i) - \sum min(X_i, Y_{i,} \sim Y)}{\sum min(X_i) - \sum min(X_i, Y_{i,} \sim Y)} \tag{4.3}$$

The standard protocol for identifying a sufficient condition is to first check if the relation reaches a high enough level of consistency. Among those that do, one then checks if also PRI is high enough. Applied to our latest soccer team example, we have already found that X reaches a high enough consistency level both for Y (0.859) and for $\sim Y$ (0.803). But if we look at PRI, we see a decisive difference: for outcome Y, condition X has a PRI of 0.583 whereas for outcome $\sim Y$ it is only 0.417. Based on this information, we have further supporting evidence for the sufficiency claim $X \to Y$ and *against* the claim $X \to \sim Y$.

PRI is symmetric. This means the following holds: $PRI_Y = 1 - PRI_{\sim Y}$. From this it follows that the closer PRI is to 0.5, the less one should be inclined to consider the given set as sufficient for a given outcome. Conditions with a PRI value lower than 0.5 should not be deemed sufficient. Note also that with a crisp-set outcome, the PRI value is always identical to the consistency score. This is because with crisp sets the second sum in both the numerator and denominator in the PRI formula is always 0.

Note that apart from a higher PRI, there is another, related argument in support of $X \to Y$ over $X \to \sim Y$. As the XY plots 4.4 and 4.5 show, there is just one deviant case consistency in kind for $X \to Y$ (Joe), but two (Ana and Jim) for $X \to \sim Y$.[4]

Criterion 4: Empirical Relevance

After a subset relation has passed the hurdles of consistency, not too many deviant cases consistency in kind, and high-enough PRI, we want to gauge how empirically important the sufficient condition is. How much of the outcome can be explained with a given sufficient condition? In QCA language, this is called coverage. When coach Susan finds that there are various reasons why her players arrive in time, she might be interested in knowing which of them

---

[3] The siblings for necessity are claims on trivial necessary conditions. In Section 3.2.3, we have introduced the parameters of coverage and, in particular, Relevance of Necessity (RoN), for tackling this problem.

[4] As a matter of fact, with simultaneous subset relations, it holds that there *must* be a deviant case consistency in kind (DCK) for at least one of the subset patterns. Any typical case for one of the pattern will become a DCK case for the other pattern. From this it follows that at least one of the two subset patterns must be less than perfectly consistent (Schneider and Wagemann, 2012, p. 237ff). In applied QCA, both subset relations tend to be less than perfectly consistent and contain deviant cases consistency in kind.

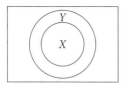

Figure 4.7 High coverage – Euler diagram

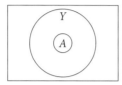

Figure 4.8 Low coverage – Euler diagram

explains most of punctual players. This information might enable Susan to choose the most effective measures to increase the number of players who arrive in time.

An intuitive way of graphically representing the notion of coverage is via an Euler diagram. Figures 4.7 and 4.8 display two perfectly consistent subset relations. Let X be the set of players living close by, A the set of players arriving by bike, and Y the outcome set of players arriving in time. Both conditions X and A are fully consistent as sufficient conditions for outcome Y. When comparing the two, which one is empirically more important for explaining Y? Or, which one covers more of Y? Clearly, living close by (X) shows the higher coverage. Among those who arrive in time (Y), fewer do so because they come by bike (A) than because they live close by (X).

The same basic notion of coverage applies to fuzzy sets. Here, it is the amount of overlap in fuzzy set membership scores in X and Y vis-à-vis the size of membership scores in Y. Graphically, in an XY plot coverage expresses itself by the closeness of cases to the diagonal. The more the cases are located far above the diagonal, the more they reduce the coverage of the condition. The XY plots for condition 'living close by' in Figure 4.9 illustrates a higher coverage (Cov.Suf: 0.616) than that for condition 'coming by bike' in Figure 4.10 (Cov.Suf: 0.303).

The coverage values are calculated using the formula displayed in Equation 4.4. Like all other formulas introduced before, it can be applied to both crisp and fuzzy sets.

$$Cov_{suf} = \frac{\sum min(X_i, Y_i)}{\sum Y_i} \tag{4.4}$$

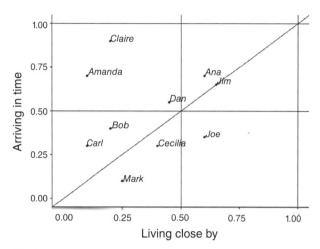

Figure 4.9 XY plot – high coverage

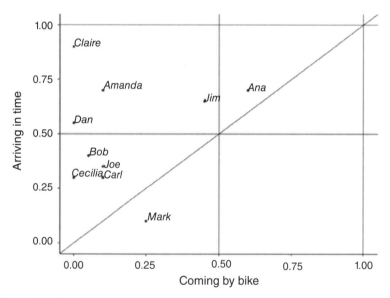

Figure 4.10 XY plot – low coverage

Just as for consistency, not all cases above the diagonal are of equal importance for coverage, even if the coverage sufficiency formula treats them as such.
From a research-practical point of view, we are interested in those players whose
punctuality we have been unable to explain. This is why, again, we advise to
complement the parameters of fit with a case perspective. Cases in the area

$X < 0.5$ and $Y > 0.5$ – such as Claire, Amanda, Dan, and Jim in Figure 4.10 – are more problematic for coverage than other cases above the diagonal (for example, Ana, Bob, or Joe). They are good examples of players who arrive in time but are not good examples of the sufficient condition (arriving by bike) that is supposed to explain their punctuality. They are called deviant cases coverage (see Schneider and Rohlfing, 2013, and Section 6.3). The more deviant cases coverage there are, the more the coverage, or explanatory power of the sufficient condition, is diminished. This is why we recommend to always reveal the number and names of deviant cases coverage.

So far, we have calculated coverage for single sufficient conditions for arriving in time (Y). Coach Susan has identified three different sufficient terms, though, and we wrote the solution as follows:

$$X + A + B * C \to Y. \tag{4.5}$$

How can we calculate the coverage for each sufficient term and how for the entire solution formula? In order to understand the answer to these questions, we can have a look at the Euler diagram in Figure 4.11. It graphically displays the hypothetical empirical situation of coach Susan. Each sufficient condition is represented by a circle within the circle for outcome Y. The size of the circle represents the empirical size of each set. With multiple sufficient conditions, there are also multiple coverage scores for the different elements of the solution formula.

First, we can calculate the so-called raw coverage for each of the sufficient conditions. We see that X (living close by) has higher coverage than A (coming by bike), which, in turn, has higher coverage than $B * C$ (females from families with punctuality as a norm). In order to obtain the coverage score for each condition, we simply use the coverage formula in Equation 4.4, substituting X with each case's membership in the sufficient condition of interest. For the

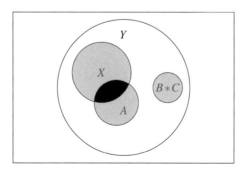

Figure 4.11 Multiple sufficient conditions – Euler diagram

sake of argument, let us say that raw coverage scores are $X = 0.3$, $A = 0.2$, and $B * C = 0.1$.

Second, we can calculate the coverage of the entire solution formula. Graphically speaking, this so-called solution coverage is the outer area of all three conditions in relation to the size of the outcome Y and expresses the overall explanatory power of our QCA solution. To calculate solution coverage, we also simply use Equation 4.4. This time, we need to replace X with each case's membership in the entire solution.[5] For the sake of argument, let us say that the solution coverage is 0.5, that is, we cover, or explain, half of the outcome set Y.

Note that the solution coverage (0.5) is less than the sum of the raw coverage for the three conditions $(0.3 + 0.2 + 0.1 - 0.6)$. Why is this the case? The reason is that separate sufficient conditions can empirically overlap. Remember from Section 2.4.1 that the logical OR (+) is a non-exclusive OR. In Figure 4.11, this is visualized by the overlap between conditions X and A in black ink. Some punctual kids live close by *and* they ride their bike to the training pitch. This means that such cases are explained by more than one sufficient condition.

Because of this overlap, we need to calculate a third form of coverage. It is called unique coverage and expresses the amount of coverage attributable to only one condition. Graphically speaking, the unique coverage of condition X in Figure 4.11 is the size of that area of X where it is *not* A. For the sake of argument, let the unique coverage of X be 0.23, lower than its raw coverage (0.3). Let the unique coverage of A be 0.13 (raw coverage was 0.2). For condition $B * C$, unique and raw coverage are identical (0.1) because it happens so that this condition does not empirically overlap with any of the other two.[6]

Based on the unique coverage scores, coach Susan concludes that 'living close by' (X) has the highest explanatory power because it displays the highest unique coverage.

We now have several parameters of fit for the evaluation of sufficiency relations at hand: consistency, PRI, and the different forms of coverage. We have also learned about different types of cases and how they matter differently for assessing the consistency and coverage of a sufficiency relation. The calculation of parameters of fit and the identification of types of cases would be quite

---

[5] For an explanation on how to calculate membership scores in complex Boolean expressions with logical OR and AND operators, see Section 2.4.1.

[6] Note that the sum of all unique coverage scores is smaller than the solution coverage. This is because the sum of unique coverage scores does not count the area of overlap between X and A, whereas the solution coverage does also include those multiple explained cases.

cumbersome if we needed to do it by hand. Luckily, there are dedicated R functions for this. We introduce them in the remainder of this and subsequent chapters.

> ### Box 4.3 Core Points – Assessing Sufficiency Patterns
>
> - There are different signs for a deviation from a perfect pattern of sufficiency.
> - Consistency expresses the amount of counter-evidence against a sufficiency statement.
> - PRI signals simultaneous subset relations (a condition being sufficient for both the outcome and its negation) and, thus, guards against untenable sufficiency claims.
> - Deviant Consistency in Kind (DCK) cases provide stronger evidence against a sufficiency claim then cases that deviate only in degree. The consistency measure should always be complemented by an assessment of DCK cases when evaluating sufficiency.
> - Sufficient conditions can vary in their empirical relevance, numerically expressed by the coverage scores.
> - Numerical parameters of fit should always be complemented by a focus on types of cases.

4.3 Truth Table Analysis: Identifying Multiple Sufficient Conditions

For didactic reasons, let us assume now that coach Susan has managed to gather data on some new players on three different possible conditions for arriving in time to the training session. How can she analyze these data to identify sufficient conditions? In this section, we explain the formal analysis of sufficiency. Key to this is the construction and analysis of a so-called truth table.

At the beginning of her investigation, coach Susan has some hunches, or even 'theories' as to what might be the reasons for punctuality (Y): living close by (X); arriving by bike rather than in their parent's car (A); and coming from a family where being punctual is taught as a virtue (C).[7] Susan gathers empirical information on all conditions and the outcome and then assigns membership scores of cases in all sets, that is, she calibrates these sets, following the principles and practices explained in Chapter 2. This yields the calibrated dataset shown in Table 4.3. We have 13 players. Each has a membership score in the three conditions and in the outcome.

---

[7] For didactic reasons, we drop 'being female' as a condition.

Table 4.3 Calibrated dataset: 13 football players, three conditions, and outcome

Player	X	A	C	Y
Amanda	0.6	0.8	0.7	0.7
Bob	0.3	0.7	0.7	0.8
Carl	0.8	1	0.3	0.9
Cecilia	0	0.6	0.2	0.3
Ana	0.9	0.1	0.2	1
Alex	0.7	0.2	0.4	0.8
Mark	0.75	0.7	0.6	0.65
Dee	0.55	0.3	0.3	0.45
Fiona	0.35	0.7	0.2	0.75
Kim	0.4	0.9	0.6	0.6
Joe	0.4	0.4	0.4	0.2
Jess	0.45	0.45	0.55	0.2
Frank	0.6	0.35	0.6	0.2

Notes: X = living close to the pitch; A = coming by bike; C = family with punctuality as virtue; Y = arriving in time.

In order to identify sets that pass the criterion of being a sufficient condition for outcome Y, we apply the so-called truth table algorithm (Ragin, 2008b). It represents data in the form of a truth table. Figure 4.12 graphically depicts the sequence of steps that lead from the calibrated data to a QCA solution formula via the construction and minimization of a truth table.

In a nutshell, the truth table algorithm works like this. The rows of the truth table consist of all logically possible combinations between the conditions specified by the researcher. In our example, there are three conditions, and each can be either present or absent.[8] The truth table therefore consists of $2^3 = 8$ rows. Based on the empirical information, each row is then either considered sufficient or not sufficient for the outcome. A third option in applied QCA is that a row is considered a logical remainder, a subject we discuss in detail in Section 4.4. Once all rows have been assigned an output value as being either sufficient, not sufficient, or a remainder, the information in the truth table is then summarized via the process of logical minimization, as indicated in step 5 in Figure 4.12. In the next section, we explain how a truth table is constructed. After that, in Section 4.3.2 we describe how logical minimization works.

---

[8] For fuzzy sets, the distinction between more present than absent is made at the 0.5 membership score.

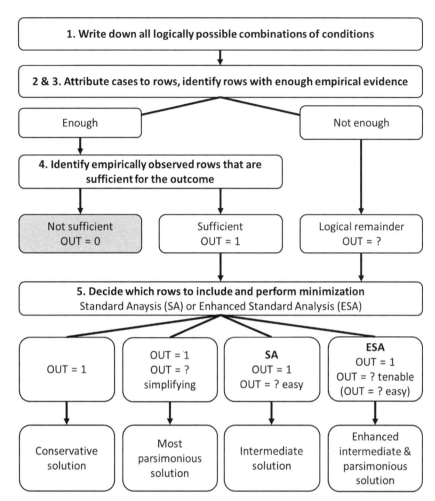

Figure 4.12 Truth table algorithm: constructing and logically minimizing a truth table

4.3.1   Constructing the Truth Table

We explain each step of the truth table algorithm in detail.

Step 1: Write down all logically possible combinations of the conditions
By writing down all logically possible combinations between conditions and their negations, we create the rows of a truth table. With three conditions X, A, C, each of which can take on two different values (1 or 0), there are $2^3 = 8$ logically possible combinations, aka truth table rows. A helpful way of thinking about truth table rows is to perceive them as ideal types located at the corners of a property space (Lazarsfeld, 1937). Each condition represents

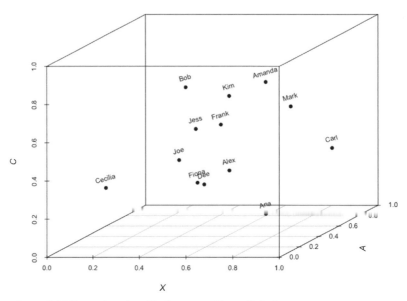

Figure 4.13 Property cube with three conditions: X, A, C

one dimension of this space. With fuzzy sets, each of these dimensions ranges from 0 to 1. In our example, we have three such dimensions, aka conditions. A three-dimensional space forms a cube with eight corners (see Figure 4.13). These corners correspond to our truth table rows and represent the ideal-typical scenarios for each of the logically possible combinations of our three conditions. For instance, row $X * A * C$ denotes the ideal typical case that lives close by, arrives by bike, and comes from a family with punctuality as a virtue. As we will see in step 2, cases populate this property space according to their set membership values in these conditions.

Step 2: For each case, determine the truth table row to which it belongs best
Each empirical case (Amanda, Bob, Carl, etc.) belongs best to one and only one of these 2^3 truth table rows/ideal types/corners of the property space. How do we figure out which row is the one that best describes a given case? In order to answer this question, note that each truth table row is, in essence, a Boolean statement. For instance, row 1, 1, 1 is the row in which all three conditions occur together in their presence, i.e., $X * A * C$. In our example, it is the ideal typical player who lives close by, always comes by bike, and whose family considers punctuality an important norm. Likewise, row 0, 1, 0 is where we have $\sim X * A * \sim C$ (players not living close by, coming by bike, not from a family that considers punctuality an important norm).

Now recall from Chapter 2 that the logical AND ($*$) operator requires that we take the minimum score across the sets to be combined. Also remember that the logical negation ($\sim$) requires that we subtract from 1 each case's score in the non-negated set.

Equipped with this, we can now calculate each case's score in all of the eight truth table rows. This is perhaps easiest for row $X * A * C$. We do not need to negate any of the conditions and simply take the minimum across each case's value displayed in Table 4.3. Take Amanda: her membership scores are $X = 0.6$, $A = 0.8$, and $C = 0.7$. The minimum across those values is 0.6. Hence, Amanda's membership in row 1, 1, 1 is 0.6. Bob's membership in row 1,1,1 is 0.3; that of Carl 0.3, and so on. Each of our 13 cases has one membership score in row 1,1,1 that ranges from 0 to 1. The same holds true for all the other truth table rows: each case has one membership score in each row. For demonstration, let us calculate Amanda's score in row 0,1,0, aka $\sim X * A * \sim C$. Since Amanda scores $\sim X = 0.4$ and $A = 0.6$ and $\sim C = 0.3$ and the minimum across these three values is 0.3, we conclude that Amanda's membership in row 0,1,0 is 0.3. We can do the same calculations for Bob, Carl, and all the others for each of the eight truth table rows.

Table 4.4 contains precisely this information: each case's membership in each truth table row. We see that each case has partial membership in each row. Then how can we identify which row a given case best belongs to, as required by step 2 of the truth table algorithm? For this, remember the crucial role of the 0.5 qualitative anchor. As explained in Chapter 2, it establishes the qualitative difference between cases that are more members of a set from those that are more non-members of a set. It turns out that each case can only have a

Table 4.4 Thirteen soccer players, membership in all truth table rows

				Truth table row							
		Conditions		1 XAC	2 $XA\sim C$	3 $X\sim AC$	4 $\sim XAC$	5 $X\sim A\sim C$	6 $\sim XA\sim C$	7 $\sim X\sim AC$	8 $\sim X\sim A\sim C$
Player	X	A	C	111	110	101	011	100	010	001	000
Amanda	0.6	0.8	0.7	**0.6**	0.3	0.2	0.4	0.2	0.3	0.2	0.2
Bob	0.3	0.7	0.7	0.3	0.3	0.3	**0.7**	0.3	0.3	0.3	0.3
Carl	0.8	1	0.3	0.3	**0.7**	0	0.2	0	0.2	0	0
Cecilia	0	0.6	0.2	0	0	0	0.2	0	**0.6**	0.2	0.4
Ana	0.9	0.1	0.2	0.1	0.1	0.2	0.1	**0.8**	0.1	0.1	0.1
Alex	0.7	0.2	0.4	0.2	0.2	0.4	0.2	**0.6**	0.2	0.3	0.3
Mark	0.75	0.7	0.6	**0.6**	0.4	0.3	0.25	0.3	0.25	0.25	0.25
Dee	0.55	0.3	0.3	0.3	0.3	0.3	0.3	**0.55**	0.3	0.3	0.45
Fiona	0.35	0.7	0.2	0.2	0.35	0.2	0.2	0.3	**0.65**	0.2	0.3
Kim	0.4	0.9	0.6	0.4	0.4	0.1	**0.6**	0.1	0.4	0.1	0.1
Joe	0.4	0.4	0.4	0.2	0.4	0.4	0.4	0.4	0.4	0.4	**0.6**
Jess	0.45	0.45	0.55	0.2	0.45	0.45	0.45	0.45	0.45	**0.55**	0.45
Frank	0.6	0.35	0.6	0.2	0.35	**0.6**	0.35	0.4	0.35	0.4	0.4
Number of cases in truth table row:				2	1	1	2	3	2	1	1

membership above 0.5 in *one*, and only one, truth table row. If one reads each line in Table 4.4, one can see that all the membership values of a single case in each truth table row are below 0.5 except in one, for which it is above 0.5. For convenience, we highlight the membership scores of higher than 0.5 in bold font. For Amanda, for instance, it is the value 0.6 in row 1,1,1; for Bob, it is 0.7 in row 0,1,1; for Carl, it is 0.7 in row 1,1,0; and so on.

A note of caution is needed here. If we assign a case a membership score of exactly 0.5 in one of the conditions, then it will not reach a membership of higher than 0.5 in any of the truth table rows. Instead, it will have exactly 0.5 membership in at least two rows. This makes sense. By assigning a 0.5 score in a condition, one essentially says, 'I cannot decide whether this case is an instance of the set or of its negation'. This ambiguity with regard to this case then travels over to the truth table, where we cannot determine to which row that case best belongs. We therefore advise thinking twice before assigning the 0.5 membership score. These cases are not dropped from the analysis as it is sometimes believed. They continue to be part of each and every calculation of parameters of fit for each truth table row and the solution formula. However, they increase the ambiguity of the analysis. In general, it holds that the closer a case's membership is to the 0.5 anchor, the more ambiguous is its conceptual status vis-à-vis the set in question. This, in turn, increases the ambiguity of statements made about those sets.

In sum, we attribute each case to the truth table row to which it best belongs by determining in which of the 2^k logically possible truth table rows it holds a membership higher than 0.5.

Step 3: For each truth table row, determine if it contains enough empirical evidence

In a truth table, the main units of interest are the truth table rows and whether or not they are sufficient for the outcome of interest. This means that we shift our attention from cases to truth table rows. This is why Table 4.5 is a more convenient depiction than Table 4.4. Its rows represent all logically possible combinations plus the names of cases in each of these truth table rows, information we obtained from Table 4.4 (last row).

Let us look at each row in Table 4.5 and ask: which rows contain enough empirical evidence? For the time being, let us translate 'enough empirical evidence' as 'at least one case must hold a membership of higher than 0.5 in it'. In other words, there must be at least one case that represents this truth table row in empirical terms. We find that all eight truth table rows contain at least one case. Some contain more than one, e.g., row 1,1,1 contains two cases (Amanda and Mark) or row 1,0,0 even three (Alex, Ana, and Dee). The frequency of cases above which a truth table row is considered to have enough empirical evidence is also called frequency cutoff.

Table 4.5 Thirteen soccer players,
sorted into truth table rows

Row	X	A	C	Cases
1	1	1	1	Amanda, Mark
2	1	1	0	Carl
3	1	0	1	Frank
4	0	1	1	Bob, Kim
5	1	0	0	Ana, Alex, Dee
6	0	1	0	Cecilia, Fiona
7	0	0	1	Jess
8	0	0	0	Joe

The fact that in this example all truth table rows are populated by at least one case is rather rare in applied QCA. Later on, we will encounter more realistic scenarios in which some (and often several) truth table rows are left without enough empirical evidence. These so-called logical remainder rows present a challenge in applied QCA and deserve a separate discussion in Section 4.4.

Step 4: For the truth table rows that contain enough empirical evidence, determine whether they are sufficient for the outcome
Now that we know that each truth table row contains enough empirical information, we need to answer the question: Which of these rows are sufficient for the outcome and which ones are not? In Section 4.2, we have learned that this question can be translated as: Which row is a subset of the outcome? In some cases, the answer to this question is straightforward. For example, in the case of crisp sets, when all cases that are members of the row are also members of the outcome, the row is clearly a subset of the outcome. However, in empirical practice, inconsistencies are likely to happen as cases might depart from a perfect sufficiency pattern. These rows are called contradictory truth table rows as, in essence, the same combination of conditions leads both to the occurrence and the non-occurrence of the outcome in different cases.

Researchers can adopt different strategies for dealing with contradictory rows, before or during the analytic moment. Before the analytic moment, researchers can attempt to resolve these contradictions by going back to their research design and changing the case selection or calibration, adding conditions, and/or re-conceptualizing the outcome.[9] Solving contradictions before the analytic moment illustrates the iterative nature of QCA involving a back-and-forth dialogue between theory and evidence (Ragin, 1987; Schneider and Wagemann, 2012). Note that making these research design changes should

---

[9] For a more extensive treatment of these strategies, see Schneider and Wagemann (2012, chapter 5.1).

Table 4.6 Truth table: 13 soccer players

Row	X	A	C	Cases	OUT
1	1	1	1	Amanda, Mark	1
2	1	1	0	Carl	1
3	1	0	1	Frank	0
4	0	1	1	Bob, Kim	1
5	1	0	0	Ana, Alex, Dee	1
6	0	1	0	Cecilia, Fiona	0
7	0	0	1	Jess	0
8	0	0	0	Joe	0

always be transparent and theoretically guided. In applied QCA, more often than not, researchers will still end up with some contradictions in their truth table due to the 'noisy' nature of social science data. Hence, during the analytic moment, researchers can resort to parameters of fit and check for deviant cases consistency in kind when making the decision if a truth table row is to be considered sufficient or not.

Going back to our example, for each of the eight rows, we need to calculate the parameters of fit (consistency and PRI) and check for deviant cases consistency in kind. If a row performs well in these tests, we consider it a sufficient condition for the outcome. Such rows obtain the value of 1 in column 'OUT' in our truth table in Table 4.6. Truth table rows that fail our sufficiency test obtain the value of 0 in column 'OUT'. Think of the truth table column 'OUT' as containing the answer to the question: 'Is the row sufficient for the outcome?' Value 1 means 'yes', and value 0 means 'no'.

We know the membership score of each case in outcome Y (arrives in time for practice) from Table 4.3, and each case's membership in each truth table row is reported in Table 4.4. To illustrate, let us investigate the status of truth table row 5 (1,0,0) as a sufficient condition for outcome Y. For this, we produce an XY plot with row 5 on the x-axis and the outcome on the y-axis. As we see in Figure 4.14, most cases are above the main diagonal.[10] The consistency score is at an acceptable level (0.830), the PRI value is fine (0.643), and out of the three 'typical' cases for this row (Alex, Ana, and Dee), only one is a deviant case consistency in kind (Dee). The consistency level above which rows are considered sufficient is also called raw consistency threshold. We therefore have reason to consider this row as sufficient for Y, and therefore assign it the value 1 in column 'OUT' of our truth table. We proceed along similar lines with all the

[10] This figure is produced with the following command: `pimplot(data = SF5, outcome = "Y", results = sol_y, ttrows = "5")`.

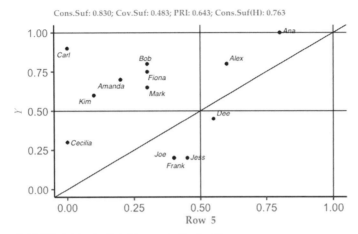

Figure 4.14 XY plot for truth table row 5 (X~A~C)

other seven truth table rows. Some will pass the sufficiency test, others will not. Once done with all rows, we have managed to create a truth table: each logically possible combination between our three conditions (X, A, C) is assigned a value in the *OUT* column as either being sufficient for Y (OUT $= 1$) or not (OUT $= 0$). As the truth table in Table 4.6 shows, four rows are considered sufficient for the outcome (rows 1, 2, 4, and 5), whereas the other rows are not sufficient for the outcome.

Box 4.4 Core Points – Constructing Truth Tables

- Any set data – crisp, fuzzy, multi-value – can be represented in a truth table.
- Each truth table row represents one of the logically possible AND combinations of conditions. In a QCA with k conditions, there are 2^k possible combinations of conditions.
- The 0.5 qualitative anchor used in calibration is crucial for assigning each case to one truth table row, that is, to a particular combination of conditions.
- Each case belongs best to one truth table row only.
- Each truth table row can contain one, multiple, or no empirical cases.
- Each truth table row is a statement of sufficiency. A row can either be sufficient for the outcome (output value $= 1$), not be sufficient for the outcome (output value $= 0$), or be a logical remainder (output value $= ?$).
- The output value of truth table rows that contain enough empirical evidence (i.e., that are not logical remainders) is determined using the protocol for identifying sufficiency patterns as explained in Section 4.2.2.
- During the analysis of truth tables, the unit of interest is the logically possible combinations of conditions, not the empirical cases.

Using R for Constructing a Truth Table

The process of representing your data in a truth table sounds rather cumbersome: write down all combinations, attribute cases to rows, and then figure out which rows are sufficient. Luckily, software is our friend and performs all these steps within less than a second. For this, we make use of the function truthTable() in package QCA. We need to specify the name of our data, the outcome, and the conditions. We also need to tell the software which levels of raw consistency (here: incl.cut = 0.8) and PRI (here: pri.cut = 0.51) are fine for us in order to deem a row sufficient for the outcome and what is the lowest number of cases in a row before it is classified as a logical remainder (here: n.cut = 1). We can make the table look nicer and be more informative if we sort it from high to low consistency (sort.by), and print the names of cases with membership above 0.5 in a row (show.cases). To show only the DCK cases in each row, one can specify dcc=TRUE (not done here due to space considerations).

C 4.1

```
# Construct truth table:

TT_y <- truthTable(data = SF5,
                   outcome="Y",
                   conditions = c("X","A","C"),
                   incl.cut = 0.8,
                   pri.cut = 0.51,
                   n.cut = 1,
                   sort.by = "incl",
                   show.cases = TRUE)
TT_y
```

The output printed on the screen shows the eight truth table rows, whether they are deemed sufficient for the outcome ('OUT'), how many cases hold a membership of higher than 0.5 in each row ('n'), the consistency ('incl') and PRI score, and the names of the cases with scores above 0.5. Note that this output can also be saved as a LaTeX, HTML, or text file using function stargazerTT() in package SetMethods.[11]

O 4.1

```
OUT: output value
  n: number of cases in configuration
incl: sufficiency inclusion score
 PRI: proportional reduction in inconsistency
```

---

[11] For example, to save as a text file: stargazerTT(truthtable = TT_y, show.cases = TRUE, type = "text", out = "myTT.txt"). To save as CSV file, type: write.csv(TT_y$tt, "myTT.csv")

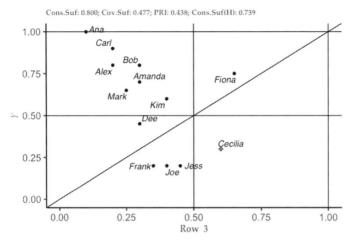

Figure 4.15 XY plot for truth table row 3 (∼XA∼C)

	X	A	C	OUT	n	incl	PRI	cases
4	0	1	1	1	2	0.862	0.625	Bob , Kim
7	1	1	0	1	1	0.859	0.613	Carl
8	1	1	1	1	2	0.857	0.613	Amanda , Mark
5	1	0	0	1	3	0.830	0.643	Ana , Alex , Dee
3	0	1	0	0	2	0.800	0.438	Cecilia , Fiona
2	0	0	1	0	1	0.773	0.286	Jess
6	1	0	1	0	1	0.754	0.370	Frank
1	0	0	0	0	1	0.753	0.269	Joe

We have chosen a consistency threshold of 0.8. Row 3 is exactly on this threshold. Its PRI value is suspiciously low and below our threshold of 0.51. Row 3 is therefore assigned the value $OUT = 0$. To check if it is the right decision not to consider it as sufficient for outcome Y, let us create a plot of row 3 to see where the only two cases with membership above 0.5 (Cecilia and Fiona) are located.[12] The XY plot in Figure 4.15 shows that Fiona confirms and Cecilia contradicts the statement of sufficiency. We therefore stick to our decision to assign this row the value 0 in column 'OUT'.

We now have a complete truth table. Each row is classified as either sufficient or not sufficient for the outcome. The next step consists in summarizing the information contained in the truth table via the process of logical minimization.

---

[12] To create a plot of row 3, one can use the command `pimplot(data = SF5, outcome = "Y", results = sol_y, all_labels = TRUE, ttrows = "3", jitter = TRUE, fontsize = 6)`. See C 4.3 for more details on using the pimplot function. Option `dcc = TRUE` of the truthTable function also shows (only) the contradictory cases in each row.

4.3.2 Logical Minimization

In essence, the truth table represents the answer to our question: Which conditions are sufficient for the outcome? The answer is: all truth table rows with value 1 in column 'OUT'. We can write this answer in Boolean terms.

$$\sim XAC + XAC + XA\sim C + X\sim A\sim C \to Y. \tag{4.6}$$

There are four different so-called primitive expressions (the truth table rows with OUT = 1). Each consists of a conjunction of conditions. In other words, we have equifinality and conjunctural causation, two trademark features of causal complexity typical in QCA. Note, though, that the Boolean formula in Formula 4.6 is overly complicated. It contains elements that are not needed for our attempt to explain the occurrence of outcome Y. In other words, there are redundancies in Equation 4.6. We now explain how to get rid of them via the process of logical minimization. This process has two steps: First, eliminate redundant conjuncts from all primitive expressions. This yields the so-called prime implicants. Second, eliminate logically redundant prime implicants.

Identify Prime Implicants

Consider the two primitive expressions XAC and $XA\sim C$. Both lead to Y, and they are identical to each other except for the value of one conjunct. In one, C is present, and in the other $\sim C$ is present. This means that as long as cases are members of XA, their membership in condition C is irrelevant for explaining the outcome. We can therefore logically minimize $XAC + XA\sim C \to Y$ to $XA \to Y$. Along similar lines, we can minimize $XA\sim C + X\sim A\sim C \to Y$ to $X\sim C \to Y$. Following the same logic, we can also summarize the first and second primitive expression as $AC \to Y$. Since no further pairwise matching of conjunctions can be done, we have identified all prime implicants.

$$XA + X\sim C + AC \to Y \tag{4.7}$$

This sufficiency statement for outcome Y is considerably simpler. There are now only three sufficient terms and each consists of only two, rather than three, conjuncts. Together, the three prime implicants cover all four primitive expressions. As long as this is maintained and as long as no truth table row with $OUT = 0$ is covered by any prime implicant, a solution formula is correct, that is, it maintains the truth value of the truth table.

However, the solution formula 4.7 is not the shortest way of summarizing the empirical information contained in our truth table. As we will see in a moment, one of the three prime implicants is not needed for covering all primitive expressions, that is, it is logically redundant.

Identifying Logically Redundant Prime Implicants

The tool for identifying logically redundant prime implicants is a so-called prime implicant chart. The columns of this chart depict all primitive expressions, and the rows all prime implicants. In order for a QCA solution to be correct, each primitive expression must be covered by at least one prime implicant. If a prime implicant can be dropped and still all primitive expressions are covered by the remaining prime implicants, then that prime implicant is logically redundant.

Table 4.7 depicts the prime implicant chart for our example. Let us start with AC, the prime implicant at the bottom of the table. Could we drop it from the solution formula? No, because then primitive expression $\sim XAC$ would no longer be covered. Similarly, we cannot drop prime implicant $X\sim C$ because it would leave primitive expression XAC uncovered. Now consider dropping prime implicant XA. Can we drop it? Yes. Both of the primitive expressions covered by XA are already covered by $X\sim C + AC$. Prime implicant XA is therefore logically redundant and can be dropped from the solution formula. We now have the most succinct summary of the reasons why some of Susan's soccer kids arrive in time for practice.

$$X\sim C + AC \rightarrow Y. \tag{4.8}$$

It is sufficient to live close by and not be from a family with punctuality as a norm ($X\sim C$) or to arrive by bike and be from a family with punctuality as a norm (AC). This is the most succinct summary of the information contained in our data in Table 4.3 and summarized in our truth table (Table 4.6).

Table 4.7 Prime implicant chart

	$\sim XAC$	XAC	$XA\sim C$	$X\sim A\sim C$
XA	–	X	X	–
$X\sim C$	–	–	X	X
AC	X	X	–	–

Box 4.5 Core Points – Logical Minimization of Truth Tables

- Step I: One-Difference Rule
  - When two primitive expressions differ in only one conjunct, that conjunct is considered redundant and dropped, simplifying the two expressions into one.
- Step II: Logically Redundant Prime Implicants
  - When a prime implicant can be dropped and still all primitive expressions are covered, then that prime implicant is redundant and can be dropped.

Using R for Logical Minimization

The process of logical minimization appears complicated. Luckily, again, we can make use of the software and a simple line of command. Function `minimize()` from package QCA is, together with the `truthTable()` function, one of the core commands for performing QCA in R. In order to obtain the solution formula, we just need to specify our truth table object as the object to be logically minimized (`input = TT_y`; see code C 4.1). Further, we ask the software to print the parameters of fit and case names for each sufficient term (`details = TRUE`). The resulting output can be saved as a LaTeX, HTML, or text file using function `stargazerSol()` in package `SetMethods`.[13]

C 4.2

```
# Logically minimize a truth table:

sol_y <- minimize(input = TT_y,
                  details = TRUE)
sol_y
```

O 4.2

```
M1: X*~C + A*C => Y
```

		inclS	PRI	covS	covU	cases
1	X*~C	0.867	0.732	0.649	0.238	Ana, Alex, Dee; Carl
2	A*C	0.882	0.733	0.596	0.185	Bob, Kim; Amanda, Mark
	M1	0.894	0.812	0.834		

---

[13] For example, to save as LaTeX: `stargazerSol(results = sol_y, outcome = "Y", type = "latex", out = "mysol.tex")`.

The software arrives at the same solution formula as we did with our manual minimization. In addition, for each of the two sufficient terms, we obtain the consistency, PRI, and coverage scores, plus the names of cases that hold a membership above 0.5 in the specific sufficient term. Furthermore, the output also reports those parameters of fit for the entire solution formula. We learn that explanation $X{\sim}C$ ('lives close by and is not from a family with punctuality as a norm')[14] fits four cases (Ana, Alex, Dee, and Carl) and that compared to the other explanation (AC, 'arriving by bike and being from a punctual family') it covers, or explains, slightly more of the outcome. It displays both a higher raw coverage ('covS') and unique coverage ('covU'). Note that the solution coverage (0.834) is less than perfect, suggesting that our solution formula does not cover all the fuzzy-set membership scores in the outcome. We probably do not explain all the cases that arrive in time.

Using R for Visualizing QCA Solution Formulas

QCA is a case-oriented method. Among many things, this means that the solution formula needs to be linked back to cases. Which cases are explained by which sufficient term? Which cases remain unexplained? And which cases contradict our sufficiency claims? The tabular presentation of the solution just shown is good for stating the Boolean expression and the accompanying parameters of fit. It is not appropriate for linking back to cases. There are several graphical tools to bring cases more to the fore and to highlight different additional aspects of the QCA solution.

When using fuzzy sets, *XY plots* are a powerful tool to display cases in relation to the solution. For this, we make use of the `pimplot()` function. It creates XY plots for each sufficient term and the entire solution formula. The function requires as arguments the data with the fuzzy-set membership scores of cases (`data = SF5`), the name of the outcome (`outcome = "Y"`), and the solution object that we have created with function `minimize()`. Argument `all_labels = TRUE` prints the labels of all cases in all plots, and `jitter = TRUE` prevents overlap of those labels.[15]

---

[14] Cases separated by a comma stem from the same truth table row, and those separated by a semicolon from different truth table rows.

[15] Note that the `pimplot()` function has multiple other functionalities: it can plot necessary disjunctions of SUIN conditions, individual truth table rows, two-by-two tables for crisp sets, etc. For different ways in which to use the `pimplot()` function, see the online appendix at https://doi.org/10.7910/DVN/S9QPM5.

C 4.3

```
# Produce XY plots of QCA solution:

pimplot(data = SF5,
        outcome = "Y",
        results = sol_y,
        all_labels = TRUE,
        jitter = TRUE,
        fontsize = 6)
```

This line of command creates the XY plots shown in Figures 4.16–4.18. For term *AC*, we see that it covers Amanda, Bob, Mark, and Kim. We call them typical cases for *AC*. For sufficient term *X~C*, Alex, Ana, and Carl are typical cases. Dee is also a member of the sufficient term *X~C*. She, however, is a deviant case consistency in kind, contradicting the sufficiency statement because she is a member of the sufficient term but not of the outcome. The XY plot for the solution formula (Figure 4.18) reveals which cases are left unexplained. These cases are in the upper-left quadrant and are called deviant cases coverage. Fiona is such an unexplained case of a punctual player. She arrives in time for reasons not captured by any of our two sufficient terms. In Section 6.3, when discussing set-theoretic multi-method research (SMMR), we will introduce an extended and more sophisticated, non-graphical way of listing these and more types of cases.

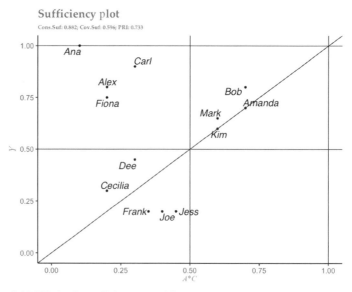

Figure 4.16 XY plot for sufficient term *AC*

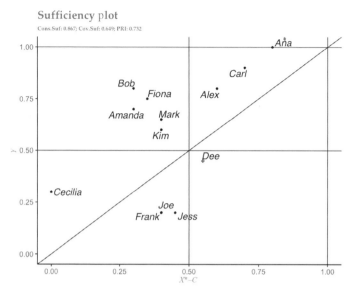

Figure 4.17 XY plot for sufficient term $X{\sim}C$

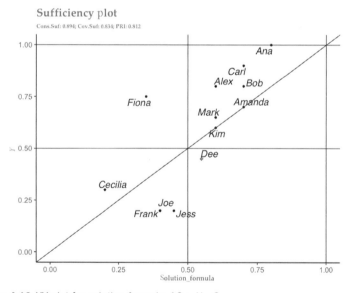

Figure 4.18 XY plot for solution formula $AC + X{\sim}C$

There are other options for graphically displaying QCA results. *Radar charts* depict the sufficient conjunctions via the size and shape of an area. This tool is particularly useful when the gist of the analysis is to detect different profiles. In our case, coach Susan might want to emphasize the profile of punctual players.

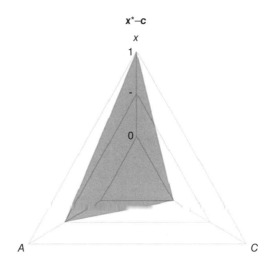

Figure 4.19 Radar chart *X*~*C*

With function `QCAradar()` such graphs can be produced. We only need to specify our QCA solution (`results = sol_y`) and the outcome (`outcome = "Y"`). From this we obtain radar charts, such as the one displayed in Figure 4.19. Each condition and its value in the sufficient term (1, 0, or logically redundant) is depicted on one of the graph's dimensions.

C 4.4

```
# Produce radar chart:

QCAradar(results = sol_y,
         outcome = "Y",
         fit = FALSE)
```

Another graphical form presents the QCA solution in a *tabular format* or a so-called Fiss-style table, as shown in Table 4.8 (Ragin, 2008b, chapter 8; Fiss, 2011). In the rows, all conditions are listed. Single columns denote the different sufficient terms and groups of columns the solution formula. The cells can contain three possible entries: a full circle denotes the presence of a condition, an empty circle the negated condition, and no cell entry signifies that the condition is logically redundant for the sufficient term in question. Additional information can be added to the table, such as the parameters of fit and the types of cases. And each sufficient term could be given a conceptually meaningful 'name'. For instance, we could label sufficient term *X*~*C* the 'convenient' path toward arriving in time, as it stipulates that living close by but not being from a punctual family is what makes those kids punctual. The other term could be

Table 4.8 Tabular presentation
of results, outcome *Y*

	Motivated *AC*	Convenient *X*~*C*
X		●
A	●	
C	●	⊖

labeled 'motivated', as kids from punctual families ride their bike to practice in order to arrive in time.

Another presentational form also requires conceptual input. For instance, coach Susan could find it curious and interesting that being from a punctual family (*C*) contributes to the outcome both in its presence and its absence. In order to highlight this aspect, the QCA solution could be presented in a *flowchart*. Flowcharts unfold their power in more complex solution formulas than the one we are using here. With more sufficient terms and more conjuncts in each of these conjunctions, a graphical presentation via a flowchart can highlight the structure of the interpretation of the findings in an effective manner.[16]

Practical Challenges: Model Ambiguity

Logical minimization as described earlier in this chapter can sometimes lead to more than one solution formula. In the literature, this phenomenon is known as model ambiguity (Baumgartner and Thiem, 2017). Model ambiguity is a problem for applied researchers, especially those who aim at interpreting their solution in a causal manner. With the data at hand, researchers cannot tell which of the multiple formulas is the 'correct' one, that is, which one depicts the true data generating process. But even for scholars who employ QCA for descriptive rather than causal purposes, model ambiguity presents a challenge. With the data at hand, more than one 'story' can be told about the conditions leading to the outcome.

For illustration, consider the following truth table. It represents data from coach Susan and some fellow coaches of other soccer teams in the neighborhood. Jointly they gathered data on 47 players. They are now curious why some

---

[16] See Schneider and Maerz (2017) and Bara (2014) for examples of flowcharts that also include higher-order concepts.

Table 4.9 Truth table: 47 soccer players, outcome ~Y

Row	X	A	C	OUT	n	incl	PRI
1	0	0	0	1	8	0.912	0.776
7	1	1	0	1	2	0.911	0.656
3	0	1	0	1	3	0.893	0.651
6	1	0	1	1	4	0.877	0.602
2	0	0	1	1	5	0.837	0.540
5	1	0	0	0	1	0.893	0.513
4	0	1	1	0	1	0.779	0.340
8	1	1	1	0	23	0.614	0.306

players do *not* arrive in time.[17] This means that column 'OUT' in the truth table shown in Table 4.9 now signals which rows are sufficient for outcome '*not arriving in time*' (rows ordered by PRI).

There are five primitive expressions (rows with OUT = 1) for outcome 'not arriving in time' ($\sim Y$). Let us use the logical minimization principle introduced in the previous section, using the `minimize()` command.[18] This yields two minimized solution formulas (M1 and M2).

C 4.5

```
# Logical minimization of truth table:

sol_ny <- minimize(tt_ny

sol_ny
```

O 4.3

```
M1: ~A*C + A*~C + (~X*~A)  => ~Y
M2: ~A*C + A*~C + (~X*~C)  => ~Y
```

Both solutions agree that players who do not arrive in time ($\sim Y$) are either not riding a bike and are from families with punctuality as a norm ($\sim AC$) or do ride a bike but are not from families with punctuality as a norm ($A\sim C$). Where they differ is with regard to a third reason for non-punctuality. M1 stipulates that it is players who do not live close by and do not come by bike ($\sim X\sim A$), whereas M2 says that it is players not living close by and not from families with punctuality as a norm ($\sim X\sim C$).

---

[17] Remember that asymmetry is a key feature of set-theoretic methods such as QCA, so we need to analyze the non-occurrence of an outcome separately from its occurrence.

[18] 'tt_ny' is the name of the truth table object.

As mentioned, model ambiguity means that there is more than one solution formula to succinctly summarize the information contained in the truth table. The best way of illustrating this is via a prime implicant chart (see Table 4.7). This chart can be obtained by accessing the sub-component 'PIChart' in our solution object 'sol_ny'.

C 4.6

```
# Display prime implicant chart:

sol_ny$PIchart
```

O 4.4

	1	2	3	6	7
~X*~A	x	x	—	—	—
~X*~C	x	—	x	—	—
~A*C	—	x	—	x	—
A*~C	—	—	x	—	x

As already mentioned, the columns of the prime implicant chart list all primitive expressions, that is, all truth table rows sufficient for the outcome (OUT = 1). In our example, these are rows 1, 2, 3, 6, and 7. The rows of the chart list all prime implicants, that is, those terms that we arrive at when performing step 1 of the logical minimization described earlier.

In order for a solution formula to be 'true', it must cover all primitive expressions. A prime implicant is redundant if it can be eliminated from the solution and still all primitive expressions are covered. Let us look at the PIChart and start with the prime implicants at the bottom. Can $A{\sim}C$ be dropped? No, because then primitive expression 7 would not be covered. Likewise, can ${\sim}AC$ be dropped? No, because then primitive expression 6 would not be covered.

What about prime implicant ${\sim}X{\sim}C$? It takes care of primitive expressions 1 and 3. Both are also taken care of by other prime implicants. This means we can drop ${\sim}X{\sim}C$ *as long as we keep* prime implicant ${\sim}X{\sim}A$. But note we could equally well drop prime implicant ${\sim}X{\sim}A$ *as long as we keep* prime implicant ${\sim}X{\sim}C$. In other words, we can summarize our data in two different ways, that is, with our models M1 and M2.

In order to decide which model to choose, researchers need to rely on additional information outside of their truth table. This information can be additional data on within-case mechanisms providing supportive evidence for one of the solution formulas, or theoretical arguments making one solution more interesting than another. Regardless of the researcher's way forward, model ambiguity should always be reported. We return to model ambiguity when discussing good practices in Chapter 7.

4.4   Analysis of Sufficiency and Limited Diversity

So far, we have been using an example in which all truth table rows contained enough empirical evidence in order to decide whether or not it can qualify as a sufficient condition for the outcome. This is rare in applied QCA. Normally what happens is that several, sometimes numerous, truth table rows remain without enough empirical evidence. We therefore cannot decide based on empirical information whether or not that row is sufficient for the outcome. Such rows are called logical remainders. In the 'OUT' column of a truth table, they are denoted with a question mark ('?'), aptly indicating that we do not know if that specific combination of conditions is sufficient for the outcome.

To illustrate, we come back to coach Susan, who, together with fellow coaches of other teams in neighboring towns, wants to further investigate the puzzle why some players arrive in time while others do not. They increase both the number of players studied to 131 and the number of potentially relevant conditions from the three we have been looking at so far to five. They add to their analysis the following two conditions: D = being a seasoned player; and E = being a goalkeeper. Furthermore, they decide to focus on explaining why players do *not* arrive in time ($\sim Y$), that is, why some of them are late.

With five conditions, there are now $2^5 = 32$ truth table rows. We have 131 cases, more than four times the number of rows. However, look at the truth table displayed in Table 4.10. More than half of the rows do not have enough empirical evidence in order to decide whether the truth table row in question is sufficient for the outcome.[19] These logical remainders are denoted with a '?' in column OUT. For instance, as row 2 shows, for some reason, there is not a single goalkeeper ($E = 1$) in the study that is a non-member of all the other four conditions (a goalie who does not live close by, does not come by bike, does not come from a punctual family, and is not a seasoned player). Because there are no such players in our study, we cannot empirically determine whether or not such a type of player would not arrive in time for practice. The same holds for the other logical remainders ($OUT =?$).

Logical remainders are a problem. We need to know whether or not a given row should be considered sufficient for the outcome (OUT = 1) or

---

[19] 'Enough' empirical evidence is here defined as 'at least two cases in a truth table row'. The football coaches choose the n.cut = 2 threshold because with such a large number of players they feel that there might be some error in their data and that they do not want to put too much faith in the fact that there is one case in a row.

whether it cannot be considered sufficient (OUT = 0). In QCA, the treatment of limited diversity is governed by the so-called Standard Analysis (Ragin, 2008b, chapter 9) and increasingly by the Enhanced Standard Analysis (Schneider and Wagemann, 2012, chapter 8). Depending on which remainder rows are included in logical minimization, we obtain different solution formulas: the conservative, the most parsimonious, or an intermediate solution. In the following, we explain how these solution formulas are obtained via the Standard Analysis. After this, we explain the logic of the Enhanced Standard Analysis.

4.4.1 Standard Analysis

In essence, the Standard Analysis (SA) protocol proposes that three different solutions are derived from truth tables with limited diversity such as that shown in Table 4.10. No matter which solution is produced, each and all of them *must* include the 'OUT = 1' rows and *cannot* include the 'OUT = 0' rows in the logical minimization. As long as this rule is adhered to, the resulting solution formula is correct. The solution types in the Standard Analysis differ in which of the remainder rows they include in the minimization and which ones they do not include. Because of this, the different solution types also differ in their degree of complexity, that is, the number of conditions and logical operators they contain.

Principles

The conservative, or complex, solution does not include any of the remainder rows into the logical minimization. As its name suggests, it is the most complex of the different solution types of the Standard Analysis. The most parsimonious solution includes all those remainder rows that contribute to obtaining the most parsimonious solution. As the name suggests, it is the most parsimonious way of representing the empirical facts contained in the truth table. And the intermediate solution includes all those remainder rows that went into the most parsimonious solution, as long as they are in line with researcher's theory-based directional expectations on single conditions. The intermediate is more complex than the most parsimonious and less complex than the conservative solution.

Practice

Let us derive the conservative solution from our truth table in Table 4.10. The conservative solution refrains from assuming that any of the 17 remainders, or possible types of players, would be late for practice if they were empirically

Table 4.10 Truth table: 131 players, five conditions, outcome $\sim Y$

	X	A	C	D	E	OUT	n	incl	PRI
19	1	0	0	1	0	1	2	0.960	0.827
11	0	1	0	1	0	1	7	0.954	0.908
5	0	0	1	0	0	1	4	0.954	0.892
25	1	1	0	0	0	1	2	0.953	0.803
3	0	0	0	1	0	1	30	0.951	0.929
1	0	0	0	0	0	1	16	0.950	0.926
7	0	0	1	1	0	1	2	0.947	0.849
20	1	0	0	1	1	1	2	0.946	0.691
22	1	0	1	0	1	1	2	0.935	0.791
4	0	0	0	1	1	1	4	0.934	0.781
12	0	1	0	1	1	1	6	0.912	0.752
24	1	0	1	1	1	0	2	0.894	0.490
28	1	1	0	1	1	0	4	0.806	0.405
32	1	1	1	1	1	0	5	0.650	0.175
30	1	1	1	0	1	0	36	0.285	0.055
17	1	0	0	0	0	?	1	0.969	0.890
21	1	0	1	0	0	?	1	0.963	0.855
13	0	1	1	0	0	?	1	0.950	0.752
15	0	1	1	1	0	?	1	0.940	0.755
6	0	0	1	0	1	?	1	0.927	0.772
26	1	1	0	0	1	?	1	0.910	0.611
14	0	1	1	0	1	?	1	0.898	0.565
2	0	0	0	0	1	?	0		
8	0	0	1	1	1	?	0		
9	0	1	0	0	0	?	0		
10	0	1	0	0	1	?	0		
16	0	1	1	1	1	?	0		
18	1	0	0	0	1	?	0		
23	1	0	1	1	0	?	0		
27	1	1	0	1	0	?	0		
29	1	1	1	0	0	?	0		
31	1	1	1	1	0	?	0		

observed. It does assume that those missing types are not sufficient for arriving late.[20]

[20] Note that this is different from claiming that those missing types are sufficient for *not* arriving in time. A logical remainder row can – and often is – considered insufficient for both the outcome and its negation; this means that it is not included in the logical minimization for either outcome Y or outcome $\sim Y$.

C 4.7

```
sol_nyc <- minimize(TT_ny,
                    details = TRUE)

sol_nyc
```

O 4.5

M1: ~X*~A*~E + ~X*~C*D + ~A*~C*D + X*~A*C*~D*E + X*A*~C*~D*~E =>
~Y

		inclS	PRI	covS	covU
1	~X*~A*~E	0.942	0.922	0.674	0.182
2	~X*~C*D	0.913	0.881	0.541	0.065
3	~A*~C*D	0.905	0.862	0.504	0.020
4	X*~A*C*~D*E	0.935	0.791	0.125	0.022
5	X*A*~C*~D*~E	0.953	0.803	0.114	0.008
	M1	0.900	0.868	0.823	

Coach Susan and her colleagues learn that there are five different ways through which players arrive late. Some combine three of their conditions, some as many as five of them. Term 1, for instance, stipulates that those kids come late who do not live close by, do not come by bike, and are not goalkeepers ($\sim X \sim A \sim E$). Conservative solutions tend to be quite complex, especially when the number of conditions is high. While this level of detail is appreciated by those who employ QCA for detailed description, it tends to make theoretical interpretation and abstraction more difficult.

The most parsimonious solution does open up the logical remainders for counterfactual claims of sufficiency. It will select all those remainders that, once included into the logical minimization as sufficient conditions, produce the simplest possible summary of the empirical facts. These specific remainders are called 'simplifying assumptions'. 'Simplest possible' means that no single conjunct can be dropped from any of the sufficient conjunctions without violating information contained in the truth table. Because of its property of non-redundancies, the most parsimonious solution is sometimes considered the only solution type that can be interpreted causally because for each of its conjuncts there is empirical evidence at the cross-case level that it does make a difference to the outcome (Baumgartner, 2008, 2015). This means if any conjunct is taken away from the most parsimonious solution, that solution is not sufficient for the outcome anymore. In order to make a solution as simple as possible, all so-called simplifying assumptions on remainders need to be included.

In order to obtain the most parsimonious solution, we use the Code 4.8.[21] The decisive difference is the argument `include = "?"`. It allows the software to use any logical remainder row for logical minimization that contributes to producing the most parsimonious solution. It does *not* mean that all `OUT = ?` rows are included in the logical minimization. To display the simplifying assumptions, we write the Code 4.9.

C 4.8

```
sol_nyp <- minimize(TT_ny,
                    details = TRUE,
                    include = "?"
                    row.dom = TRUE)
sol_nyp
```

O 4.6

```
M1: ~X + ~E + ~A*~C + ~A*~D => ~Y
```

		inclS	PRI	covS	covU
1	~X	0.905	0.877	0.832	0.033
2	~E	0.914	0.886	0.829	0.024
3	~A*~C	0.905	0.870	0.676	0.007
4	~A*~D	0.927	0.897	0.398	0.021
	M1	0.875	0.839	0.929	

The most parsimonious solution consists of only four sufficient terms. Half of them consist of only one condition and the other two combine only two conjuncts – clearly more parsimonious than the conservative solution. Players who arrive late either do not live close by ($\sim X$), or are not goalies ($\sim E$), or do not arrive by bike, and either are not from punctual families ($\sim A \sim C$), or not seasoned players ($\sim A \sim D$). This is the shortest way of summarizing the empirical information contained in our truth table.

In order to arrive at this conclusion, we have included 16 simplifying assumptions. All of them have been assumed to be sufficient for the outcome 'not arriving in time'.

C 4.9

```
# Display simplifying assumptions:

sol_nyp$SA
```

---

[21] The argument `row.dom = TRUE` is used in this example to avoid model ambiguity (see Section 4.3.2), a topic unrelated to the (Enhanced) Standard Analysis.

0 4.7

```
$M1
    X A C D E
2   0 0 0 0 1
6   0 0 1 0 1
8   0 0 1 1 1
9   0 1 0 0 0
10  0 1 0 0 1
13  0 1 1 0 0
14  0 1 1 0 1
15  0 1 1 1 0
16  0 1 1 1 1
17  1 0 0 0 0
18  1 0 0 0 1
21  1 0 1 0 0
23  1 0 1 1 0
27  1 1 0 1 0
29  1 1 1 0 0
31  1 1 1 1 0
```

The intermediate solution injects substantive knowledge into the selection of logical remainder rows. Based on theoretical considerations and often plain common sense, a distinction is made among all simplifying assumptions as to whether they represent easy counterfactuals or difficult counterfactuals. In order to establish this distinction, researchers need to formulate directional expectations on their conditions (Ragin, 2008b, chapter 9). For each condition, they need to express whether they expect it to contribute to the outcome when the condition is present, when it is negated, or whether they cannot tell, that is, whether they do not have any directional expectation for a given condition.

Susan and her colleagues, based on having read some literature and their own experience-based hunches, expect that all but one of their conditions contribute to the outcome 'arriving late' when they are negated. Only for condition D ('being a seasoned player') do they expect that it contributes to arriving late when it is present.[22] In R, we express these directional expectations via the argument dir.exp = "~X, ~A, ~C, D, ~E". R identifies easy counterfactuals during logical minimization. For example, we empirically observe that row 28 is sufficient for the outcome: XA~CDE. LR row 27 is identical to this empirically observed row only that E is negated: XA~CD~E. Based on our directional expectation ~E-> Y we can plausibly assume that ceteris paribus, row 27 too would result in the outcome: it is an easy counterfactual.

---

[22] Susan and her fellow coaches feel sure that those players know that there are no real sanctions for not showing up in time.

C 4.10

```
sol_nyi <- minimize(TT_ny,
                    details = TRUE,
                    include = "?",
                    dir.exp = "~X, ~A, ~C, D, ~E",
                    row.dom = TRUE)
sol_nyi
```

O 4.8

From C1P1:

M1:   ~A*~C + ~A*~D | 0| D | Y⫽ ⫽⫽F + ~X*~C*D => ~Y

		inclS	PRI	covS	covU
1	~A*~C	0.905	0.870	0.676	0.010
2	~A*~D	0.927	0.897	0.398	0.043
3	~C*~E	0.920	0.894	0.735	0.042
4	~X*~A*~E	0.942	0.922	0.674	0.018
5	~X*~C*D	0.913	0.881	0.541	0.014
	M1	0.887	0.854	0.893	

The intermediate solution is slightly more complex than the most parsimonious solution. It has five rather than just four terms and each term consists of at least two conjuncts. At the same time, the intermediate solution is more parsimonious than the conservative solution, which had sufficient terms consisting of three to four conjuncts.

In order to display the easy counterfactuals that have been used to produce the intermediate solution, we use the Code 4.11. We see that only seven of the 16 simplifying assumptions qualify as easy counterfactuals in light of our directional expectations (logical remainder rows 2, 6, 9, 17, 18, 21, and 27 from Table 4.10).

C 4.11

```
# Display easy counterfactuals:

sol_nyi$i.sol$C1P1$EC
```

O 4.9

```
   X A C D E
2  0 0 0 0 1
6  0 0 1 0 1
9  0 1 0 0 0
17 1 0 0 0 0
18 1 0 0 0 1
21 1 0 1 0 0
27 1 1 0 1 0
```

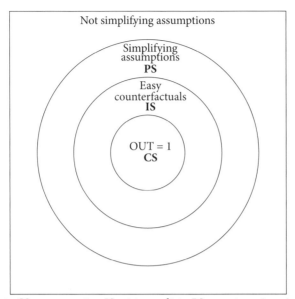

Note: CS = conservative; IS = intermediate; PS = most parsimonious.

Figure 4.20 Types of counterfactuals – Standard Analysis

The relation between the three solution types and the treatment of logical remainders according to the Standard Analysis can be graphically represented as shown in Figure 4.20. The innermost circle denotes all truth table rows that are deemed sufficient for the outcome based on empirical evidence (OUT = 1). The rectangle denotes all logical remainder rows (OUT = ?). Among them, we can distinguish between those that provide for simplifying assumptions, and those that do not. If all simplifying assumptions are included, we obtain the most parsimonious solution (PS). Among simplifying assumptions, we can further distinguish between easy and difficult counterfactuals. If we only include easy counterfactuals, then we obtain the intermediate solution (IS). If no remainder is included in the logical minimization, we obtain the conservative solution (CS). Figure 4.20 nicely illustrates that the three solutions are in a set relation. The conservative solution is a subset of the intermediate, which, in turn, is a subset of the most parsimonious solution. Along similar lines, the most parsimonious solution is, well, the most parsimonious expression to summarize the empirical evidence at hand, followed by the intermediate, and then the conservative solution.

The Standard Analysis provides applied researchers with a set of strategies of how to confront the virtually omnipresent phenomenon of limited empirical diversity. Depending on the research goal, different solution types are more adequate. The conservative solution describes cases in greater detail, whereas the most parsimonious solution prioritizes that no redundancies are included. The intermediate solution aims at striking a balance between these goals and the sound counterfactual reasoning. In the concluding Chapter 7, we discuss in further detail the various goals that can be pursued with QCA.

Box 4.6 Core Points – Standard Analysis

- Logical remainders (LR) are truth table rows without enough empirical evidence and for which we cannot assess whether or not they are sufficient for the outcome.
- The Standard Analysis protocol proposes three different solution formulas, depending on whether and which assumptions are made on these LR rows: conservative, most parsimonious, or an intermediate solution.
- The conservative solution does not include any LR row and is based only on the rows with OUT = 1.
- The most parsimonious solution includes all those LR rows that contribute to making the Boolean expression of the solution more parsimonious. The LR rows used in the most parsimonious solution are called simplifying assumptions.
- The intermediate solution includes only those simplifying assumptions that represent easy counterfactuals, based on the researcher's directional expectations on how the conditions contribute to the outcome.
- The three solutions never contradict the empirical evidence contained in the truth table rows with empirical information (OUT = 1) as they always include these rows for minimization and never include rows with OUT = 0.
- The three solutions are in a subset relation to each other as the conservative solution is a subset of the intermediate, which, in turn, is a subset of the most parsimonious solution.
- The three solutions can also be ordered in their level of complexity, with the most parsimonious solution being the simplest, followed by the intermediate, and then the conservative solution.

4.4.2   Enhanced Standard Analysis

The design of the Standard Analysis does not rule out that researchers inadvertently make untenable assumptions. Assumptions are untenable if they are logically contradictory or run counter to basic and uncontested knowledge of how the world works. For example, by introducing both conditions 'tall' and 'small player' in a research setup, we might inadvertently include a logical remainder denoting the 'tall AND small player' combination. As we will see later in this section, this is only one of the different types of untenable assumptions one can make. In order to rule out this possibility of including such untenable assumptions, the Enhanced Standard Analysis (ESA) has been proposed (Schneider and Wagemann, 2012, section 8.2).

The basic logic of ESA is straightforward. Prior to producing the three solution types defined by the Standard Analysis, make sure to block all

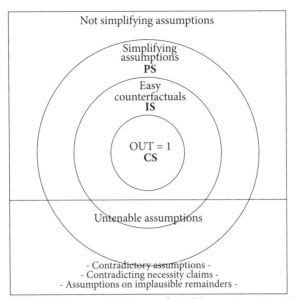

Note: CS = conservative; IS = intermediate; PS = most parsimonious.

Figure 4.21 Types of counterfactuals – Enhanced Standard Analysis

those logical remainder rows from being included into the process of logical minimization that would amount to untenable assumptions. Figure 4.21 graphically displays the argument of ESA. The figure is similar to Figure 4.20, which depicts the Standard Analysis. The only difference is that with ESA, we identify a subset of the logical remainder rows that would yield untenable assumptions if included into the logical minimization. As Figure 4.21 shows, those untenable assumptions could be simplifying or even easy counterfactuals. In other words, as we will soon show, the Standard Analysis does not prevent by default that untenable assumptions are made.

What makes the inclusion of a remainder row into the minimization process an untenable assumption? There are three different sources: (1) counterfactuals making statements on the conditions for the opposite outcome; (2) counterfactuals contradicting statements of necessity and (3) basic logic. We discuss each of them in turn. No matter what the source for untenability is, the solution is always the same and straightforward: block those remainders from being included in the logical minimization process.

Ironically, untenable assumptions can occur whenever researchers follow standards of good practice: when both the outcome and its negation are analyzed in separate analyses and when claims of necessity are made based on separate analyses of necessity. The third source of untenable assumptions stems from introducing into the analysis conditions that are mutually exclusive, such as for instance, 'tall players' and 'small players'.

Susan and her colleagues followed the standards of good QCA practice and performed an analysis of necessity for their outcome 'arriving late' ($\sim Y$). They identify two SUIN conditions (see Section 3.3.2 for how to analyze SUIN conditions). 'Not living close by' or 'not arriving by bike' are interpreted as functional equivalents of the higher-order concept 'playground not fast to reach' (T). T is necessary for $\sim Y$.

$$T = \sim X + \sim A$$
$$T \leftarrow \sim Y. \qquad (4.9)$$

The coaches also perform a sufficiency analysis for the opposite outcome 'arriving in time' (Y). This produces the three solution formulas in Equation 4.10.

$$
\begin{aligned}
Conservative: \quad & XACE+ \quad XCDE+ \quad XADE \rightarrow Y \\
Parsimonious: \quad & XAE+ \quad XCE \qquad\qquad\quad \rightarrow Y \\
Intermediate: \quad & XAE+ \quad XCDE \qquad\qquad\;\; \rightarrow Y.
\end{aligned} \qquad (4.10)
$$

Nothing seems wrong with making those sufficiency and necessity statements about outcomes Y and $\sim Y$. As we show now, however, Susan and her colleagues' most parsimonious and intermediate solutions on why players do not arrive in time ($\sim Y$) rest on untenable assumptions.

Contradictory Simplifying Assumptions

Contradictory simplifying assumptions (CSA) occur when the same logical remainder row is included in the logical minimization for the occurrence of the outcome (Y) and its non-occurrence ($\sim Y$). Doing this amounts to the nonsensical statement that one and the same truth table row X is sufficient for both Y and $\sim Y$. Such logical fallacies must be avoided by excluding such remainder rows from either the minimization for Y, or $\sim Y$, or both.

Let us check if the simplifying assumptions used for the most parsimonious solutions for outcomes Y and $\sim Y$ overlap, that is, if we used some of the remainder rows for both minimization procedures. For this, we use the LR.intersect() command in package SetMethods.

C 4.12

```
# Identify contradictory simplifying assumptions:

CSA <- LR.intersect(sol_nyp, sol_yp)
CSA
```

O 4.10

```
[1] "23" "31"
```

We discover that remainder rows 23 and 31 have been used as simplifying assumptions for both outcomes.[23] In order to avoid such contradictory simplifying assumptions, we need to exclude them from the minimization of at least one of the outcomes, Y or $\sim Y$. For the sake of illustration, we exclude them from the minimization of outcome $\sim Y$, the one Susan and her colleagues are primarily interested in.

In R, the handling of untenable assumptions according to ESA is performed with function esa() in package SetMethods. It requires the specification of the truth table in which we want to block untenable assumptions (oldtt = TT_ny). Then the function needs to be told which remainder rows constitute contradictory simplifying assumptions (contrad_rows = c(CSA)). We save the resulting new truth table in the new object TT_nyesa.

C 4.13

```
# Avoid contradictory simplifying assumptions:

TT_nyesa <- esa(oldtt = TT_ny,
                contrad_rows = c(CSA))
```

If we look at the new truth table, we see that it is identical to the old one, except for the values in column 'OUT' for rows 23 and 31. They used to be OUT = ? and are now OUT = 0. This means they can no longer be used for logical minimization. This prevents Susan and her colleagues from making contradictory simplifying assumptions when producing their enhanced most parsimonious and enhanced intermediate solutions based on the new truth table.

Assumptions Contradicting Claims of Necessity

Susan and the others make the following claim of necessity $\sim X + \sim A \leftarrow \sim Y$. Even if not directly visible, both their most parsimonious and their intermediate solution for outcome $\sim Y$ contradict this necessity claim. One sign of this logical contradiction is that in both of these solution formulas, there are sufficient terms that do *not* show any of the two SUIN conditions $\sim X$ or $\sim A$.[24] This cannot be. If these SUIN conditions are to be considered necessary for the outcome, then there should be no sufficient path toward that outcome without at least one of these SUIN conditions involved.

---

[23] Note that the numbering of the truth table rows for outcome Y and $\sim Y$ is identical.

[24] It even contradicts their conservative solution, but for a reason unrelated to logical remainders; see the next footnote for an explanation.

Why do the SUIN conditions disappear from some of the sufficient terms? This is because truth table rows have been included in the logical minimization that contradict the necessity claim. Which rows contradict the necessity claim? The answer is all rows that do not contain any SUIN condition, that is, rows without either $\sim X$ or $\sim A$. Another way of stating this is all rows that are not a member of the disjunction $\sim X + \sim A$. We know that these are the rows displaying the combination $X * A$ (see Section 2.4.3).

If we go back to the simplifying assumptions in Output O 4.7, we do notice that there are several remainder rows (27, 29, 31) that contain the presence of both X and A. When looking at the easy counterfactuals (Output O 4.9), we see that remainder 27 is even considered an easy counterfactual.

In order to prevent these untenable assumptions contradicting the statement of necessity, we use the nec.cond argument in the esa() function and specify our necessity claim in it $(\sim X + \sim A)$. This will set all truth table rows with $X * A$ in it to OUT $= 0$.[25] In other words, we assume that these rows are NOT sufficient for the outcome and therefore not included in the logical minimization.

C 4.14

```
# Avoid contradictory simplifying assumptions and statements
  contradicting claims of necessity:

TT_nyesa <- esa(TT_ny,
                contrad_rows = c(CSA),
                nec_cond = "~X+~A")
```

Assumptions on Impossible Remainders

Impossible remainders are combinations of conditions that cannot exist. For instance, if our football coaches were interested in whether both tall players (T) and small players (S) arrive in time, then there are some truth table rows that denote the impossible small-tall player $(T * S)$.[26] Obviously, such a player does not exist because the two conditions are mutually exclusive.

---

[25] Since the necessary SUIN combination was not perfectly consistent, in our example, it happens that there is also one *observed* truth table row that contains $X * A$ (row 25) and is deemed sufficient for $\sim Y$ (OUT = 1). This row, too, is set to OUT = 0 by the esa() command; otherwise, the sufficiency and necessity statements contradict each other.

[26] Remember here our discussions on sets and their calibration in Chapter 2. The negation of a set is not necessarily the same as its conceptual opposite. Applied to our example here, the negation of the set 'tall players' is simply 'not-tall players'. This is a different set than the set of 'small players'. Just think of all the medium-sized players. They are not members of either the set of tall players, or of small players. Hence, it often makes sense to include mutually exclusive sets into one truth table.

Impossible remainders can come in more subtle forms.[27] For the sake of methodological argument, let us pretend that in our soccer example, it is impossible for fundamental reasons to ever find a player who is not living close by yet coming by bike, while neither from a punctual family nor a seasoned player ($\sim X * A * \sim C * \sim D$). In order to exclude any such impossible remainder row, we use the argument `untenable_LR` = "$\sim X * A * \sim C * \sim D$".

C 4.15

```
# Avoid contradictory simplifying assumptions, statements
    contradicting claims of necessity, and assumptions on
    impossible remainders:

TT_nyesa <- esa(TT_ny,
                contrad_rows = c(CSA),
                nec_cond = "~X+~A",
                untenable_LR = "~X*A*~C*~D")
```

Obtaining the Enhanced Solution Formulas

At this point, we have blocked all three sources of untenable assumptions. None of the still available remainders in the updated truth table can contradict our statement of necessity, none has been used in the analysis for the opposite outcome (Y), and none constitutes an impossible remainder. The resulting truth table in shown in Output 0 4.11.

0 4.11

```
OUT: output value
  n: number of cases in configuration
incl: sufficiency inclusion score
 PRI: proportional reduction in inconsistency
```

	X	A	C	D	E	OUT	n	incl	PRI
19	1	0	0	1	0	1	2	0.960	0.827
5	0	0	1	0	0	1	4	0.954	0.892
11	0	1	0	1	0	1	7	0.954	0.908
25	1	1	0	0	0	0	2	0.953	0.803
3	0	0	0	1	0	1	30	0.951	0.929
1	0	0	0	0	0	1	16	0.950	0.926
7	0	0	1	1	0	1	2	0.947	0.849
20	1	0	0	1	1	1	2	0.946	0.691
22	1	0	1	0	1	1	2	0.935	0.791
4	0	0	0	1	1	1	4	0.934	0.781
12	0	1	0	1	1	1	6	0.912	0.752
24	1	0	1	1	1	0	2	0.894	0.490

[27] For an example, see the study by Ragin et al. (2003).

28	1	1	0	1	1	0	4	0.806	0.405
32	1	1	1	1	1	0	5	0.650	0.175
30	1	1	1	0	1	0	36	0.285	0.055
17	1	0	0	0	0	?	1	0.969	0.890
21	1	0	1	0	0	?	1	0.963	0.855
13	0	1	1	0	0	?	1	0.950	0.752
15	0	1	1	1	0	?	1	0.940	0.755
6	0	0	1	0	1	?	1	0.927	0.772
26	1	1	0	0	1	0	1	0.910	0.611
14	0	1	1	0	1	?	1	0.898	0.565
2	0	0	0	0	1	?	0	–	–
8	0	0	1	1	1	?	0	–	–
9	0	1	0	0	0	0	0	–	–
10	0	1	0	0	1	0	0	–	–
16	0	1	1	1	1	!	0		
18	1	0	0	0	1	?	0	–	–
23	1	0	1	1	0	0	0	–	–
27	1	1	0	1	0	0	0	–	–
29	1	1	1	0	0	0	0	–	–
31	1	1	1	1	0	0	0	–	–

From the initial 17 logical remainders, only 10 are still available for logical minimization. ESA, by definition, reduces the number of available logical remainders. Let us produce the enhanced solution formulas.

We start with the enhanced conservative solution. This might come as a surprise to some, given that the conservative solution, by definition, does not include any of the logical remainders, while ESA is about excluding specific remainder rows. There is one exception, which the present example illustrates. The truth table for outcome $\sim Y$ contains an empirically observed OUT = 1 row that contradicts Susan's claim of necessity. Row 25 in Table 4.10 contains the negation of Susan's necessary condition, i.e., it claims that $X * A$ is sufficient for $\sim Y$ when the necessity claim $\sim X + \sim A \leftarrow \sim Y$ states the exact opposite. Observed rows, such as row 25, also need to be excluded from the logical minimization by setting them to OUT = 0. Conveniently, when using the nec_cond argument in the esa() function, this is automatically done.

C 4.16

```
sol_nycesa <- minimize(TT_nyesa,
                  details = TRUE)

sol_nycesa
```

O 4.12

```
M1: ~X*~A*~E + ~X*~C*D + ~A*~C*D + X*~A*C*~D*E => ~Y
```

		inclS	PRI	covS	covU
1	~X*~A*~E	0.942	0.922	0.674	0.191
2	~X*~C*D	0.913	0.881	0.541	0.067
3	~A*~C*D	0.905	0.862	0.504	0.024
4	X*~A*C*~D*E	0.935	0.791	0.125	0.024
	M1	0.901	0.868	0.815	

Compared to the non-enhanced conservative solution, there are now only four rather than five sufficient terms. The sufficient term that has been dropped is precisely the one that did not include at least one of our two SUIN conditions. The enhanced conservative solution now features either $\sim X$ or $\sim A$ in all of its four sufficient terms, just as it is required if a claim of necessity is made.

The enhanced most parsimonious solution looks as follows.

C 4.17

```
sol_nypesa <- minimize(TT_nyesa,
                       details = TRUE,
                       include = "?"
                       row.dom = TRUE)
sol_nypesa
```

O 4.13

```
M1: ~X + ~A*~C + ~A*~D => ~Y
```

		inclS	PRI	covS	covU
1	~X	0.905	0.877	0.832	0.139
2	~A*~C	0.905	0.870	0.676	0.022
3	~A*~D	0.927	0.897	0.398	0.033
	M1	0.886	0.853	0.905	

The enhanced most parsimonious solution also has one sufficient term less than the non-enhanced solution. All contain one of the two SUIN conditions. If we look at the simplifying assumptions made, we see that none constitutes an untenable assumption: none contains the negated necessary condition ($X *$ A), none is a contradictory simplifying assumption, and none is made on an impossible remainder ("$\sim X * A * \sim C * \sim D$").

C 4.18

```
sol_nypesa$SA
```

O 4.14

```
$M1
    X A C D E
2   0 0 0 0 1
6   0 0 1 0 1
8   0 0 1 1 1
15  0 1 1 1 0
16  0 1 1 1 1
17  1 0 0 0 0
18  1 0 0 0 1
21  1 0 1 0 0
```

Last but not least, the enhanced intermediate solution looks as follows. Again, all terms are in line with our necessity claim, and because all other sources of untenable assumptions have also been blocked, we can be sure that the enhanced intermediate solution does not contradict statements we are making at other stages of our analysis.

C 4.19

```
sol_nyiesa <- minimize(TT_nyesa,
                       details = TRUE,
                       include = "?",
                       dir.exp = "~X, ~A, ~C, D, ~E")

sol_nyiesa
```

O 4.15

From C1P1:

M1:   ~A*~C + ~A*~D + ~X*~A*~E + ~X*~C*D => ~Y

		inclS	PRI	covS	covU
1	~A*~C	0.905	0.870	0.676	0.026
2	~A*~D	0.927	0.897	0.398	0.043
3	~X*~A*~E	0.942	0.922	0.674	0.018
4	~X*~C*D	0.913	0.881	0.541	0.067
	M1	0.894	0.862	0.851	

If we compare the easy counterfactuals made for the enhanced and the non-enhanced intermediate solution, we see that the latter was based on several tenable and easy counterfactuals (remainders 2, 6, 17, 18, 21). Conversely, rows 9 and 27 (see O 4.9) no longer appear: they were easy but untenable counterfactuals. ESA makes sure that untenable assumptions are prevented.

C 4.20

```
# Display  tenable  easy  counterfactuals :

tenable_EC <- LR.intersect(sol_nyi, sol_nyiesa)
tenable_EC
```

O 4.16

```
[1] "2"   "6"   "17"  "18"  "21"
```

Box 4.7 Core Points – Enhanced Standard Analysis

- The design of the Standard Analysis does not rule out that researchers can make untenable assumptions on remainders, that is, assumptions that are logically contradictory or run counter to basic and uncontested knowledge of how the world works.
- The Enhanced Standard Analysis has the goal of preventing these untenable assumptions by blocking all untenable LR rows from being included in the minimization process before producing the three solution types.
- There are three different types of untenable assumptions:
  - Assumptions contradicting claims of necessity;
  - Contradictory simplifying assumptions that are used in the minimization process for both the outcome and its negation;
  - Assumptions on impossible remainders representing combinations of conditions that cannot exist.

4.5 Summary

The analysis of sufficient conditions is the analytic core of QCA. In fact, a study without an analysis of sufficiency cannot be called a QCA.

Crucial for the analysis of sufficiency is the truth table. Constructing such a truth table is of great importance because any 'wrong' information will travel through all the logical minimization, and thus will be part of any solution formula. Applied researchers therefore need to dedicate all the time and energy needed to get the truth table 'right'. This iterative process of going back and forth between initial ideas and newly gathered empirical evidence (Ragin, 1994) involves everything from the calibration of conditions and the outcome, to the selection of cases and conditions. Contradictory truth table rows, that is, rows that contain cases with different qualitative membership in the outcome, should be seen as a heuristic tool: Are some conditions missing from the analysis? Is perhaps the membership score of one or more cases in a condition or the outcome erroneous? Or do some cases not belong to the universe of cases and should be dropped from the analysis? Before a truth table is subjected to logical minimization, all these questions should be asked and answered as best as possible (Schneider and Wagemann, 2012, section 5.1). Inspecting the truth table is simple, thanks to the `truthTable()` command and its various arguments that we have introduced in this chapter.

The process of logical minimization, while relatively simple in principle, tends to be quite complicated in practice. This is why this task should be delegated to the appropriate software. The `minimize()` command and its arguments provide all the options needed for this task. When confronted with limited empirical diversity – that is, in about 99 per cent of applied QCA – we should pay attention to the treatment of logical remainders. We have introduced the Enhanced Standard Analysis and the related `esa()` function for tackling this task.

Finally, we introduced various ways of presenting QCA results. The display of the Boolean expression, together with the parameters of fit, is the bare minimum. Beyond this, researchers are encouraged to use graphical tools, such as XY plots, tables, or charts. By using more than one presentational form, they can make sure that all important pieces of information generated by their QCA are presented: sufficient conditions (Boolean expression), their empirical fit (parameters of fit), and the location of cases (typical and deviant cases). We return to issues regarding the presentation of results in Section 7.4.3 (see also Rubinson, 2019).

Part IV

After the Analytic Moment

5 Rounding Up a Solid QCA

5.1 Introduction and Learning Goals

Throughout the previous chapters, we learned how to perform a QCA, starting from research design basics and the process of calibrating sets, to the main analytic moment consisting of finding necessary and sufficient solutions for an outcome of interest. However, a solid QCA does not end with the analytic moment. On the one hand, researchers must make several analytic decisions at various stages in the analysis (such as choosing calibration thresholds, choosing raw consistency thresholds, etc.), some with more confidence than others. On the other hand, researchers might also be confronted with data that are structured in analytically relevant ways that are, however, not accounted for in the truth table analysis. For example, cases might group into different geographic, substantive, or temporal clusters, or there might be relevant causal dependencies or sequences among conditions, yet these structures are assumed not to matter for the outcome during the logical minimization procedure.

This chapter aims to introduce the different robustness and diagnostic tools available in R to assess QCA results. It is designed to enable the reader to investigate to what extent their QCA results are robust against equally plausible analytic decisions regarding the selection of calibration anchors or consistency and frequency cut-offs. In Section 5.2, we discuss the notion of robustness in QCA and how it can be approached analytically. We present recently posited possibilities to assess robustness in R, using a more formalized and automated technique introduced by Oana and Schneider (n.d.) and implemented in R package `SetMethods`. Additionally, the chapter also introduces diagnostic and modeling tools available when confronted with structured data, such as when cases belong to different groups, or when the timing and sequence of conditions is relevant. In Section 5.3, we deal with the issue of clustered data and introduce tools for diagnosing such clusters. In Section 5.4, we discuss strategies for dealing with timing and temporality, including two-step QCA, and introduce 'coincidence analysis' (CNA) as the most formalized way of analyzing sequences and causal chains with a method similar to QCA.

Box 5.1 Learning Goals – Rounding Up a Solid QCA

- Basic understanding of different approaches to diagnosing and assessing QCA results.
- Familiarity with how the robustness of QCA results to different analytical decisions can be assessed.
- Familiarity with proposals on how to assess QCA results in the presence of clustered data.
- Familiarity with how to integrate temporality into QCA, including sequences and causal chains.

5.2   Assessing Robustness in QCA

As seen in the previous chapters, performing any QCA analysis involves a series of analytic decisions to be taken by the researcher, some with more confidence than others. Researchers decide on where to place the different calibration anchors, the different raw consistency thresholds, or the frequency cut-off for truth table rows to be considered as having enough empirical evidence.[1] When conceptual borders are easily definable, when cases cluster neatly in truth table rows, or when the number of cases in the analysis is rather small, these decisions can be straightforward and the consequences of changing them are easier to gauge. However, in applied QCA, using social science data and having more than a handful of cases, this is hardly ever the case. Conceptual borders might be imprecise, and calibration anchors might become harder to place. Cases might be numerous and they might not all cluster neatly into truth table rows. All this makes the choice of a particular calibration anchor, raw consistency threshold, or frequency cutoff less than straightforward. In such situations, we argue that researchers should apply systematic robustness tests to assess the consequences of changes in their various analytic decisions.

In general, for tackling the notion of robustness, we need to engage with two questions: 'robustness against what?' and 'how are robust results defined?'.

---

[1] Note that the approaches to robustness discussed here do not assess alterations in the conditions chosen or the cases included for analysis. Questions of case selection and scope conditions pertain to the domain of QCA as an approach and constitute more radical changes to the research design of a QCA analysis, whereas the focus of the robustness protocol introduced here is on QCA as a technique and the solution formulas that are produced.

Existing literature on robustness[2] offers several answers to the two questions. Regarding robustness against what, authors have focused on the various analytic decisions that can have consequences for QCA results, for example, changes in raw consistency, changes in calibrations, or changes in the frequency cutoff. Regarding how robust results are defined, the focus has been equally diverse. Some consider a result as robust when there is no change in the Boolean solution formula, others when parameters of fit are rather stable, yet others when solutions differ in terms of formulas or fit, but they maintain a set relation with each other.

Each of these different sources of and consequences for robustness could be studied independently, 'by hand', through performing changes to each analytic decision and evaluating the new solutions. However, considering the sheer number of different analytical decisions that one can make within substantively plausible ranges, the comparison of the different solutions created can get quickly out of hand. In order to ease the process of evaluating robustness, Oana and Schneider (n.d.) introduce a more comprehensive Robustness Test Protocol, complete with functions for easy R implementation. The protocol allows us to assess both the various sources of robustness (changes in calibration, raw consistency threshold, and frequency cutoff) and their various consequences for QCA sufficient solutions (Boolean expression, parameters of fit, subset relations, and types of cases) in a more systematic and automated fashion.[3] As the protocol involves the evaluation of multiple sources of robustness in their various consequences for QCA solutions, robustness is essentially considered more than a yes or no question, but rather a matter of degree and involving more than one aspect. Solutions can be "less than perfectly robust" in multiple ways that can be comprehensively and transparently detailed by using this protocol.

The three main steps of the protocol consist of evaluating sensitivity ranges, evaluating fit-oriented robustness, and evaluating case-oriented robustness. We introduce each of these notions of robustness in the following subsections. We then illustrate how the protocol can be implemented with a set of functions from the SetMethods package that eliminate the need for time-consuming and often inconclusive manual robustness checks.

---

[2] See, among others, Arel-Bundock (2019); Baumgartner and Thiem (2020); Cooper and Glaesser (2016a); Emmenegger et al. (2014); Hug (2013); Krogslund et al. (2014); Rohlfing (2015, 2016); Schneider and Wagemann (2012); Skaaning (2011); Thiem et al. (2016).

[3] We focus here only on the analysis of sufficiency due to the fact that for necessary conditions the consequences of such changes are easier to assess.

5.2.1   Sensitivity Ranges

The first step in our QCA Robustness Test Protocol consists of evaluating sensitivity ranges for the solution obtained. Sensitivity ranges represent those ranges for the various sources of robustness (changes in calibration, raw consistency threshold, and frequency cutoff) within which the Boolean expression for the solution remains unchanged. Sensitivity ranges are obtained by gradually increasing and decreasing the values chosen for the qualitative anchors, the raw consistency threshold, and the frequency cutoff until the Boolean expression of the solution changes. In this way, obtaining sensitivity ranges allows researchers to assess how 'sensitive' a particular QCA solution is to the various analytic choices taken. The wider those ranges, the less sensitive and more robust the solution.

Note that sensitivity ranges are calculated by assessing alternative analytic choices in isolation, while keeping all other parameters constant at their original values. Therefore, with this procedure we obtain separate ranges for each of the calibration anchors of each of the conditions and the outcome, for the raw consistency threshold, and for the frequency cutoff. While performing each sensitivity range in isolation is informative in itself, frequently we also want to assess how robust our solution is when we simultaneously change several analytic decisions. Additionally, substantively *plausible* analytical changes might be outside of these *empirically derived* sensitivity ranges, and one should perform robustness tests against those substantively plausible ranges. The next steps in the robustness protocol are specifically designed to cope with this more research-realistic situation.

5.2.2   The Initial Solution, the Test Set, and the Robust Core

Alternative analytic decisions outside of the sensitivity ranges obtained in the previous step can still often be substantively plausible. Additionally, alternative analytic decisions could be taken simultaneously, rather than in turn. In such a situation, the number of possible alternative solutions created becomes rather high and comparing each of them in turn can get out of hand.

To overcome this issue, Oana and Schneider (n.d.) propose aggregating these alternative solutions by combining them into a so-called Test Set TS. This Test Set TS, therefore, represents the space of all other possible solutions generated based on changes in analytical decisions that fall within the range of substantive plausibility. Test solutions are aggregated into a minimal ($minTS$) and a maximal ($maxTS$) Test Set by creating the intersection, or respectively, the union of the various alternative solutions. Rather than comparing the Initial Solution IS chosen by the researcher with each of the solutions obtained during

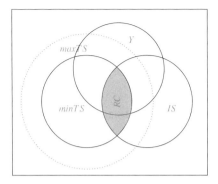

Figure 5.1 Initial Solution (IS), Test Set (TS), and the Robust Core (RC)

Note: minTS - Minimal Test Set; maxTS - Maximal Test Set; RC - Robust Core; IS - Initial Sol.; Y - Outcome
Source: adapted from Oana and Schneider (n.d.)

the robustness checks separately, one only needs to compare the *IS* with the *minTS* and *maxTS*.[4] Another concept introduced by the protocol is that of the Robust Core *RC*: it represents the intersection between *IS* and all the alternative solutions (hence, the *minTS*). The Robust Core, therefore, represents the part of the Initial Solutions *IS* that withstands all of the robustness tests performed.

Figure 5.1 illustrates the logic of our robustness approach by depicting the initial solution *IS*, the minimal and maximal Test Set (*minTS* and *maxTS*), and the outcome *Y*. Additionally, it also shows the robust core *RC* situated at the intersection between *IS* and *minTS*. The robustness of the initial solution changes depending on how much the *IS*, the *minTS*, the *maxTS*, and *RC* overlap. The perfect robustness situation would be when they perfectly coincide (*minTS* = *IS* = *RC* = *maxTS*). As soon as the overlap becomes less than perfect, robustness decreases. When the overlap between the *IS* and the *minTS* becomes less than perfect, the robust core *RC* becomes smaller than either the *IS*, or the *minTS*, or both. When the overlap between the *IS* and the *maxTS* is less than perfect, the *RC* need not be affected, but new cases that are part of the *maxTS* become additional, possible cases to be taken into consideration for robustness, as we shall see in Section 5.2.4 when looking at case-oriented robustness.

By evaluating the various degrees of overlap between the *IS*, *minTS*, *RC*, and *maxTS*, Oana and Schneider (n.d.) offer a way of evaluating the robustness of the initial solution in both a fit-oriented and a case-oriented perspective.

---

[4] In some cases, researchers might not have a best bet for substantive interpretation and, hence, there is no *IS*, but only several equally plausible decisions. In these cases, the procedure described here can still be used for assessing overlaps between alternative plausible solutions by randomly picking one solution as the *IS*.

5.2.3   Fit-Oriented Robustness

The fit-oriented perspective on robustness essentially involves the comparison of various parameters of fit for the Initial Solution (*IS*), the Robust Core (*RC*), and the minimal and maximal Test Set (*minTS* and *maxTS*). As previously mentioned, the *minTS* represents the intersection of all alternative solutions considered by the researcher, whereas the *maxTS* represents the union of all these solutions. The *RC* constitutes the part of the initial solution that withstands all these alterations and is obtained by intersecting the *minTS* with the *IS*. With this fit-oriented perspective, researchers can compare how well the Robust Core *RC* fares in comparison to the *IS*, but also whether and how much the *minTS*, *maxTS* and the *IS* overlap.

There are four different parameters of fit relevant for robustness. The first two, *Robustness Fit Consistency* (*RF_cons*)[5] and *Robustness Fit Coverage* (*RF_cov*),[6] essentially involve the comparison of the consistency and coverage of the *IS* and the *RC*. These two parameters allow us to compare how well the *RC*, that is, the part of the solution that withstands all changes, fares in terms of consistency and coverage in comparison to the entire initial solution *IS*. In other words, the more *IS* and *RC* overlap, the higher the value of these parameters, and the higher the robustness of the initial solution. In addition to these two parameters, two other parameters of fit are needed for evaluating the degree of overlap between the *minTS* and *maxTS* more generally and the *IS*. While the initial solution could perfectly coincide with the robust core, there might still be other cases included by the minimal and maximal test set that the initial solution does not cover. To evaluate this, the *Robustness Fit Set Coincidence* parameters (*RF_SC_minTS* and *RF_SC_maxTS*)[7] express the set coincidence (Ragin and Fiss, 2016) between the initial solution and the aggregated test sets. While we do not go into detail regarding the calculation of these parameters, it suffices to say that all four range from 0 to 1, with higher values indicating higher robustness.

5.2.4   Case-Oriented Robustness

While parameters of fit allow us to assess the subset relation or the degree of overlap among the *IS*, *RC*, *minTS*, and *maxTS*, they do not allow us to spot which and how many cases turn from typical cases to deviant cases or vice versa when robustness tests are performed. This is important information, and the

---

[5] $RF_{cons} = Cons_{IS}/Cons_{RC}$.
[6] $RF_{cov} = Cov_{RC}/Cov_{IS}$.
[7] $RF_{SC\_minTS} = \sum min(IS_i, minTS_i) / \sum max(IS_i, minTS_i)$
$RF_{SC\_maxTS} = \sum min(IS_i, maxTS_i) / \sum max(IS_i, maxTS_i)$.

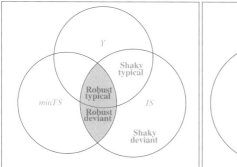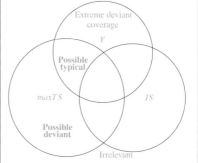

Figure 5.2 Robustness – relevant case types
Source: adapted from Oana and Schneider (n.d.)

case-oriented perspective on robustness identifies and quantifies these changes in case types.

The Venn diagram in Figure 5.2 displays where each case type is located in the overlapping areas among the *IS*, *minTS*, *maxTS*, and the outcome *Y*. Cases that are members of the robust core can be either *robust typical* ($Y \geq 0.5$) or *robust deviant* ($Y \leq 0.5$), depending on their membership in the outcome *Y*. Cases that are members only of the *IS*, but are not part of the *RC* (and, hence, the *minTS*), are considered *shaky* as their status as typical or deviant can change when alternative analytical decisions are made. Finally, cases that are members only of *maxTS*, but not of the *IS*, are considered *possible* as they are 'newly' covered by alternative solutions when making changes in analytical decisions and, therefore, they become possible typical or possible deviant depending on their membership in the outcome *Y*. We consider all those cases covered by the union of alternative solutions (*maxTS*), but not by the *IS*, as possible ones because we want to take into consideration all those cases that might end up being relevant for the analysis had one solution been chosen over another. Finally, cases that are not covered by either *IS* or the *maxTS*, which are called irrelevant ($Y \leq 0.5$) and extreme deviant coverage ($Y \geq 0.5$), are of little concern for assessing the robustness of the *IS*.

In the case of fuzzy sets, the relevant types of cases for robustness can also be visualized using XY plots of the *IS*, the *minTS*, and the *maxTS*. Figure 5.3 illustrates a robustness plot with the Initial Solution on the *x*-axis and the two Test Sets on the *y*-axis. Each of the four quadrants in this plot represents particular types of cases. Depending on the type, membership in either the *minTS* or the *maxTS* is taken into account. In such a plot, the robust cases are always located in the upper-right quadrant as these cases are more in than out (≥ 0.5) both of *minTS* and *IS*. The round markers denote cases that are more in than

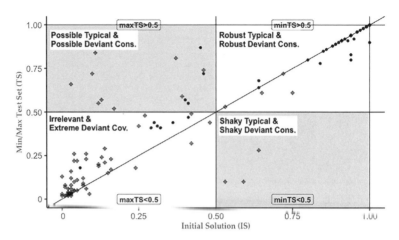

Figure 5.3 Robustness XY plot – types of cases

out of the outcome ($\geq$ 0.5), hence robust typical cases, while the empty cross markers denote cases that are more out than in of the outcome ($\leq$ 0.5), hence robust deviant consistency cases. Similarly, the upper-left quadrant denotes the possible typical and deviant consistency cases ($maxTS \geq 0.5$ & $IS \leq 0.5$), whereas the lower-right quadrant denotes shaky typical and deviant consistency cases ($IS \geq 0.5$ & $minTS \leq 0.5$). The lower-left quadrant, instead, is of little interest for robustness, as these cases are neither members of IS nor of $maxTS$.

The two shaded quadrants (where possible and shaky cases are located) are most informative for robustness. The more cases they contain, the lower the robustness of our initial solution. Moreover, if we find cases in both areas, this indicates that not only does the IS contain shaky cases, but it also omits possible cases. Generally, robustness of the IS is higher if cases are located only in one of the two shaded quadrants, the fewer cases we have in these two quadrants, and the closer these cases are to the diagonal.

The case-oriented perspective on robustness allows researchers not only to identify the specific cases located in each of these intersections, but also to look at their relative frequencies. These relative frequencies are relevant for expressing the robustness of the IS: the more robust cases there are in comparison to the other types of cases, the higher the robustness of the IS. There are three case-oriented robustness parameters. First, the Robustness Case Ratio for typical cases RCR_{typ}[8] are used for comparing the number of robust typical cases to all typical cases (robust, shaky, and possible). Just like the other parameters, this ratio varies from 0 to 1, with values of 1 being

---

[8] $RCR_{typ} = robust_{typical}/(shaky_{typical} + possible_{typical} + robust_{typical})$.

Table 5.1 Initial Solution *IS*

	inclS	PRI	covS	covU
GG*AH	0.883	0.844	0.741	0.616
HE*~GG*HI*HW	0.871	0.400	0.207	0.082
Solution	0.877	0.824	0.823	

obtained when the *minTS*, *maxTS*, and *IS* perfectly overlap, that is, when all the typical cases are of the robust kind. Second, the Robustness Case Ratio for deviant cases consistency RCR_{dev}[9] works in a similar manner for the deviant consistency in kind cases: the closer its value is to 1, the more robust is our initial QCA solution. Third, we summarize the various relations between the *IS* and the *min/maxTS* in terms of cases into four ranks (*Rob_Case_Rank*). Rank 1 indicates the best robustness situation in which all relevant cases are robust and, hence, there are no shaky or possible cases. The next best situation is rank 2 where there are no shaky cases, but there are possible cases. In rank 3, there are shaky cases, but no possible cases. Finally, in rank 4 there are both types of unrobust cases simultaneously. Therefore, the Rob_Case_Rank parameter take values from 1 to 4, with higher values indicating worse robustness.

5.2.5 Performing Robustness Tests with `SetMethods`

The Robustness Test Protocol that we have described can be easily implemented in practice using a series of functions from the `SetMethods` package. To illustrate how they work, we use the example from Paykani et al. (2018) on the conditions for explaining high life expectancy (*HL*). Their data consist of fuzzy-set membership scores on the conditions of high-quality education, good governance, affluent health system, high income inequality, and high wealth for explaining the outcome set of high life expectancy for 131 countries around the globe (see Box 5.2). Using a raw consistency threshold of 0.87 and a frequency cutoff of two cases per truth table row, we create the initial QCA solution *IS* using the `minimize()` function. We find that having good governance (*GG*) and an affluent health system (*AH*) or having high-quality education (*HE*), not good governance (~*GG*), high income inequality (*HI*), and high wealth (*HW*) is sufficient for having a high life expectancy (Table 5.1).[10]

---

[9] $RCR_{dev} = robust_{deviant}/(shaky_{deviant} + possible_{deviant} + robust_{deviant})$.

[10] This is the most parsimonious solution, but all the robustness tests are independent of the solution type.

Box 5.2 Empirical Example – Conditions for High Life Expectancy (Paykani et al., 2018)

- *Research question*: Which structural conditions explain high life expectancy?
- *Cases*: 131 countries
- *Outcome:* High life expectancy (*HL*)
- *Conditions*: High-quality education (*HE*); Good governance (*GG*); Affluent health system (*AH*); High income inequality (*HI*); High wealth (*HW*)
- *Additional factors:* Region; Year
- *Sets*: Fuzzy
- *Source*: Paykani et al., 2018. A fuzzy-set qualitative comparative analysis of 131 countries: which configuration of the structural conditions can explain health better? *International Journal for Equity in Health*, 17(1), 10.

Sensitivity Ranges in Practice

To calculate the sensitivity ranges within which this Boolean formula for the sufficient solution stays the same, we use functions `rob.inclrange()`, `rob.ncutrange()`, and `rob.calibrange()`. These functions work similarly to the `minimize()` function, but have some additional options. With the `step` argument, we specify the value with which the particular threshold is increased and decreased, and with the `max.runs` option we specify the number of times for which that threshold is increased/decreased for finding the upper and lower bounds of the sensitivity range. Additionally, for the `rob.calibrange()` function, we need to specify the raw data (`raw.data`), the calibrated data (`calib.data`), the name of the condition chosen for testing the ranges in these two datasets (`test.cond.raw and test.cond.calib`), and the initial thresholds used for calibrating this conditions (`test.thresholds`).

   In the following example, we test the sensitivity ranges for the calibration of condition *HW* (high wealth) based on the average GDP per capita of the country. We do this by adding and subtracting the step value 500 (in this case, US$) from each of the initially selected thresholds for a maximum of 40 runs.

C 5.1

```
# Create an object storing the conditions names:

conds <-  c("HE","GG","AH","HI","HW")

# Determine sensitivity ranges for qualitative calibration
    anchors of condition HW:
```

```
rob.calibrange(raw.data = PAYR,
               calib.data = PF,
               test.cond.raw = "WEAL",
               test.cond.calib = "HW",
               test.thresholds = c(3000,10500,28500),
               step = 500,
               max.runs = 40,
               outcome = "HL",
               conditions = conds,
               incl.cut = 0.87,
               n.cut = 2,
               include = "?")
```

O 5.1

```
Exclusion:  Lower bound  3000 Threshold  3000 Upper bound  10000
Crossover:  Lower bound  10000 Threshold  10500 Upper bound
    11000
Inclusion:  Lower bound  10500 Threshold  28500 Upper bound  NA
```

In Output 5.1, we see that for the 0.5 crossover threshold, the Boolean formula for the sufficient solution remains the same no matter where we place the threshold within the lower bound 10,000 and the upper bound 11,000 US$. For the inclusion thresholds, note that the Output 5.1 shows a missing value – "NA". This means that the algorithm could not find the value for a threshold from which onward the initial solution would change. For example, for the inclusion threshold, this means that by adding the 500 step value 40 times (the maximum runs specified), the software could still not find an upper range where the solution changes. Increasing the value for the max.runs can eliminate these "NAs".

When it comes to the raw consistency threshold and frequency cutoff, we see that the Initial Solution is relatively sensitive to changes. The Boolean formula of the solution stays the same only when the raw consistency threshold is placed within the 0.85–0.87 range and when the frequency cut-off is fixed at two cases.

C 5.2

```
# Determine sensitivity range for raw consistency threshold:

rob.inclrange(data = PF,
              step = 0.01,
              max.runs = 20,
              outcome = "HL",
              conditions = conds,
              incl.cut = 0.87,
              n.cut = 2,
              include = "?")
```

O 5.2

Raw Consistency T.:   Lower bound   0.85 Threshold   0.87 Upper
bound   0.87

C 5.3

```
# Determine sensitivity range for frequency cut-off:

rob.ncutrange(data = PF,
              step = 1,
              max.runs = 20,
              outcome = "HL",
              conditions = conds,
              incl.cut = 0.87,
              n.cut = 2,
              include = "?")
```

O 5.3

N.Cut: Lower bound   2 Threshold   2 Upper bound   2

Fit-Oriented Robustness in Practice

The sensitivity ranges give us information on when the Boolean formula stays
the same when we make one change at a time for each parameter separately
while holding all other parameters constant. Sensitivity range tests, therefore,
do not allow us to assess how multiple, simultaneous changes affect the robustness of our solution. This is an important limitation because it is far away
from what applied QCA researchers need: testing their QCA solution against
multiple changes in their analytic setup. As a solution to this problem, we have
introduced the notion of the Test Set TS, which aggregates the changes triggered
by various robustness checks.

   For illustration, we continue with the Paykani et al. data and create several
alternative solutions. For $TS1$, we modify the raw consistency threshold to
0.75; for $TS2$, we modify the calibration of condition HW using the qualitative anchors 0–1000, 0.5–9 000, and 1–37 000; and for $TS3$, we lower the
frequency cutoff to one case and combine it with the modified calibration of
condition HW.[11] Note that the modifications to the analytic decisions should
be located within the substantively plausible limits, but they can be outside of

---

[11] Note that one can produce as many alternative test solutions as desired, including test solutions
that contain more than one modification.

the sensitivity ranges that we found earlier. In practice, we advise researchers to attempt to build tests that are as challenging as substantively plausible by varying parameters not only within sensitivity ranges, but within their wider substantive plausibility ranges and by testing various combinations of analytic changes. To create these various alternative solutions, we simply use the `minimize()` function introduced in Chapter 4 with the previous specifications. We then combine these alternate solutions in a Test Set *TS* using the `list()` function. After this, we can obtain the three robustness parameters by using the `rob.fit()` function, in which we specify the test set just created (`test_sol =`), the initial solution (`initial_sol =`), and the outcome (`outcome =`).

C 5.4

```
# Create the test set in a list:

TS <- list(TS1, TS2, TS3)

# Calculate robustness parameters:

RF <- rob.fit(test_sol = TS,
              initial_sol = IS,
              outcome = "HL")
RF
```

We see that RF_{cov} and RF_{cons} are less than 1. This means that the *IS* does not perfectly overlap with the *RC*. However, their values are very high, thus indicating that their overlap, while not perfect, is still substantial. A similar inference can be drawn from the still high but slightly lower values of RF_{SC_minTS} and RF_{SC_maxTS}, which indicate a reasonable degree of set coincidence between *IS*, the *minTS*, and the *maxTS*. All in all, we can conclude that while the sensitivity ranges for the raw consistency threshold and frequency cutoff are rather narrow, the solution is quite robust (though not perfectly so) in terms of fit measures when tested against a series of plausible analytic changes.

O 5.4

	RF_cov	RF_cons	RF_SC_minTS	RF_SC_maxTS
Robustness_Fit	0.917	0.966	0.883	0.752

Case-Oriented Robustness in Practice

In order to specifically identify which and what types of cases make the robustness of our initial solution less than perfect, we should also look at case-oriented robustness by using an XY plot, identifying types of cases, and calculating robustness case ratios. To obtain a robustness plot, we use the `rob.xyplot()` function, where we need to specify the test set (`test_sol =`), the initial solution (`initial_sol =`), and the outcome (`outcome =`). Additionally, we can jitter (`jitter = TRUE`) the case names and determine the font size (`fontsize =`) for better visualization. Option `all_labels = FALSE` shows only labels for the problematic cases in the upper-left and lower-right quadrants, while option `area_lab = TRUE` can be used to further label whether membership in *minTS* or *maxTS* is taken into consideration for the position of cases in each particular quadrant of the plot.

C 5.5

```
# Plotting the initial solution against the test set:

rob.xyplot(test_sol = TS,
           initial_sol = IS,
           outcome  = "HL",
           all_labels = FALSE,
           fontsize = 3.5,
           jitter=TRUE,
           area_lab=TRUE)
```

In the robustness plot (Figure 5.4), we see that indeed many of the cases are located on the diagonal. This means there is a high degree of overlap among *IS*, *minTS*, and *maxTS* – a graphical support of the findings generated with the robustness fit parameters used. However, there are quite a few cases

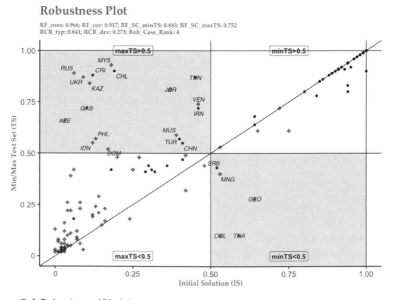

Figure 5.4 Robustness XY plot

in the problematic upper-left quadrant (possible cases). Some are possible typical (e.g., TUN, IRN, CRI), while some are possible deviant (e.g., PHL, AZE, RUS). Additionally, there are also a few cases located in the problematic lower-right quadrant (shaky cases): one shaky typical (SRB) and four shaky deviant consistency (MNG, GEO, COL, THA) cases. Since there are cases in both the upper-left quadrant and the lower-right quadrant, the *Rob_Case_Rank* parameter indicates that we are in the lowest case robustness rank. It therefore takes the value 4, indicating that the *IS* not only contains shaky cases, but there are also other possible cases that are part of the *maxTS* that could be typical or deviant consistency in kind had alternative decisions been made.

The names of the various types of cases that are created when intersecting *min/maxTS* and *IS*, together with their ratios, can also be identified using the `rob.cases()` function in which we specify the test set, the initial solution, and the outcome. At the beginning of Output 5.5, we find the three robustness case parameters.

C 5.6

```
# Obtaining names of case types and robustness case parameters:

rob.cases(test_sol = TS,
          initial_sol = IS,
          outcome = "HL")
```

By looking at *RCR_typ*, we see that the ratio of typical cases which are robust is close to 1, thus very high. Of all typical cases, 84.1 per cent are members of both *IS* and *minTS* and, therefore, robust. The ratio of robust deviant consistency cases *RCR_dev*, on the other hand, is very low. Of the deviant consistency cases, 27.3 per cent are robust for both *IS* and *minTS*, while the rest are, as we saw from the plot, shaky deviant consistency cases or possible deviant consistency cases. Finally, the last part of the output (*Rob_Case_Rank*) takes the value of 4 indicating that we simultaneously have cases that fall into both categories 'shaky' and 'possible'. This was already visible in Figure 5.4.

Below the three case-based parameters, the output also reports the names of the cases for each type. Due to its length, we only list the Robust Typical Cases (IS*minTS and Y > 0.5) and the Robust Deviant Cases (IS*minTS and Y < 0.5).

O 5.5

```
CaseParameters
                      RCR_typ  RCR_dev  Rob_Case_Rank
Robustness_Case_Ratio   0.841    0.273              4

CaseNames
Robust Typical Cases (IS*MIN_TS and Y > 0.5) :
```

Boolean Expression: GG*AH*HE + HE*~GG*HI*HW*AH

Cases in the intersection / Total number of cases: 37 / 131 =
    28.24 %
Cases in the intersection / Total number of cases Y > 0.5:   37 /
    52 = 71.15 %

Case Names:
ARG AUS AUT BRB BEL CAN HRV CYP CZE DNK EST FIN FRA DEU GRC HUN
    ISL IRL ISR ITA JPN KOR LUX MLT MNE NLD NOR POL PRT SVK SVN
    ESP SWE CHE GBR USA URY

Robust Deviant Cases (IS*MIN_TS and Y < 0.5) :

Boolean Expression: GG*AH*HE + HE*~GG*HI*HW*AH

Cases in the intersection / Total number of cases: 6 / 131 = 4.58
    %
Cases in the intersection / Total number of cases Y < 0.5:   6 / 79
    = 7.59 %

Case Names:
BRA BGR LVA LBN LTU ROM

Box 5.3 Core Points – Robustness

- For assessing the robustness of their QCA sufficient solution to various changes in analytic decisions, researchers can adopt a three-step protocol consisting of evaluating sensitivity ranges, fit-oriented robustness, and case-oriented robustness.
- Sensitivity ranges represent those ranges within which changes in calibration anchors, raw consistency threshold, and frequency cutoff can be made, in turn, without modifying the Boolean expression of the solution.
- Fit-oriented robustness allows researchers to evaluate how robust their initial solution is to multiple, simultaneous changes by assessing through parameters of fit the intersection between various alternative solutions created.
- Case-oriented robustness allows researchers to identify different types of cases (robust cases, shaky cases, and possible cases) in the intersection between various alternative solutions created.
- The functions for QCA robustness tests in R are `rob.inclrange()`, `rob.ncutrange()`, `rob.calibrange()`, `rob.fit()`, `rob.xyplot()`, and `rob.cases()`.

5.3   Cluster Diagnostics

Having introduced the reader to the possibilities of testing robustness with `SetMethods`, we now turn to the issue of clustered data.

5.3.1   The Problem

Researchers are frequently confronted with data that are structured in analytically relevant ways. For example, cases might be subgrouped into different geographic, substantive, or temporal clusters. When there is no condition in the truth table that captures these clusters, one effectively assumes that the difference between them is analytically irrelevant. In other words, in such situations researchers simply 'pool' the data across subgroups and assume that the 'pooled' result holds for all clusters. This, however, might not be true. Some clusters could be very different from others, and the general sufficiency pattern (the QCA solution and its parameters of fit) might vary widely across them. For instance, going back to our coach Susan example, imagine that the students she analyzed come from different neighborhoods in the city. While these neighborhoods could be of similar distance to the pitch, some have better bike lanes, others are better connected by public transportation, and so on. It could well be that the QCA solution we found when looking at all the players together does not apply equally well to players from specific neighborhoods. The pooled result would then be a mere artifact of having thrown into one basket cases that follow different causal recipes.

This section introduces a diagnostic tool that researchers can use when confronted with such structured data. This tool can be used to check whether the sufficiency pattern (or necessity, for that matter) holds across the different clusters in the data and whether pooling the data is a good analytic strategy. For this, the cluster diagnostics tool reports three different types of consistency (and also coverage) measures (García-Castro and Arino, 2016). It first reports the pooled consistency, which is the consistency of the solution formula and each of its terms for the entire pooled dataset. It then reports the between consistency, which is the consistency of the solution within each cluster. Finally, it also reports the within consistency, which is the consistency score of the solution and its terms for each case. This last measure, the within consistency, is only meaningful when a case is part of multiple clusters, such as when dealing with time series data where the different points in time are the clusters, and a case is measured at more than one time point.

Cluster diagnostics essentially consists of comparing these different consistency measures for identifying clusters within which the QCA solution does not hold. As we will see in the practical example in the next subsection, comparing the pooled consistency with the between consistency in each cluster can be done both by looking at a standardized distance measure of how much these differ, and by plotting the consistency values across clusters in order to spot the ones that deviate from the pattern. The same procedure is applied to within consistencies if this measure is meaningful, such as when the same case is measured across multiple clusters (e.g., in panel or time-series cross-sectional data).

5.3.2 Performing Cluster Diagnostics with `SetMethods`

To illustrate how cluster diagnostics tools works in practice, we again use the example of Paykani et al. (2018) on the conditions for explaining high life expectancy (see Box 5.2). Cases are 131 countries which belong to different regions around the globe. One could inquire into whether the QCA solution obtained from the pooled data applies to all different world regions. One way of investigating this could be by adding to our truth table a (multi-value) condition that captures each case's region. This, however, would make the already huge truth table even bigger.

Instead, researchers can test whether the pooled result holds across the various world regions by using the `cluster()` function from the `SetMethods` package. To use this function, the data must be saved in the so-called long format: if a case is measured across multiple clusters, these different measures are treated as separate cases and constitute separate rows in the data (for instance, when a case is measured at multiple time points). Additionally, the data needs to have a column containing the case names and a column with the cluster name for each case.

Within the `cluster()` function, we first need to specify the QCA result we obtained (`results = PS`). This is the result obtained using the `minimize()` function from the `QCA` package (as detailed in Chapter 4). We then need to specify the name of the calibrated dataset used (`data = PAYF`) and the name of the outcome (`outcome = "HL"`). Finally we specify the name of the column containing the case names (`unit_id = "COUNTRY"`) and the name of the column containing the cluster names (`cluster_id = "REGION"`).

C 5.7

```
# Determine robustness of results across clusters:

CS <- cluster(results = PS,
              data = PAYF,
```

```
              outcome  = "HL",
              unit_id  = "COUNTRY",
              cluster_id = "REGION",
              wicons   = FALSE)
CS
```

Output 5.6 reports consistencies, distance measures, and coverages for all sufficient terms of the solution for the pooled data, and between each cluster. By using the option `wicons = FALSE`, we do not print here within consistencies and coverages. In this example within consistencies do not make sense because each case (here: countries) is only part of one cluster, in this example, global regions. Looking first at the consistency distance measure ('From Between to Pooled'), we can see that it is rather small, thus indicating that the clusters do not differ too much and the pooled solution does adequately apply to each world region. Looking at the parameters of fit for each cluster, we see that this is indeed the case, and that, in general, consistencies for regions are at similar levels to the pooled consistency. There is one notable exception: the African Region appears to be an outlier, as its consistency score (0.376) strongly deviates from the pooled consistency (0.883). This means that the explanation for high life expectancy found for other world regions does not apply in the African Region. It further suggests that one might need to study this region separately: pooling it together with other world regions seems to produce misleading results in this particular research design.

O 5.6

Consistencies:

	GG*AH	HE*~GG*HI*HW
Pooled	0.883	0.871
Between African Region (33)	0.376	0.297
Between Eastern Mediterranean Region (8)	1.000	0.916
Between European Region (46)	0.918	1.000
Between Region of the Americas (26)	0.828	0.927
Between South–East Asian Region (8)	1.000	0.817
Between Western Pacific Region (10)	0.863	0.882

Distances:

	GG*AH	HE*~GG*HI*HW
From Between to Pooled	0.105	0.119

Coverages:

	GG*AH	HE*~GG*HI*HW
Pooled	0.741	0.207

Between African Region (33)	0.674	0.380
Between Eastern Mediterranean Region (8)	0.262	0.782
Between European Region (46)	0.919	0.079
Between Region of the Americas (26)	0.453	0.362
Between South−East Asian Region (8)	0.322	0.691
Between Western Pacific Region (10)	0.691	0.183

Additionally, after inspecting consistencies, one can also look at between coverage values. Even if the solution is consistent in each cluster, it could turn out that it empirically covers only very few cases in that group. In such a scenario, when the coverage is very low for both sufficient terms in a cluster, one might want to look for a missing sufficient term that more adequately captures the causal recipe that those cases follow. In the preceding example, we see that for most regions at least one of the sufficient terms has quite high coverage. However, in the Americas the coverage of both terms is slightly lower than for other regions. While this does not constitute reason for concern on its own, as the solution is still quite consistent in this region, one could look for a missing sufficient term to improve the empirical coverage of cases in the American region. If coverage of one sufficient term is particularly high for one cluster (here: the world region), one might use this information for labeling that term accordingly. For instance, coverage of term $\sim$ GG $*$ HI $*$ HW is much higher in the Eastern Mediterranean region than in the pooled data.

The function cluster.plot() displays the same information visually. The function works by inputting the result of the cluster diagnosis above (cluster.res = CS). Additionally, it has some options for better visualization: labs = for whether or not we want the names/labels of the clusters printed, size = for adjusting the size of these labels, angle = for rotating the labels, and wicons = FALSE for not displaying within consistency plots. We obtain plots for each sufficient term (see Figure 5.5). The plots display the consistency value across each cluster (the between consistency values) and a horizontal line at the pooled consistency benchmark to which we are comparing the between cluster values. We can see in this plot that while most regions are around the horizontal line for both sufficient terms, the African Region deviates from the pattern.

C 5.8

```
# Plot results of cluster diagnostics:

cluster.plot(CS,
             labs = TRUE,
             size = 7,
             angle = 15,
             wicons = FALSE)
```

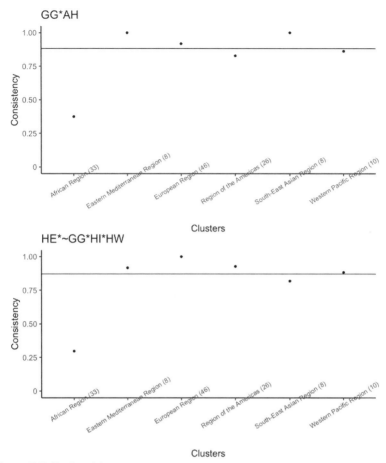

Figure 5.5 Cluster plot

Box 5.4 Core Points – Cluster Diagnostics

- Cluster diagnostics are used to check whether the subset pattern holds across different subgroups (clusters) of cases in the data and, therefore, whether pooling the data is a feasible analytic strategy or needs to be revised.
- The diagnostics consists of comparing the consistency of the sufficient solution across the entire data (pooled consistency) with the consistency of the solution in each cluster of cases (between consistency).
- The presence of clusters in which the solution consistency deviates strongly from the pooled consistency might indicate that pooling the data is not a good analytic strategy and that separate QCAs might be required for different clusters of cases.
- The functions for QCA cluster tests in R are `cluster()` and `cluster.plot()`.

5.4 Integrating Time and Temporality

Despite its (increasing) algorithmic and computational sophistication, QCA continues to be seen as a method with great affinities to qualitative approaches. One strength of qualitative approaches is their focus on the temporal dimension in describing and explaining social phenomena. Yet, QCA, in its standard form, does not emphasize the temporal dimension. In fact, most applied QCA seem to assume that time, timing, sequencing, or other aspects of the temporal dimension do not matter. For instance, in our recurrent example of coach Guenn trying to understand the reasons why some players arrive in time, while others do not, no notion of temporality has been included in the analysis. We disregarded any information on how long a player has already been living close by, whether a player was first a goalkeeper and then joined the team or vice versa, just to mention a few potentially relevant analytic features related to the temporal dimension.

Several strategies exist for injecting time into QCA (Schneider and Wagemann, 2012, section 10.3; Fischer and Maggetti, 2017; Verweij and Vis, 2020). They are summarized in Box 5.5. As it will become clear, while all of them represent an improvement over completely ignoring the temporal dimension, none of them comes close to the level of complexity and sophistication that characterizes good qualitative case study research and its handling of time. We therefore take the position that, ultimately, the combination of QCA with within-case analysis is needed in order to do justice to the complexities introduced by the temporal dimension. In Section 6.3, we spell out the details on how to combine QCA with case studies in so-called set-theoretic multi-method (SMMR) designs Schneider (2022).

Box 5.5 Core Points – Injecting Temporal Aspects into QCA

Before the analytic moment, calibrate sets expressing:
- information aggregated over time
- sequences of events
- changes over time

During the analytic moment, perform:

- separate truth table analyses for each temporal block
- temporal QCA (tQCA)
- two-step QCA
- coincidence analysis (CNA)/ causal-chain QCA

Box 5.5 (Cont.)

After the analytic moment, perform:

- cluster diagnostics

5.4.1 Calibration, Temporal QCA, Two-Step QCA

Before the analytic moment, one easy yet seldom used strategy incorporates temporality via the *calibration of sets*. Whenever researchers have empirical information at hand about the temporal order of their sets, they can use this in order to calibrate sets that capture this information. For instance, Paykani et al. (2018), in their QCA on the conditions for high life expectancy, use the average Gini value over the years 2010–2015 in order to calibrate their condition 'high income inequality'. By using the average, they throw out potentially useful information. Using the same raw data, one could also calibrate, for instance, the set 'increase in income inequality'. Cases with higher Gini in 2015 than in 2010 would be members of this set.

Another calibration-related strategy creates sets that express the *temporal order* between two (or more) sets. For instance, Paykani et al. (2018) use the two sets 'high wealth' and 'good governance'. Because raw data over time exist for both sets, it would be possible to distinguish those cases that first achieved good governance and then high wealth from those that display the opposite sequence. This difference can be captured in a set called 'first good governance, then high wealth'. We can add this 'sequence set' into the truth table next to the sets 'good governance' and 'high wealth'. Cases that display the sequence have a membership of 1, those that display the opposite sequence score 0, and all cases that are not members of either 'good governance' or 'high wealth' receive a 'don't care' score (-) in the sequence condition. This strategy of handling (short) sequences is called *temporal QCA* (tQCA) (Caren and Panofsky, 2005; Ragin and Strand, 2008). Provided empirical information is at hand, tQCA is a potentially useful strategy during the analytic moment, which should be applied more often than it currently is. A truth table coded in the way described here can easily be logically minimized with function `minimize()`, and the result we obtain will reveal sufficient terms that express sequences of conditions.

A third strategy for incorporating the temporal dimension, to be applied during the analytic moment, is to run a *separate QCA* for cases measured at different points in time. The study by Paykani et al. (2018) can again serve as an example here. They possess raw data over multiple years for all their conditions and the outcome. Rather than averaging this information for each set, one could run a separate QCA for each year in which data are available.

This strategy would be recommended if and when it is of interest to assess whether at different points in time the outcome occurs for different reasons. If there are time-point-sensitive solutions for the same outcome, one could go on and intersect the year-specific QCA solutions in order to obtain the part that explains the outcome that are robust over time. Note that when QCA is performed on data that is pooled over different time periods (or any other potentially analytically relevant cluster), we recommend using the `cluster()` function from package `SetMethods`. As explained in Section 5.3, this function tests whether pooling the data is warranted. If it is not, then the strategy of running separate QCAs is one way forward.

A fourth strategy that can be used for incorporating the temporal dimension is *two-step* QCA (Schneider and Wagemann, 2006; Schneider, 2019). This strategy is based on the distinction between remote and proximate conditions analyzed in separate steps. One element of remoteness is often the temporal distance to the outcome. In a first step, only remote conditions are analyzed. The second step then consists of an analysis of proximate conditions together with those remote conditions that 'survived' the first step. The updated two-step QCA approach (Schneider, 2019) requires that step 1 on remote conditions is an analysis of necessity, and step 2 an analysis of sufficiency. The type of sequence that two-step QCA can identify is when temporally remote conditions (step 1) are necessary conditions for proximate configurations to be sufficient for the outcome (step 2). Similarly to tQCA, two-step QCA can reveal sequences that lead to the outcome.

5.4.2   Coincidence Analysis (CNA), Causal Chains, and Common causes

A fifth strategy for incorporating temporality, also during the analytic moment, is the most formalized way of analyzing sequences with a method similar to QCA. This strategy has been decisively developed by Baumgartner (2009, 2013).

Principles

Under the label of *coincidence analysis* (CNA), an algorithm has been formulated that aims at uncovering two types of structure in the data: common causes and sequences. Common cause structures mean that one or more sets share the same condition(s). Sequences, or causal chains, represent structures in the data in which conditions lead to other conditions in a successive pattern.

Figures 5.6 and 5.7 provide a graphical representation of both types of structure. For the sake of illustration, let us return to our coach Susan mock example.

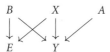

Figure 5.6 Common cause structure

Figure 5.7 Causal chain structure

As a reminder (see Box 4.1), the letters stand for the following conditions: X = living close by; A = arriving by bike; B = being a female player; E = being a goalkeeper; and Y = arriving in time.[12]

Figure 5.6 represents a common cause structure: 'being a goalkeeper' (E) and 'arriving in time' (Y) have similar conditions: both are brought about by 'being female' (B) or 'living close by' (X). 'Arriving in time' has the alternative condition of 'arriving by bike' (A). Expressed in Boolean terms, this common cause structure can be written as in expression 5.1.

$$(B + X + A < - > Y) * (B + X < - > E). \qquad (5.1)$$

Figure 5.7, instead, represents a causal chain, running from 'living close by' (X) or 'being female' (B) leading to 'being a goalie' (E), which, in turn, leads to 'arriving in time' (Y). An alternative route toward arriving in time consists of simply arriving by bike (A). This causal chain can be written as in expression 5.2.

$$(A + E < - > Y) * (B + X < - > E). \qquad (5.2)$$

Practice

How do we uncover such structures in our data? Baumgartner has devised both an algorithm of logical minimization and the R package cna for this task, together with a terminology that differs in several respects from the standard QCA speak as captured, for instance, in the glossaries in Rihoux and Ragin (2009) or Schneider and Wagemann (2012). Adrian Dusa, the author of the R package QCA, has implemented the function causalChain() and

---

[12] Figures 5.6 and 5.7 are adapted from Baumgartner and Thiem (2015, figure 1).

demonstrates that this function produces the same results as the corresponding functions in package cna[13] (Dusa, 2018, section 10.2). In the following, we choose the function causalChain() from package QCA over functions from package cna simply because it allows us to stay within the terminology and packages used throughout this book, and because we assume the typical reader of our book is an applied QCA researcher. We briefly demonstrate how to uncover the two types of dependencies outlined earlier.

In a standard QCA, users specify the outcome set and the condition sets. When uncovering sequences or causal chains, users need to show more flexibility: conditions might be the outcome of other conditions, and the outcome might actually be a condition for other conditions. In principle, one can leave it open and allow any of the sets involved to be considered the outcome and the remaining sets the conditions. In practice, though, some temporal order is usually known prior to the start of the logical minimization. In our coach Susan example, for instance, it is known prima facie that 'being female' cannot be the outcome of any of the other conditions. This means, 'being female' can only be at the beginning of a causal chain, not in the middle or at the end.

Let us illustrate the practical details with the example from Paykani et al. (2018). In its original version, the set 'high life expectancy' HL is the outcome and there is no temporal ordering among the five conditions. It could be argued, though, that the conditions used in Paykani et al. (2018) are of a quite different temporal nature. For example, having a 'high-quality educational system' HE could potentially be a condition for having 'good governance' GG in place.

If we want to see if there are any 'causal dependencies' among conditions, we use the argument ordering in function causalChain() to let the software know that in our analysis set 'high life expectancy' HL cannot be the cause for any of the other sets involved. In addition, for illustrative purposes, we impose the ordering that 'high wealth' (HW) cannot be the cause for 'good governance' GG. Beyond this, the function allows us to also specify a minimum threshold for the consistency (sol.cons) and coverage of the solution term(s) (sol.cov), the same as for the consistency of the prime implicants (pi.cons).[14] We are interested in the most parsimonious solution (include = "?") and set the number of cases required per truth table row to minimum 2 (n.cut = 2).[15]

---

[13] Baumgartner (personal conversation) provides evidence for diverging results in specific data scenarios.

[14] If these options are not specified, the default value for the argument sol.cov is 1, whereas the default for the argument pi.cons is 0.

[15] The argument row.dom = TRUE is used in order to limit model ambiguity.

C 5.9

```
# Detect temporal dependencies:

PAK_chain <- causalChain(data = PAYF,
                         ordering = "GG < HW < HL",
                         sol.cons = 0.8,
                         sol.cov = 0.7,
                         pi.cons = 0.8,
                         include = "?",
                         n.cut = 2,
                         row.dom = TRUE,
                         strict = TRUE)
PAK_chain
```

O 5.7

```
...
M2: AH <-> GG

...
M2: GG <-> HW
...


...
...
M4: HE*~HI + HE*HW <-> HL
```

The algorithm identifies three outcomes: good governance (*GG*), high wealth (*HW*), and high life expectancy (*HL*). For each outcome, there is model ambiguity and we report only one model in the output. According to this, an affluent health system (*AH*) leads to good governance (*GG*), which, in turn, leads to high wealth (*HW*). High wealth combined with high-quality education (*HE*) leads to high life expectancy (*HL*), but this ultimate outcome can also be brought about by combining *HE* with not-high income inequality (~*HI*).[16] Graphically, this can be represented as shown in Figure 5.8.

In principle, the idea of relaxing assumptions on the causal ordering of sets is both plausible and exciting. And in practice, the implementation of this approach to QCA has become much easier thanks to the existence of dedicated functions. However, giving up the assumption that there is only one outcome and no ordering among conditions significantly increases the complexity of the analysis. This, in turn, increases the sensitivity of results to analytic decisions. For instance, different orderings as specified in argument `ordering` lead to different results. Perhaps even more problematic from a point of view of

---

[16] We remind the reader that this example, just like all the others we are using in the book, is constructed for purely didactic purposes and without any ambition of contributing to the substantive topic.

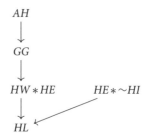

Figure 5.8 Causal chain – 'high life expectancy'

robustness is that results seem to strongly depend on the choice of the various thresholds for consistency and coverage. Strong theoretical priors are needed to adjudicate which ordering is superior to others and thorough robustness tests must be performed to gauge how sensitive the results are to the thresholds chosen. In addition, further conceptual questions need to be elaborated in order to link this relatively new approach to standard concerns in QCA. For instance, can or should causal orderings distinguish between necessity and sufficiency? Or, can untenable assumptions on remainders occur and, if so, be prevented?

In sum, several tools are at the applied QCA researcher's disposal for integrating different notions of time and temporality before, during, and after the analytic moment. All of them should be used more than they currently are. There is, however, a limit to what can be done before the complexity of the truth table and its logical minimization gets out of control. This is one reason why it is so fruitful to combine QCA, injected with notions of temporality, with within-case analyses, because the heavier lifting in terms of grappling with the time dimension can and should be done at the within-case level.

5.5 Summary

In this chapter, we have presented several tools for building a solid QCA that goes beyond the analytic moment. Researchers make several analytic decisions at various stages of their QCA; they are often confronted with cases that are grouped in analytically relevant ways; and they face situations in which timing and temporality might matter for explaining their outcome of interest. The tools introduced here allow researchers to deal with these issues in a transparent way, with the goal of improving the quality of inferences drawn from their QCA.

The first set of tools aimed at assessing the robustness of QCA results. The Robustness Test Protocol we presented consists of three steps: sensitivity ranges, fit-oriented robustness, and case-oriented robustness. Sensitivity ranges are the ranges within which calibration thresholds, raw consistency thresholds, and the frequency cutoff for truth table rows can be modified, in turn, without changing the Boolean formula of the sufficient solution. Fit-oriented robustness and case-oriented robustness, on the other hand, allow researchers to evaluate how robust their initial solution is to multiple, simultaneous, substantively plausible changes. Fit-oriented robustness comprises a series of parameters of fit for assessing the intersection between various alternative solutions created, whereas case-oriented robustness allows us to identify types of cases in these intersections. All three steps of the protocol can be implemented with functions available in the `SetMethods` package.

The second set of tools is designed for situations in which readers are confronted with clustered data. As some clusters might be very different from others, the clustering diagnostics tools introduced here can be used to check whether the sufficiency pattern is stable across the different clusters in the data and whether pooling the data is a good analytic strategy. The functions `cluster()` and `cluster.plot()` in package `SetMethods` provide the information for these diagnostics.

Finally, the last set of tools presented in this chapter aimed at dealing with time and temporality. After presenting various ways of dealing with time before, during, and after the analytic moment, we focused on coincidence analysis (CNA) as the most formalized way of analyzing sequences and causal chains. The `QCA` package offers the functionality for analyzing causal chains with the `causalChain()` function.

6 Post-QCA Tools

6.1 Introduction and Learning Goals

As discussed in Chapter 1, it significantly strengthens the inferences drawn based on QCA results if we connect these results to theoretical knowledge and within-case evidence before, during, and after the analysis (see Figure 1.6). In this chapter, we discuss two prominent tools of doing so after the analytic moment: set-theoretic theory evaluation and set-theoretic multi-method research (SMMR). Theory evaluation is a form of re-assessing theoretical hunches based on the results generated by QCA. While it can also be used for the identification of interesting cases for follow-up case studies, this task is better achieved with SMMR. The latter is a tool for identifying typical and deviant cases for comparative or single within-case analysis. In this chapter, we first demonstrate the use of theory evaluation and then turn to SMMR.

Box 6.1 Learning Goals – Post-QCA Tools

- Basic understanding of what theory evaluation and set-theoretic multi-method research are.
- Familiarity with how to apply formal set-theoretic theory evaluation for re-assessing theoretical hunches based on the results generated by QCA.
- Familiarity with how to use SMMR for the identification of cases for follow-up case studies after QCA.
- Ability to implement theory evaluation and SMMR in R.

6.2 Formal Set-Theoretic Theory Evaluation

This chapter introduces formal theory evaluation, a procedure for re-examining theories in light of empirical results generated with QCA. The goal of theory evaluation is to identify those elements of a theory that are supported by empirical evidence and those that are not, and to highlight ways in which the theory should be amended. Theory evaluation can also be used as a tool for selecting cases for within-case analysis. The notion of theory evaluations originates in Ragin (1987, pp. 118–121) and is further refined in Schneider and Wagemann (2012, chapter 11.3). The goal of this chapter is to enable readers to perform set-theoretic theory evaluation using the `theory.evaluation()` function in the R package `SetMethods`, and to interpret its output.

6.2.1 What Is Formal Theory Evaluation?

QCA has a close affinity with qualitative methods. It involves an iterative process of going back and forth between theory and evidence (Ragin, 2000). In this process, initial theoretical hunches play an important role in various crucial steps of the analytic process: in calibrating set membership scores, choosing cases and conditions, and specifying directional expectations for the intermediate solutions. This inherently iterative nature of the analytic process, plus the usually rather complex solution formulas make QCA incompatible with the logic of standard hypothesis testing (Schneider and Wagemann, 2012, section 11.3).

Ragin (1987, pp. 118–121) introduced formal set-theoretic theory evaluation as a way for QCA researchers to compare previously formulated theoretical expectations with empirical QCA findings. Unlike traditional hypothesis testing, it is a procedure for identifying which parts of the theory are supported by empirical evidence and which ones are not. When both a researcher's theory (T) and the empirical results (S) obtained via QCA are represented in Boolean terms, we can create four logically possible scenarios. Specifically, we can look at four intersections of T (our expectations), S (our findings), $\sim T$ (what we did not expect), and $\sim S$ (what we did not find). These areas represent parts of the theory that are in line with empirical findings, and parts in which the theory should be expanded or restricted in line with these findings. First, the intersection $T * S$ tells us the parts of our expectations that the results support. Second, we can look at those aspects of our theoretical expectations that the results do not support: the intersection $T * \sim S$. Third, we may also get findings that we did not expect ($\sim T * S$). And finally, the intersection $\sim T * \sim S$ tells us what we neither expected nor found.

Schneider and Wagemann (2012, chapter 11.3) refine theory evaluation and show how accounting for less-than-perfect consistency and coverage of QCA results can add leverage to these evaluations. This is an important addition, since nowadays in applied QCA deviations from perfect set relations are the rule rather than the exception. These findings usually allow for some degree of inconsistency, that is, some cases covered by a QCA solution do not show the outcome. Likewise, findings usually do not show a perfect coverage, leaving

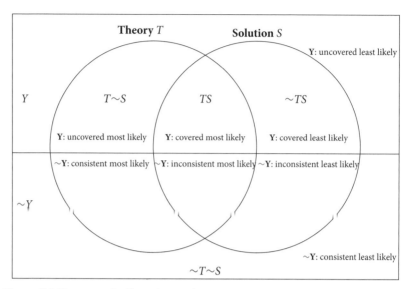

Figure 6.1 Theory evaluation – types of cases
Source: adapted from Oana and Schneider (2018)

some cases with the outcome unexplained. For theory evaluation, this means that in addition to each case's membership scores in T and S, also their membership in the outcome Y must be taken into account. This gives rise to eight different areas. Each area can be again expressed in Boolean terms and each area defines a different type of case.

Figure 6.1 displays the eight areas and the types of cases they contain. For example, only those cases in area $T * S$ that also display the outcome (Y) actually support the theory. We call these the 'covered most likely cases' as they are covered by the solution and also likely to have the outcome according to theoretical expectations. The more cases there are in this area, the stronger the support for the theory. In contrast, cases in the $T * S$ intersection that do not display the outcome ($\sim Y$) contradict both our theoretical expectations and our empirical findings. We call these 'inconsistent most likely', as they are inconsistent with the solution and were theoretically expected to display the outcome, but did not. These cases are puzzling and if they are numerous, the empirical support for the theory is undermined.

All cases in the $\sim T * S$ intersection are 'least likely' cases because they are not expected by the theory but part of the solution. They come in two variants 'covered' (Y) or 'inconsistent' ($\sim Y$) least likely. 'Covered least likely' cases suggest a need to expand the theory to include these types of cases, whereas 'inconsistent least likely' cases are both not in line with the theory and contradict our empirical solution. Furthermore, all cases in the $T * \sim S$

intersection are 'most likely', because they are expected by the theory but not part of the solution. They, too, come in two variants: 'uncovered most likely' (Y) cases support the theory, but contradict the solution. 'Consistent most likely' ($\sim Y$) cases are in line with the solution, but suggest a delimitation of the theory. Finally, cases in the $\sim T * \sim S$ intersection are neither expected by the theory nor part of the solution. When they display the outcome Y, they are 'uncovered least likely'; when they do not ($\sim Y$), they are 'consistent least likely'. Uncovered least likely cases are particularly puzzling as neither theory nor the solution suggest that they should display the outcome, yet they do.

6.2.2 Performing Theory Evaluation with `SetMethods`

In this section, we show how to obtain for each intersection (a) the Boolean expression; (b) the number and percentage of cases; and (c) the names of cases in each intersection. We also point to other useful options, such as handling model ambiguity and obtaining parameters of fit for the intersections between theory and empirics. Function `theory.evaluation()` in package `SetMethods` returns all this information.

For showing the implementation and interpretation of theory evaluation, we use the empirical example from Thomann (2015) (Box 6.2). This study looks at how and why countries which are fully compliant with EU directives 'customize' these directives to their own domestic particularities. The dataset is comprised of 76 veterinary drug regulations in Austria, France, Germany, and the United Kingdom (UK), and the outcome represents extensive customization of these regulations (*CUSTOM*). Six conditions are used for explaining this outcome: responsiveness to domestic adaptation of EU regulatory modes (*RESP*), the salience of the issue being regulated (*SAL*), domestic resistance (*RES*), the existence of numerous veto points (*VPO*) and veto players (*VPL*), and having a coercive interventionist style in the use of policy instruments (*COERC*).

Box 6.2 Empirical Example – Member State Implementation of EU Law (Thomann, 2015)

- *Research question*: Why do EU member states customize EU food safety policies?
- *Cases*: 76 veterinary drug regulations in Austria, France, Germany, and the UK
- *Outcome:* Extensive customization (*CUSTOM*)
- *Conditions*: Responsiveness to domestic adaptation of EU regulatory modes (*RESP*); High issue salience (*SAL*); Strong domestic resistance (*RES*); Numerous veto points (*VPO*); Numerous veto *players* (*VPL*); Coercive domestic interventionist style (*COERC*)

Box 6.2 (Cont.)

- *Sets*: Fuzzy and crisp
- *Source*: Thomann, Eva. 2015. Customizing Europe: transposition as bottom-up implementation. *Journal of European Public Policy*, 22(10), 1368–1387.

Two things are needed for using the `theory.evaluation()` function. First, we need the QCA solution as calculated with the `minimize()` function in the QCA package and stored into an object (here: `C_int`). This solution object is then input in the argument `empirics` of function `theory.evaluation()`. Second, we need to summarize our theoretical expectations (or our 'hunches') as a Boolean expression. Negated sets must be indicated with a '~', conjunctions with '*', and disjunctions with '+'. In our empirical example, Thomann (2015) derives several expectations from Europeanization theory. For the outcome CUSTOM, she specifies her theoretical hunches as follows: *RESP * SAL * RES * VPO + RESP * SAL * RES * VPL + RESP * COERC*. For the sake of clarity, it is advisable to store these hunches in an object (here: `TCUSTOM`). This theory object can be used in the argument `theory`. It is also possible to directly enter the Boolean expression for the hunches in this argument.

The `theory.evaluation()` function has several useful options. If the solution (conservative, parsimonious, or intermediate) presents model ambiguity at any stage, the option `"sol ="` identifies which model of the solution should be used (see Section 4.3.2 on model ambiguity). If the option `print.data =` is set to TRUE, the function will first return the membership of all cases in the solution, the theory, and the different intersections between them. Additionally, if the option `"print.fit ="` is set to TRUE, the function will also return the parameters of fit for the different intersections between theory and empirics (more information on these parameters of fit are provided later in this section). Setting `"print.data ="` and `"print.fit ="` to FALSE skips these parts of the output. We opt for this, due to space limitations.

C 6.1

```
# Summarize the theory in Boolean terms:

TCUSTOM <- "RESP*SAL*RES*VPO + RESP*SAL*RES*VPL + RESP*COERC"

# Perform theory evaluation:

TEV <- theory.evaluation(theory = TCUSTOM,
                    empirics = C_int,
                    outcome = "CUSTOM",
                    print.fit = FALSE,
                    print.data = FALSE)
TEV
```

Output 6.1 consists of the identification of cases in each of the eight intersections between the theory, solution, and outcome. The type of cases that each intersection represents (for example, intersection $T * S * Y$ contains covered most likely cases), the Boolean expression of the intersection, and the names of cases that populate this intersection are reported. For fuzzy sets, this means that the cases' membership in this particular intersection (say $\sim T * S * Y$) is higher than 0.5. Additionally, we see the number and percentage of cases in the intersection out of the total number of cases; as well as out of the total number of cases that display the outcome. In other words, the output provides a list of the covered and uncovered cases (by the empirical solution), whether they are most or least likely cases, as expected by the theory, whether they have membership above or below 0.5 in the outcome, and their percentage relative to the total number of cases.

From Output 6.1 we learn, for instance, that 52.94 per cent of the extensively customized policies in Thomann's study support the expectations of EU compliance theory (covered most likely cases in intersection $T * S * Y$).[1] These cases are described by the combination of conditions: $RESP * SAL * RES * VPO + RESP * SAL * RES * VPL + RESP * COERC * SAL * RES + RESP * COERC * VPO + RESP * COERC * SAL * VPL$. However, 23.53 per cent of cases do not conform to the expectations of compliance theory (covered least likely cases in intersection $\sim T * S * Y$), which leads her to conclude that customization follows partly different dynamics than compliance. Additionally, we can also notice there are even several uncovered least likely cases ($\sim T * \sim S * Y$), such as a3au, a3ge, etc., which comprise almost one fourth of all cases that are members of the outcome. These cases are members of the outcome contrary to what both theory and empirical findings would suggest. Within-case analysis of such cases is often a fruitful avenue for refining both the theoretical hunches and the empirical analysis.

O 6.1

```
CASES:
**********************

Covered  Most  Likely  (T*S  and  Y > 0.5)  :
_____

Boolean  Expression:  RESP*SAL*RES*VPO  +  RESP*SAL*RES*VPL  +  RESP*
     COERC*SAL*RES  +  RESP*COERC*VPO  +  RESP*COERC*~SAL*VPL

Cases  in  the  intersection/Total  number  of  cases:  27 / 76 = 35.53
      %
Cases  in  the  intersection/Total  number  of  cases  Y > 0.5:   27 /
      51 = 52.94 %
```

---

[1] The output is only partly presented here due to space limitations. In its full version, the output presents all eight types of cases rather than just the three presented here.

Case Names:
a4fr a4ge a5fr a5ge d10au d10fr d10ge d12au d12fr d12ge d13au
    d13fr d13ge d1au d1fr d1ge d2au d2fr d2ge d4au d4ge d6au
    d6fr d6ge d7au d7fr d7ge

Covered Least Likely (~T*S and Y > 0.5) :

Boolean Expression : ~SAL*~RESP*VPL*COERC + ~SAL*~COERC*~RESP*VPO
    + ~RES*~COERC*RESP*SAL + ~VPO*~VPL*~COERC*RESP*SAL

Cases in the intersection / Total number of cases: 12 / 76 = 15.79
    %
Cases in the intersection / Total number of cases Y > 0.5:   12 /
    51 = 23.53 %

Case Names:
a1au a1fr a1ge a3fr a4au d10uk d12uk d13uk d2uk d6uk d7uk d9fr

Uncovered Most Likely (T*~S and Y > 0.5) :

Boolean Expression : RESP*COERC*~SAL*~VPO*~VPL + RESP*COERC*~RES*
    ~VPO*SAL + RESP*COERC*~RES*~VPO*~VPL

Cases in the intersection / Total number of cases: 0 / 76 = 0 %
Cases in the intersection / Total number of cases Y > 0.5:   0 / 51
    = 0 %

Case Names:
No cases in this intersection

Uncovered Least Likely (~T*~S and Y > 0.5) :

Boolean Expression : ~RESP*SAL + ~VPO*~VPL*~RESP + ~RESP*COERC*~
    VPL + ~VPO*~RESP*~COERC + ~SAL*~COERC*~VPO + ~VPO*~SAL*~
    COERC + ~SAL*~COERC*RESP

Cases in the intersection / Total number of cases: 12 / 76 =
    15.79 %
Cases in the intersection / Total number of cases Y > 0.5:   12 /
    51 = 23.53 %

Case Names:
a3au a3ge a3uk d3au d3fr d3ge d5au d5ge d8uk d9au d9ge d9uk

One of the advanced options of the theory.evaluation() function reports the parameters of fit of the different intersections between theory and empirics. If the argument "print.fit =" is set to TRUE, the function returns these parameters of fit in the first part of the output, before reporting the cases. Output 6.2 shows only this first part of the output. It reports consistency, coverage, and PRI for each sufficient path of the solution chosen (*RESP * SAL * RES*, *RESP * SAL * ~COERC*, etc.), for the entire solution formula, for the theory alone, and for the different intersections between the two. Note, however, that these parameters must be interpreted cautiously because the cases' membership in these intersections is typically highly skewed. For example, the parameters of fit will not necessarily tell us beyond any doubt if an intersection is populated by deviant cases consistency in kind. Hence, reporting the percentage of cases with membership above or below 0.5 in the outcome is a more attractive piece of information that researchers should take into account when evaluating their theories.

O 6.2

```
FIT:
**********************

                        Cons.Suf  Cov.Suf    PRI
RESP*SAL*RES              0.8810   0.3450   0.8360
RESP*SAL*~COERC          0.8870   0.2080   0.8220
RESP*VPO*COERC           0.9040   0.3790   0.8480
~SAL*VPL*COERC           0.8260   0.2370   0.7050
~RESP*~SAL*VPO*~COERC    0.7959   0.0654   0.4262
Sol.Formula              0.8240   0.7220   0.7540
Theory                   0.8570   0.5390   0.8030
T*S                      0.8860   0.5180   0.8380
~T*S                     0.8240   0.3520   0.6920
T*~S                     0.9070   0.1630   0.7830
~T*~S                    0.4520   0.4070   0.2680
```

Box 6.3 Core Points – Set-Theoretic Theory Evaluation

- Set-theoretic theory evaluation is a tool for comparing previously formulated theoretical expectations summarized in a Boolean form with empirical QCA findings.
- Unlike traditional hypothesis testing, this procedure is used for assessing which parts of the theory are supported by empirical empirical evidence and which ones not by assessing the Boolean intersection of the theory and the empirical findings.

> **Box 6.3 (Cont.)**
>
> • The procedure essentially consists of identifying different types of cases in the areas when intersecting theoretical expectations with empirical findings.
> • The function for performing set-theoretic theory evaluation in R is `theory.evaluation()`.

6.3   Set-Theoretic Multi-Method Research (SMMR)

QCA is a case-oriented method. Case knowledge and a focus on cases come into play at all stages of performing a QCA. As explained in Chapter 1, before the analytic moment, both the delimitation of the relevant universe of cases and meaningful calibration depend on what researchers have already learned about their (potential) cases. Likewise, during the analytic process (see Chapters 3 and 4), standards of good QCA practice demand that cases do not disappear behind Boolean expressions and parameters of fit. The topic we are turning to now is how we can bring cases back into the picture *after* a QCA result has been produced. We frame this task under the label of set-theoretic multi-method research (SMMR; Schneider and Rohlfing, 2013, 2016, 2019; Rohlfing and Schneider, 2013, 2018; Beach and Rohlfing, 2018). For a detailed book-long treatment of SMMR, see Schneider (2022).

6.3.1   What Is SMMR?

To illustrate what SMMR is about, take the QCA result displayed in Table 6.1, based on data from Paykani et al. (2018) (Box 5.2). It looks like, and in fact is, a perfectly normal QCA result: equifinality, conjunctural causation, and a less-than-perfect fit of this Boolean expression with the underlying data from which it has been derived. However, just presenting the solution formula leaves questions unanswered. Which mechanism(s) link these sufficient terms to the outcome? Which cases are typical for each sufficient term? Which cases contradict our sufficiency claims? And which cases remain unexplained by our QCA solution? One effective way to answer these questions is through studying specific cases. SMMR is based on the premise that QCA-based inference becomes stronger if and when we add within-case evidence.

One first step in the right direction is presenting the result in the form of XY plots, as shown in Figures 6.2 and 6.3.[2] In fact, XY plots should belong to

---

[2] For reason of space, we only display the XY plot of one sufficient term and the solution formula.

Table 6.1 Intermediate solution for outcome 'High Life Expectancy'

	consS	PRI	covS	covU
HE * GG * HW	0.901	0.864	0.800	0.579
HE * AH * HI * HW	0.914	0.793	0.246	0.025
Solution	0.898	0.858	0.826	

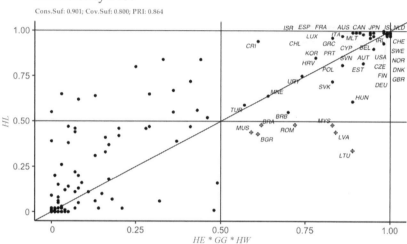

Figure 6.2 Sufficient term HE * GG * HW

the standard graphical tools for visualizing QCA results. It is difficult, however, to read the case labels in XY plots when several dozens of cases are analyzed. Additionally, the plot on its own does not actually tell us which of these cases we should study in depth and for which analytic purposes. Guiding these decisions is precisely what SMMR is about: based on a QCA result, it identifies the best available cases for within-case analysis. SMMR, therefore, is the formalized framework within which the analysis of a truth table via QCA (cross-case level) is combined with process tracing[3] (within-case level).

This combination can come in two sequences. Either we start with process tracing followed by a QCA, or vice versa, we start with a QCA followed by process tracing (Beach and Rohlfing, 2018). In this chapter, we focus on the QCA-first variant of SMMR, that is, we treat it as a tool to be used after the analytic moment.[4]

---

[3] We adopt a broad conception of process tracing and causal mechanisms here.

[4] The process tracing-first variant of SMMR is a tool that belongs to the stage before the analytic moment.

Sufficiency Plot

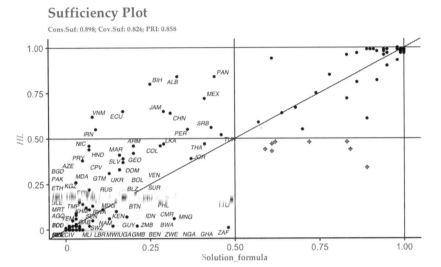

Figure 6.3 XY plot – QCA solution formula

The analytic goals of SMMR are (a) to identify the within-case mechanisms that explain why a given cross-case sufficient term identified via QCA does produce the outcome of interest and (b) to use within-case evidence on mechanisms to identify which elements (conjuncts or entire conjunctions) are missing from the QCA solution. The first goal of SMMR – the identification of causal mechanisms – probes into the causal properties of our QCA solution. The question is whether a sufficient term not only makes a difference to the outcome of interest, but whether it does so by also making a difference to a within-case causal mechanism. With regard to the second goal, SMMR can be used to improve our QCA model by identifying conditions that we have omitted because consistency and solution coverage are not perfect (see the QCA solution in Table 6.1). This use is similar, but not identical, to the pre-analytic moment stage of QCA, where we aim at solving contradictory truth table rows by respecifying the model (adding conditions), concepts (re-calibrating), and scope conditions (adding or dropping cases) (see step 4 in Section 4.3.1).

6.3.2   Identifying Typical and Deviant Cases

In order to pursue each of these two goals of SMMR – model specification and causal inference – researchers must choose the appropriate types of cases for within-case analysis. Case types are defined by the QCA solution formula. Depending on a case's membership in the outcome Y, a sufficient term T or the solution formula S, cases count as typical, individually irrelevant, deviant

Table 6.2 Types of cases in SMMR

Membership in sufficient		Type of case
$T > 0.5$	$Y \geq T$	(1) Typical
$T > 0.5$	$Y < T$	(2) Deviant consistency in degree
$T > 0.5$	$Y < .5$	(3) Deviant consistency in kind
$S < 0.5$	$Y > .5$	(4) Deviant coverage
$S < 0.5$	$Y < .5$	(5) Individually irrelevant (IIR)

Note: S = solution; T = term; Y = outcome.

Source: Schneider and Rohlfing (2019, table 2).

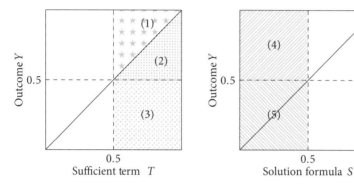

Figure 6.4 XY plot – types of cases
Source: Oana and Schneider (2018, figure 2)

consistency, or deviant coverage. Table 6.2 lists all the main types of cases in SMMR.[5] Figure 6.4 provides the same information in graphical form. Note that for typical cases and for deviant consistency cases, the point of reference is the sufficient term. Why? Because we need to know for which configuration the case is typical or deviant. In contrast, for deviant coverage cases and for individually irrelevant cases, the point of reference is the entire solution term (Schneider and Rohlfing, 2013). Why? Because we need to know which cases are left unexplained by *all* our sufficient terms in the QCA solution, not just unexplained by one or some terms.

Figure 6.2 displays the XY plot for the sufficient term $HE * GG * HW$. For this term, there are many typical cases in the upper triangle in the upper-right quadrant, such as Canada (CAN) or Italy (ITA). Deviant consistency cases in kind are Romania (ROM) or Lithuania (LTU). They are puzzling because they

---

[5] We limit ourselves to QCA solutions of sufficiency. Please see Schneider and Rohlfing (2013) and Rohlfing and Schneider (2013) for more details on SMMR based on necessary conditions.

have membership in the sufficient term but not in the outcome. Cases such as Hungary (HUN) or Slovakia (SVK) are deviant cases consistency in degree. They are members of both the sufficient term and the outcome, but they fall below the main diagonal and are therefore inconsistent cases for the sufficiency statement. This case type can only occur when fuzzy sets are used. They are not useful for within-case analysis because they can neither count as typical, nor as deviant cases.[6]

The XY plot in Figure 6.3 shows the entire solution rather than a single sufficient term. When taking the entire solution as the point of reference, we are mostly interested in the cases located in the left-hand side of the plot. This is because the goal of looking at the entire solution is to find out which cases are left unexplained by all our sufficient terms together. We, therefore, identify deviant cases coverage in the upper-left quadrant (for instance, Albania [ALB] or Mexico [MEX]) and individually irrelevant (IIR) cases in the lower left quadrant (for instance, Egypt [EGY] or Rwanda [RWA]). The former are puzzling because they have membership in the outcome but are not explained by any of the sufficient terms of the QCA solution. IIR cases in and of themselves are not of interest. They do play an important role in some forms of comparative within-case analyses that we discuss later.

6.3.3   Types of Cases and Analytic Goals

Now that we have our types of cases defined, the question is which of them should be chosen for either model improvement or causal inference SMMR designs. We answer this question by first assuming that a researcher is performing a single within-case study. After that, we turn to comparative within-case studies.

Single Within-Case Analysis

Box 6.4 Core Points – Conjuncts and Conjunctions

- A conjunct is a set that together with other sets forms a conjunction. For instance, A is a conjunct in the conjunction $A * B * C$.
- If a conjunction can be interpreted as sufficient for an outcome $A * B * C \rightarrow Y$, then we often call it a sufficient conjunction or sufficient term.
- If the conjunction is deemed sufficient, then a conjunct like A is also often labeled as an INUS condition.

---

[6] Due to limitations of space, we base our discussion on fuzzy sets. Unless explicitly pointed out, everything we explain holds for both fuzzy and crisp (and multi-value) sets.

Table 6.3 Types of cases and analytic goals in SMMR

Type of case	Goal of within-case analysis
Typical uniquely covered	Inference on mechanism
Deviant consistency (degree)	Not recommended
Deviant consistency (kind)	Identify missing conjunct
Deviant coverage	Identify missing conjunction
IIR	Not useful for single within-case analysis

Source: adapted from Oana and Schneider (2018).

Table 6.3 summarizes the link between the type of case and the goals of single within-case analyses. Typical cases should be chosen when the goal is to identify the causal mechanism (M) that links the sufficient term (T) to the outcome (Y). A typical case is uniquely covered if it is typical for only one sufficient term in the equifinal solution formula. The analysis of the two types of deviant cases – consistency and coverage – pursues the goal of improving the QCA model. When analyzing deviant consistency cases, we want to identify INUS conditions that should be part of a sufficient term produced by the QCA. In turn, by analyzing deviant coverage cases, we can identify entire omitted sufficient terms. Within-case analysis on individually irrelevant (IIR) cases is, as the name suggests, not relevant for single-case process tracing.[7]

Single within-case studies have a long tradition in social science research. Almost unavoidably, they often require the use of counterfactuals. How would the outcome in my case change if the purported cause changed? Or, what if a specific event had not taken place? Would this have changed the mechanism in my case? These and similar questions on hypothetical scenarios are valuable and should follow the rules for counterfactuals formulated in the literature (e.g., Lebow, 2010; Emmenegger, 2012). Yet, if empirical data are at hand, comparative case studies seem superior because they help us avoid having to speculate about what would have happened. Therefore, well-crafted comparisons should, if not replace, then at least complement counterfactual reasoning.

Comparative Within-Case Analysis

In SMMR, much of the needed comparative evidence might be at hand because it builds on QCA, and QCA is, by definition, a comparative method. There are four forms of comparison in SMMR. They are listed in Table 6.4, together with the analytic goal associated with each within-case comparison.

---

[7] This is because one principle of SMMR stipulates that in order to learn something about the conditions of an outcome, at least one case under analysis must be a member of either the condition or the outcome or both (Schneider and Rohlfing, 2013).

Table 6.4 Forms of comparisons and their goals in SMMR

Comparison	Inferential goal
Typical – IIR	Causal properties of mechanism
Typical – typical	Generalizability of mechanism
Typical – deviant consistency	Identify omitted conjunct
IIR – deviant coverage	Identify omitted conjunction

Source: adapted from Schneider and Rohlfing (2019, table 3).

The comparison of a typical case with an IIR case aims at testing the causal properties that link a specific sufficient term (T) to the outcome (Y). In our within-case analysis, we want to find out whether the sufficient condition T not only causes Y, but also triggers mechanism M that then leads to Y. The comparative within-case analysis of two typical cases helps us to establish whether the causal mechanism found in these cases can be generalized to all cases that are typical for the sufficient term under investigation. The remaining two forms of comparison serve the purpose of identifying elements omitted from the QCA. We compare a typical case with a deviant case consistency in order to identify an omitted INUS condition from a sufficient term that is already part of our QCA solution formula. We compare an IIR case and a deviant case coverage, in turn, in order to identify an entire new conjunction that we could not identify with our QCA. Figure 6.5 visualizes the four feasible forms of comparative within-case analyses and their analytic goals.

For applied QCA, we need to go one step further and answer the question: How do we know which cases in our data are the best ones for within-case analysis? For example, look at the XY plot in Figure 6.3. There are multiple deviant coverage and IIR cases. This raises the question which (pair) of them is the best one available for within-case analysis. Likewise, which of the many typical cases in Figure 6.2 is the most appropriate for process tracing on the mechanism linking the sufficient term and the outcome? Visual inspection quickly reaches its limits. Moreover, we do not necessarily see from the plot many of the selection principles developed in the SMMR literature (Rohlfing and Schneider, 2013, 2018; Schneider and Rohlfing, 2013, 2016, 2019; Schneider, 2022) by which the best available case or pair of cases is identified. What we need is a dedicated set of functions that perform the job of identifying the best available cases. The smmr() function in package SetMethods does precisely this. It has all of the case selection criteria implemented. We now show how to use this function and explain any additional selection criterion if and when it is necessary to understand the output of the smmr() function.

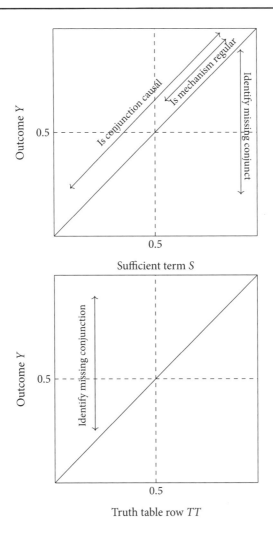

Figure 6.5 Forms of feasible comparisons

Source: adapted from Oana and Schneider (2018, figure 1)

6.3.4   Performing SMMR with `SetMethods`

As input, the `smmr()` function requires information on whether the goal is a single-case or a comparative within-case analysis. This information is provided in the argument `match`. If set to FALSE, case selection is done for single within-case analysis; if set to TRUE, case pairs for comparative within-case analysis are identified. Furthermore, within each of these two SMMR forms, we need to specify which single-case or comparative analysis we want to perform.

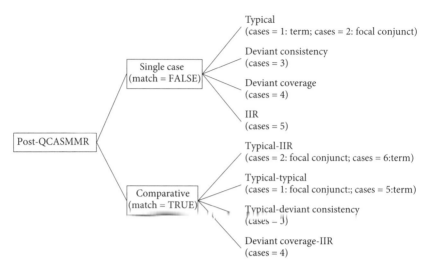

Figure 6.6 Forms of SMMR as specified in function `smmr()` in `SetMethods`
Source: Oana and Schneider (2018)

This is done by the argument `cases`. Figure 6.6 displays how this works. A numeric value assigned to the argument `cases` determines which single-case or comparative within-case types will be displayed. For instance, if we wish to obtain a list of the best available deviant consistency cases for single within-case analysis, we need to set argument `match = FALSE` and argument `cases = 3`.

Continuing with our example of the conditions for outcome 'high life expectancy' by Paykani et al. (2018) (see Box 5.2), the intermediate solution formula shown in Table 6.1 is produced with the following R code.

C 6.2

```
sol_yi <- minimize(TT_y,
                   details = TRUE,
                   include = "?",
                   dir.exp = c(HE, GG, AH, ~HI, HE))
sol_yi
```

Performing Single Within-Case SMMR

In order to identify typical cases for single within-case analysis, function `smmr()` needs to be specified as follows. The argument `term` determines which of the four sufficient terms we are focusing on. By choosing `term = 1`, we select the first sufficient term $HE * GG * HW$.

C 6.3

```
# Identify  typical  cases  for  single  within-case  analysis:

typ_y <- smmr(results = sol_yi,
               outcome = "HL",
               sol = 1,
               match = FALSE,
               cases = 2,
               term = 1,
               max_pairs = 7)
typ_y
```

With argument `cases` set to 2 and max_pairs = 7, `smmr()` lists the first seven best typical cases for within-case analysis.[8] The sufficient term we are focusing on consists of three conjuncts (*HE*,*GG*, and *HW*). In order to establish the causal properties of the sufficient term, we need to investigate whether conjunction $HE * GG * HW$ makes a difference to outcome *Y* by making a difference to mechanism *M*. This, in turn, requires that we investigate whether taking away any one of the three conjuncts also makes the within-case mechanism *M* disappear (Schneider and Rohlfing, 2019). This is why we need to perform process tracing separately on cases that are typical for focal conjunct *HE*, for *GG*, and for *HW*, respectively. When we probe the causal properties of one conjunct, it is considered the focal conjunct. All other remaining conjuncts in the conjunction are called complementary conjuncts.

O 6.3

```
Typical  Cases - Focal  Conjunct  HE :
```

	FocalConj ConsFC	Outcome MostTypTerm	CompConj	Term	UniqCov	Best	MostTypFC	Rank
CYP	0.94 TRUE	0.96 FALSE	0.97	0.94	TRUE	0.10	FALSE	1
MLT	0.92 TRUE	0.98 FALSE	0.96	0.92	TRUE	0.20	FALSE	1
LUX	0.90 TRUE	0.99 FALSE	1.00	0.90	TRUE	0.28	FALSE	1
TUR	0.57 TRUE	0.59 FALSE	0.60	0.57	TRUE	0.47	FALSE	1
HRV	0.78 TRUE	0.85 FALSE	0.84	0.78	FALSE	0.36	FALSE	1
FRA	0.99 TRUE	0.99 FALSE	0.98	0.98	TRUE	0.02	TRUE	2

[8] If researchers wish to see more typical cases, they can set argument `max_pairs` to a number higher than the default value 5.

	FocalConj ConsFC	Outcome	CompConj MostTypTerm	Term	UniqCov	Best	MostTypFC	Rank
JPN	0.99 TRUE	1.00	0.98 FALSE	0.98	TRUE	0.04	FALSE	2

Typical Cases — Focal Conjunct GG :

	FocalConj ConsFC	Outcome	CompConj MostTypTerm	Term	UniqCov	Best	MostTypFC	Rank
NLD	0.99 TRUE	0.99	1.00 TRUE	0.99	TRUE	0.01	TRUE	1
FRA	0.98 TRUE	0.99	0.99 FALSE	0.98	TRUE	0.04	FALSE	1
JPN	0.98 TRUE	1.00	0.99 FALSE	0.98	TRUE	0.06	FALSE	1
ESP	0.95 TRUE	0.99	0.96 FALSE	0.95	TRUE	0.13	FALSE	1
KOR	0.94 TRUE	0.99	0.96 FALSE	0.94	TRUE	0.16	FALSE	1
GRC	0.86 TRUE	0.97	0.90 FALSE	0.86	TRUE	0.36	FALSE	1
ISR	0.91 TRUE	0.99	0.96 FALSE	0.91	FALSE	0.25	FALSE	1

Typical Cases — Focal Conjunct HW :

	FocalConj ConsFC	Outcome	CompConj MostTypTerm	Term	UniqCov	Best	MostTypFC	Rank
SVN	0.95 TRUE	0.97	0.96 FALSE	0.95	TRUE	0.09	FALSE	1
PRT	0.94 TRUE	0.98	0.95 FALSE	0.94	TRUE	0.14	FALSE	1
CHL	0.83 TRUE	0.96	0.90 FALSE	0.83	TRUE	0.43	FALSE	1
CRI	0.61 TRUE	0.94	0.88 FALSE	0.61	TRUE	1.05	FALSE	1
URY	0.74 TRUE	0.75	0.80 FALSE	0.74	FALSE	0.28	FALSE	1
AUS	0.99 TRUE	0.99	0.99 TRUE	0.99	TRUE	0.01	TRUE	2
CAN	0.99 TRUE	0.99	0.99 TRUE	0.99	TRUE	0.01	TRUE	2

For each group of typical cases, the function lists several pieces of information (see Output 6.3). The best available case is always listed first: the case's membership in the focal conjunct (*HE* when we focus on *HE*); in the outcome, in the intersection of the complementary conjunct(s), that is, the other conjuncts that make up the term of interest (*GG * HW* when we focus on *HE*); and in the term under investigation (here *HE * GG * HW*). Column 'UniqCov' shows whether the case is typical for only the sufficient term *HE * GG * HW* or also for any other sufficient term in our solution formula. The next column shows whether the case is the best available typical case.[9] Column MostTypFC states whether the case obtains the smallest value in column 'Best'. The next column reports the rank to which the case belongs. In general, cases from higher ranks are better than from lower ranks.[10] The column 'ConsFC' indicates whether a case's membership in the focal conjunct is smaller than its membership in the outcome, that is, whether it is consistent with a sufficiency claim. The last column shows whether a case is the most typical case if we look at the entire sufficient term instead of its individual conjuncts. From the output, we thus learn that Cyprus is the best available typical case for process tracing on focal conjunct *HE*, Netherlands for focal conjunct *GG*, and Slovenia for focal conjunct *HW*.

To identify the best available deviant consistency case, we do not need to distinguish between focal and complementary conjuncts. Instead, the selection is straightforwardly based on the entire term. The specification of the function smmr() looks as follows.

C 6.4

```
# Identify deviant consistency cases for single within−case
    analysis:

dcon_y <− smmr(results = sol_yi,
               outcome = "HL",
               sol = 1,
               match = FALSE,
               cases = 3)
dcon_y
```

We do not have to specify which term we are interested in because the function automatically lists deviant consistency cases for each term and ranks them from best to worst. For sufficient term $HE * GG * HW$, Lithuania is the most deviant consistency case, for $HE * AH * HI * HW$ it is Lebanon. As before, the output reports each case's membership in the term of interest and the outcome. The column 'Best' displays each case's score on the formula that calculates how much it approaches the ideal-typical deviant consistency case.[11] The column 'most_deviant' simply reports whether the case in question displays the smallest value in 'Best', and thus is the most deviant consistency case in the data.

---

[9] The values in the column 'Best' and in similar columns for other types of cases are calculated based on formulas that are explained in detail in Oana and Schneider (2018); Schneider and Rohlfing (2019); and updated in Schneider (2022).

[10] The details of how ranks are constructed are explained in Schneider and Rohlfing (2019) and further explicated in Schneider (2022).

[11] Simply put, the ideal-typical deviant consistency case is located in the lower-right corner of an XY plot and shows the maximum different membership score in the term and the outcome (Schneider and Rohlfing, 2013).

O 6.4

```
Deviant Consistency Cases :

     Cases         Term TermMembership Outcome Best MostDevCons
21   LBN  HE*AH*HI*HW          0.61    0.47 1.25        TRUE
11   BRA  HE*AH*HI*HW          0.53    0.48 1.42       FALSE
4    LTU   HE*GG*HW            0.89    0.34 0.56        TRUE
3    LVA   HE*GG*HW            0.84    0.44 0.76       FALSE
5    MYS   HE*GG*HW            0.83    0.48 0.82       FALSE
7    ROM   HE*GG*HW            0.72    0.48 1.04       FALSE
2    BGR   HE*GG*HW            0.61    0.43 1.21       FALSE
1    BRA   HE*GG*HW            0.62    0.48 1.24       FALSE
6    MUS   HE*GG*HW            0.59    0.44 1.26       FALSE
```

The last type of case relevant for single-case SMMR is the deviant coverage case. We obtain this list by setting argument `cases` to the value 4.

C 6.5

```
# Identify deviant coverage cases for single within−case
    analysis:

dcov_y <− smmr(results = sol_yi,
               outcome = "HL",
               sol = 1,
               match = FALSE,
               cases = 4)
dcov_y
```

Deviant coverage cases are puzzling because our QCA solution could not explain why the outcome occurred in these cases. Within-case analysis in these cases therefore aims at identifying hitherto overlooked combinations of conditions. Analytically, the best place to start this discovery is by identifying the truth table to which a deviant coverage case belongs (Schneider and Rohlfing, 2013). This is why the function smmr() lists the best available deviant coverage cases for each truth table row that does contain at least one such case. In addition, Output 6.5 shows each case's membership in the solution formula, its score in the formula 'Best', its membership in the truth table row and the outcome and whether these two scores are consistent with a claim of sufficiency, and, finally, whether in its truth table row it is the most deviant coverage case. For each truth table row, cases are ranked based on whether their truth table row membership is smaller than in the outcome (the column 'Cons_TT') and then their value in the column 'Best'.

0 6.5

Deviant Coverage Cases :

	Case	SolMembership	TT_HE	TT_GG	TT_AH	TT_HI	TT_HW	TT_row_membership	Outcome	Best
1	ALB	0.33	0	0	0	0	0	0.53	0.84	0.47
12	VNM	0.08	0	0	0	0	0	0.82	0.62	0.18
4	ECU	0.17	0	0	0	1	0	0.58	0.65	0.42
9	PER	0.36	0	0	0	1	0	0.56	0.55	0.44
5	IRN	0.09	0	0	0	1	1	0.54	0.55	0.46
2	BIH	0.25	0	0	1	1	0	0.54	0.80	0.46
6	JAM	0.29	0	1	0	1	0	0.59	0.65	0.41
8	PAN	0.44	0	1	0	1	1	0.56	0.84	0.44
7	MEX	0.41	0	1	0	1	1	0.53	0.72	0.47
10	SRB	0.43	0	1	1	0	1	0.52	0.56	0.48
3	CHN	0.31	1	0	0	1	0	0.55	0.64	0.45
11	TUN	0.46	1	1	0	0	0	0.53	0.52	0.47

	MostDevCov	ConsTT
1	FALSE	TRUE
12	TRUE	FALSE
4	TRUE	TRUE
9	FALSE	FALSE
5	TRUE	TRUE
2	TRUE	TRUE
6	TRUE	TRUE
8	TRUE	TRUE
7	FALSE	TRUE
10	TRUE	TRUE
3	TRUE	TRUE
11	TRUE	FALSE

Among other things, we see that there are two cases in the truth table row with all conditions negated (row 0,0,0,0,0). Among them, Albania is the best available deviant coverage case because Vietnam, the second case in this row, displays a smaller value in the column 'Best'. However, its membership in the truth table row exceeds that in the outcome and is therefore not consistent with a claim of sufficiency.[12]

Performing Comparative Within-Case SMMR

We specify the four forms of comparative within-case analysis via the `smmr()` function by setting the argument `match = TRUE`. For the comparison between a typical and an individually irrelevant case, the argument `cases` needs to be set to 2. With the argument `term`, we specify which sufficient term in the QCA solution we want to focus on.

C 6.6

```
# Identify best-matching pair of typical and IIR cases for
     comparative within-case analysis:

typiir_y <- smmr(results = sol_yi,
                 outcome = "HL",
                 sol = 1,
                 match = TRUE,
                 cases = 2,
                 term = 1)

typiir_y
```

Let us continue to focus on the same term 1 ($HE * GG * HW$). Because the goal of the comparison of a typical and an IIR case is probing the causal properties of mechanism M, we again have to perform separate within-case analyses for each focal conjunct in turn. In order to be causal, each focal conjunct in the conjunction must make a difference to mechanism M. In other words, each conjunct must be a necessary element of the conjunction – that is, it must be an INUS condition. When looking at focal conjunct HE, we learn that Cyprus (typical case) and Botswana (IIR case) form the best-matching pair for this analytic purpose. This pair belongs to the best rank (rank 1), Cyprus is a uniquely covered typical case, and Botswana is a globally uncovered IIR case. This means Botswana is not a member of any of the two sufficient terms in our QCA solution. Cyprus' membership in the focal conjunct is smaller than its membership in the outcome (column 'ConsFC'), but it is neither the most typical case for the entire term nor the focal conjunct. There are other pairs of cases that fulfill these criteria. However, among all of them, the pair Cyprus–Botswana displays the best (aka smallest) value on the 'Best' measure. For the

---

[12] The function `smmr()` can also display all IIR cases, sorted by the truth table to which they best belong. For this, the argument `cases` needs to be set to value 5. Since, however, IIR cases are not useful for single within-case SMMR, we do not show them here.

other two focal conjuncts, other pairs of cases qualify as best-matching (NLD–RUS for focal conjunct *GG*, and SVN–JOR for focal conjunct *HW*).

O 6.6

```
Focal Conjunct HE :
```

	Typical	IIR	UniqCov	GlobUncov	Best	PairRank	ConsFC
	MostTypTerm	MostTypFC					
182	CYP BWA	TRUE		TRUE	0.90	1	TRUE
	FALSE	FALSE					
1304	CYP SUR	TRUE		TRUE	0.91	1	TRUE
	FALSE	FALSE					
191	MLT BWA	TRUE		TRUE	0.97	1	TRUE
	FALSE	FALSE					
1313	MLT SUR	TRUE		TRUE	0.98	1	TRUE
	FALSE	FALSE					
190	LUX BWA	TRUE		TRUE	1.08	1	TRUE
	FALSE	FALSE					

```
Focal Conjunct GG :
```

	Typical	IIR	UniqCov	GlobUncov	Best	PairRank	ConsFC
	MostTypTerm	MostTypFC					
1183	NLD RUS	TRUE		TRUE	0.40	1	TRUE
	TRUE	TRUE					
1173	FRA RUS	TRUE		TRUE	0.42	1	TRUE
	FALSE	FALSE					
1178	JPN RUS	TRUE		TRUE	0.43	1	TRUE
	FALSE	FALSE					
1186	ESP RUS	TRUE		TRUE	0.48	1	TRUE
	FALSE	FALSE					
1179	KOR RUS	TRUE		TRUE	0.51	1	TRUE
	FALSE	FALSE					

```
Focal Conjunct HW :
```

	Typical	IIR	UniqCov	GlobUncov	Best	PairRank	ConsFC
	MostTypTerm	MostTypFC					
701	SVN JOR	TRUE		TRUE	1.24	1	TRUE
	FALSE	FALSE					
700	PRT JOR	TRUE		TRUE	1.27	1	TRUE
	FALSE	FALSE					
685	CHL JOR	TRUE		TRUE	1.53	1	TRUE
	FALSE	FALSE					
686	CRI JOR	TRUE		TRUE	2.15	1	TRUE
	FALSE	FALSE					
704	URY JOR	FALSE		TRUE	1.49	1	TRUE
	FALSE	FALSE					

In order to identify the best-matching pair of two typical cases, we set the argument `cases` to 1. Similarly to the previous output, case pairs are listed from better to worse and we are provided with the information on the pair's formula value (column 'Best'), whether or not each of the two typical cases is uniquely covered, whether the pair belongs to rank 1 or lower, whether each case's membership in the focal conjunct is consistent, and whether they are the most typical for the term and for the focal conjunct, respectively. In essence, the idea is to compare the most typical with a just-so typical case.[13] We learn that Cyprus and Turkey form the best-matching pair of two typical cases for focal conjunct HE if the goal is to test the generalizability of the causal mechanism M of the sufficient term $HE * GG * HW$. Along similar lines, the pair France–Netherlands is the best available when analyzing focal conjunct GG, and Uruguay–Slovenia when analyzing focal conjunct HW.

C 6.7

```
# Identify best-matching pair of two typical cases for
    comparative within-case analysis:

tytyp_y <- smmr(results = sol_yi,
                outcome = "HL",
                match = TRUE,
                cases = 1,
                term = 1,
                max_pairs = 3)
tytyp_y
```

O 6.7

```
Focal Conjunct HE :
```

	Typical1	Typical2	UniqCov1	UniqCov2	Best	PairRank	ConsFC1
	ConsFC2	MostTypTerm1	MostTypTerm2				
446	CYP	TUR	FALSE	FALSE	0.71	1	TRUE
	TRUE		FALSE		FALSE		
455	MLT	TUR	FALSE	FALSE	0.78	1	TRUE
	TRUE		FALSE		FALSE		
454	LUX	TUR	FALSE	FALSE	0.89	1	TRUE
	TRUE		FALSE		FALSE		

	MostTypFC1	MostTypFC2
446	FALSE	FALSE
455	FALSE	FALSE
454	FALSE	FALSE

```
Focal Conjunct GG :
```

	Typical1	Typical2	UniqCov1	UniqCov2	Best	PairRank	ConsFC1
	ConsFC2	MostTypTerm1	MostTypTerm2				

---

[13] A just-so typical case displays the smallest membership values above 0.5 in the outcome and the condition of interest (Schneider and Rohlfing, 2019).

149	NLD	FRA	TRUE	FALSE	1.02		1	TRUE
	TRUE		TRUE		FALSE			
259	NLD	JPN	TRUE	FALSE	1.05		1	TRUE
	TRUE		TRUE		FALSE			
435	NLD	ESP	TRUE	FALSE	1.08		1	TRUE
	TRUE		TRUE		FALSE			

	MostTypFC1	MostTypFC2
149	TRUE	FALSE
259	TRUE	FALSE
435	TRUE	FALSE

Focal Conjunct HW :

	Typical1	Typical2	UniqCov1	UniqCov2	Best	PairRank	ConsFC1
	ConsFC2	MostTypTerm1	MostTypTerm2				
481	SVN	URY	FALSE	FALSE	0.79	1	TRUE
	TRUE	FALSE		FALSE			
480	PRT	URY	FALSE	FALSE	0.82	1	TRUE
	TRUE	FALSE		FALSE			
393	SVN	PRT	FALSE	FALSE	1.13	1	TRUE
	TRUE	FALSE		FALSE			

	MostTypFC1	MostTypFC2
481	FALSE	FALSE
480	FALSE	FALSE
393	FALSE	FALSE

The comparative within-case analysis of a typical case and a deviant consistency case is performed by setting the argument cases to 3. The output displays the rank order of best-matching pairs for each of the four sufficient terms. For instance, Japan (typical) and Lithuania (deviant consistency) form the best matching pair for term $HE * GG * HW$. For our term $HE * AH * HI * HW$, the best-matching pair involves Israel paired with the deviant consistency case of Lebanon.

C 6.8

```
# Identify best-matching pair of typical and deviant consistency
    cases for comparative within-case analysis:

typdcon_y <- smmr(results = sol_yi,
                  outcome = "HL",
                  sol = 1,
                  match = TRUE,
                  cases = 3)
typdcon_y
```

O 6.8

Term HE*GG*HW :

	Typical	DevCons	Best	MostTypTerm	MostDevCons

1	JPN	LTU 0.56	FALSE	TRUE
2	AUS	LTU 0.57	TRUE	TRUE
3	CAN	LTU 0.57	TRUE	TRUE
5	ISL	LTU 0.57	TRUE	TRUE
10	NLD	LTU 0.57	TRUE	TRUE

Term HE*AH*HI*HW :

	Typical	DevCons Best	MostTypTerm	MostDevCons
1	ISR	LBN 1.26	FALSE	TRUE
2	USA	LBN 1.32	TRUE	TRUE
3	HRV	LBN 1.40	FALSE	TRUE
4	ISR	BRA 1.43	FALSE	FALSE
5	USA	BRA 1.49	TRUE	FALSE

Finally, the best-matching pair of deviant coverage and IIR cases is obtained by setting argument `cases` to 4. For each truth table row that contains at least one deviant coverage case and IIR case, respectively, the output reports the distance of this pair in the column 'Best' (the smaller the value, the better), the truth table row to which they belong, and whether the deviant coverage case's membership in the truth table is consistent, that is, smaller than its membership in the outcome.[14] We learn that the pairing Albania (deviant coverage) with Mali, Liberia, Burundi, or Tanzania (IIR) form equally best-matching pairs for truth table row 0,0,0,0,0, only slightly ahead of another pair that involves Albania as the deviant coverage case and Ethiopia as the IIR case. For truth table row 0,0,0,1,0, there are again several equally best-matching pairs, all of which involve Ecuador as the deviant coverage case.

C 6.9

```
# Identify best-matching pair of deviant coverage and IIR cases
    for comparative within-case analysis:

dcoviir_y <- smmr(results = sol_yi,
                  outcome = "HL",
                  sol = 1,
                  match = TRUE,
                  cases = 4)
dcoviir_y
```

O 6.9

Matching Deviant Coverage-IIR Cases :

	DevCov	IIR	TT_HE	TT_GG	TT_AH	TT_HI	TT_HW	Best	ConsTT_DCV
1	ALB	MLI	0	0	0	0	0	1.10	TRUE
2	ALB	BDI	0	0	0	0	0	1.10	TRUE
3	ALB	TZA	0	0	0	0	0	1.10	TRUE
4	ALB	LBR	0	0	0	0	0	1.10	TRUE

[14] The output of this function is only partly displayed here due to space limitations.

5	ALB	ETH	0	0	0	0	0	1.11	TRUE
6	ECU	ZWE	0	0	0	1	0	1.19	TRUE
7	ECU	AGO	0	0	0	1	0	1.19	TRUE
8	ECU	BEN	0	0	0	1	0	1.19	TRUE
9	ECU	NGA	0	0	0	1	0	1.19	TRUE
10	ECU	GMB	0	0	0	1	0	1.19	TRUE
11	IRN	GAB	0	0	0	1	1	1.45	TRUE
12	IRN	VEN	0	0	0	1	1	1.76	TRUE
13	IRN	DOM	0	0	0	1	1	1.78	TRUE
14	BIH	UGA	0	0	1	1	0	1.12	TRUE
15	JAM	GHA	0	1	0	1	0	1.17	TRUE
16	JAM	NAM	0	1	0	1	0	1.19	TRUE
17	JAM	BTN	0	1	0	1	0	1.27	TRUE
18	JAM	BLZ	0	1	0	1	0	1.34	TRUE
19	JAM	CPV	0	1	0	1	0	1.48	TRUE
20	PAN	BWA	0	1	0	1	1	1.06	TRUE
21	PAN	ZAF	0	1	0	1	1	1.13	TRUE
22	MEX	BWA	0	1	0	1	1	1.24	TRUE
23	MEX	ZAF	0	1	0	1	1	1.25	TRUE
24	PAN	TTO	0	1	0	1	1	1.30	TRUE
25	CHN	PHL	1	0	0	1	0	1.32	TRUE
26	TUN	JOR	1	1	0	0	0	1.81	FALSE

6.3.5 Summary SMMR

SMMR should become a standard tool in applied QCA. Combining a cross-case and a within-case perspective strengthens the inferences drawn – if and when this combination of methods follows a coherent logic and set of principles.[15] SMMR, performed with the function smmr(), offers such coherence. In applied QCA, it is unavoidable to make compromises in the choice of cases. Cases that are best from a methodological point of view might not be the ones that a researcher feels most comfortable with, for instance because they do not speak the language, have no research networks there, or because it is a dangerous place to do research. There are, in other words, often non-methodological, practical considerations for choosing cases. Furthermore, it might be impossible to perform in one research project all the within-case analyses that are stipulated in the SMMR framework, especially if the project takes the form of a journal article. Despite these limitations, it is important that researchers be aware of which cases they should choose in principle, so that they can realistically assess what they have achieved in practice. Even if practical considerations influence the choice of cases available for within-case analysis, the tools of SMMR presented here help researchers determine what inferences they can, and cannot, draw based on the cases they have chosen for within-case analyses.

[15] The complete list of SMMR principles and formulas can be found in Schneider (2022).

Box 6.5 Core Points – SMMR

- Set-theoretic multi-method research (SMMR) is the formalized framework within which the analysis of a truth table via QCA (cross-case level) is combined with process tracing (within-case level).
- The goal of post-QCA SMMR is to strengthen the inferences drawn by identifying best available (pairs of) cases for within-case analysis according to different analytical goals.
- Post-QCA single case studies and comparative case studies can be used for either (a) identifying or inquiring about the causal properties of the QCA solution or for (b) identifying which elements (conjuncts or entire conjunctions) are missing from the QCA solution.
- While methodological rules spelled out in SMMR should be followed as best as possible, practical constraints might lead to the choice of sub-optimal cases. If so, this should be taken into account when drawing inferences.
- The function for performing SMMR in R is smmr().

6.4   Summary

Complementary analyses performed after the logical minimization of the truth table significantly increase the quality of a QCA-based study. Two tools are theory evaluation and set-theoretic multi-method research. Both help in shedding more light on the observable implications of QCA results.

Theory evaluation is a formalized way through which QCA researchers can compare previously formulated theoretical expectations with their empirical findings. There are eight possible intersections between theory, empirical findings, and the outcome. Each of them defines a different type of case by distinguishing whether they are covered or uncovered by the solution, whether the theory expects them to be most likely or least likely members of the outcome, and whether or not they display the outcome. The number of cases in these areas determines how strongly specific parts of the theory are corroborated or undermined by the QCA results. The function theory.evaluation() in the package SetMethods provides all the information needed for this evaluation.

Set-theoretic multi-method research is a formalized process of identifying the best available cases for within-case process tracing in a given data set. Based on the QCA results, cases are classified as either typical, deviant, or individually irrelevant. For all the analytically relevant comparative within-case analyses, the best-matching pairs of cases are identified. The function smmr() in the package SetMethods provides all the tools for performing these analyses and, thus, to systematically connect QCA with case studies.

7 Summary and Outlook

7.1 Introduction

Now that the reader has gained an understanding of QCA and its implementation in R before, during, and after the analytic moment, we can further consolidate the links between these analytic steps. Accordingly, this last chapter has four goals. The first is consolidation: we summarize the protocol for analyzing set relations of necessity and sufficiency. The second goal is to broaden the perspective: we discuss the diverse variants, uses, and analytic goals of QCA in different research designs. Third, we summarize good practices for conducting QCA and presenting its results. Lastly, we map exciting developments that are likely to shape the field in the foreseeable future.

> **Box 7.1 Learning Goals – Summary and Outlook**
>
> - Consolidated knowledge of the analytic protocol of QCA.
> - Overview of different uses of QCA, their analytic goals, and corresponding tools.
> - Overview of recommendations for good practice and transparency before, during, and after the analytic moment.
> - Outlook of possible developments in the field.

7.2 Analytic Protocol

We analyze set relations to learn about facts we do not know by using the facts we do know – that is, to establish inferences (King et al., 1994). Figure 7.1 summarizes the main analytic steps of QCA before, during, and after the analytic moment. In practice, the sequence of the steps of QCA often is not linear. As argued and demonstrated throughout the book, the QCA analytic process tends to be iterative. Indeed, the application of QCA to 'noisy' social science data requires that the researcher take core analytic decisions that typically involve a back-and-forth dialogue between theory and evidence so as

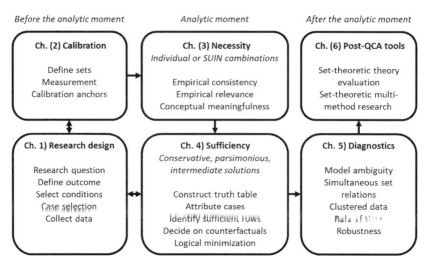

Figure 7.1 Analytic steps in QCA

to yield robust and valid inferences (Ragin, 1987; Schneider and Wagemann, 2012). In particular, there tends to be interaction between the processes before and during the analytic moment.[1] As a result, the processes of research design, calibration, and the analyses of necessity and sufficiency might be reiterated several times during a QCA project.

With regard to research design, we are now able to specify appropriate case selection strategies for research using QCA (see also Berg-Schlosser and De Meur, 2009; Mello, 2021). As Table 7.1 illustrates, case selection can be based on two main considerations (see Levi-Faur, 2006). First, the question is whether cases with similar outcomes are compared (the so-called method of agreement), or cases that differ in outcomes (method of difference) (Mill, 1872). When comparing cases with the same outcome, this only enables us to detect necessary conditions that these cases have in common. To distinguish necessary from sufficient conditions, we need to also examine cases that do not display the outcome. Thus, typically with QCA we compare cases that differ in the outcome.

A second question is whether we compare cases from similar contexts (most similar systems design) or cases that vary on contextual conditions (most different systems design) (Przeworski and Teune, 1970). Comparing contextually similar cases has the advantage that we rule out an influence

---

[1] The processes that take place after the analytic moment, such as diagnostic and post-QCA tools, may also interact with other steps. For example, clustered diagnostic tools might draw attention to the need to do separate QCAs in different groups of cases, or post-QCA case studies (SMMR) might draw attention to omitted conditions.

Table 7.1 Case selection strategies for QCA

		OUTCOME	
		Similar	**Different**
CONTEXT	Most similar systems	Dealing with similarities in similar cases	Dealing with differences in similar cases
		Not usually suitable	*Typical QCA design*
	Most different systems	Dealing with similarities in different cases	Dealing with differences in different cases
		Only necessary conditions	*Needs to account for contextual effects*

Source: Own illustration inspired by Levi-Faur (2006)

of contextual conditions on the results, and 'zoom in' on selected conditions that we deem relevant. In QCA, this is often something we want to do, as it helps us reduce the number of conditions in the truth table and thereby tackle the problem of limited empirical diversity (Section 4.4; Berg-Schlosser and De Meur, 2009).[2] However, comparing most similar systems often comes at the expense of generalizability. Conversely, the logic behind a most different system design is to find relations between the conditions and the outcome that are robust even across different contexts (Levi-Faur, 2006). The challenge for QCA researchers here is to take into account the influence of context on the outcome, e.g., by use of two-step QCA (Section 5.4; Schneider, 2019) or cluster diagnostics (Section 5.3). In sum, the comparison of most similar cases with different outcomes (the so-called MSDO design) is the most suitable – and the most frequent – research design for QCA studies.

Despite technical differences between the analyses of necessity and sufficiency, we ask the same essential questions in order to conclude the existence or non-existence of a set relation. Based on Chapters 3 and 4, we can formulate an integrated protocol for analyzing set relations, as summarized in Figure 7.2. This protocol bases inferences on cross-case patterns, knowledge of individual cases, and external knowledge (adapted from Thomann, 2019; see also

---

[2] Of course, this strategy makes less sense when combined with the method of agreement, as we will already know that the context conditions amount to the necessary conditions; we could still analyze the presence of necessary disjunctions, though.

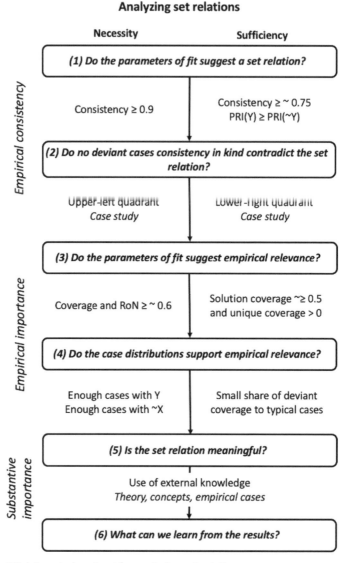

Analyzing set relations

Necessity   Sufficiency

Empirical consistency

(1) Do the parameters of fit suggest a set relation?

Consistency ≥ 0.9

Consistency ≥ ~ 0.75
PRI(Y) ≥ PRI(~Y)

(2) Do no deviant cases consistency in kind contradict the set relation?

Upper-left quadrant
Case study

Lower-right quadrant
Case study

Empirical importance

(3) Do the parameters of fit suggest empirical relevance?

Coverage and RoN ≥ ~ 0.6

Solution coverage ~≥ 0.5
and unique coverage > 0

(4) Do the case distributions support empirical relevance?

Enough cases with Y
Enough cases with ~X

Small share of deviant
coverage to typical cases

Substantive importance

(5) Is the set relation meaningful?

Use of external knowledge
Theory, concepts, empirical cases

(6) What can we learn from the results?

Figure 7.2 Integrated protocol for analyzing set relations

Schneider, 2018). It follows three main steps: determining empirical consistency, empirical importance, and substantive importance.

We suggest some hands-on thresholds for acceptable values of parameters of fit. These thresholds are indicative rather than set in stone. Parameters of fit can be very sensitive to concrete features of the measurement, calibration, and the number and distribution of cases. As they can therefore be misleading on their own, we suggest always complementing the interpretation of parameters of fit with an analysis of actual case distributions and the presence of deviant cases.

To determine *empirical consistency*, we start by looking at whether the parameters of fit suggest the existence of a set relation (consistency). We also want to avoid simultaneous subset relations (PRI). If this is the case, we check if there are deviant cases consistency in kind, with a different qualitative membership in the condition and the outcome set. If so, it is recommended to study these cases in more depth (Section 6.3). Why does this case deviate from the set relation? Does it make us conclude that no set relation exists, or can we learn something else from the case? For instance, this stage may help us discover one or more alternative relevant conditions for an outcome that we failed to consider. It sometimes happens that the case study also reveals idiosyncrasies of specific cases, without however casting overall doubt on the set relation. The results of this step can make the researcher return to earlier stages and engage in additional data collection or a reconceptualization of the sample, explanatory framework, concepts, or calibration.

After a set relation is considered as empirically consistent, we next seek to determine how empirically important the set relation is. An empirically important sufficient condition covers a large share of the outcome set (Section 4.2.2). An empirically important necessary condition should be non-trivial, as the condition set is neither much bigger than the outcome set, nor does it approximate a constant (Section 3.2.3; Schneider and Wagemann, 2012, section 9.2; Mahoney and Vanderpoel, 2015). Thus, the third question is if the parameters of fit (coverage and RoN) suggest empirical importance. If so, in a fourth step we check again for the existence of deviant cases coverage. In the framework of SMMR, case studies of such deviant cases can provide important insights into necessary refinements of the research design or calibration, alternative explanations for an outcome, or idiosyncrasies of cases (Section 6.3). These insights may potentially lead to a reiteration of parts of the analytic cycle.

Finally, if a set relation is both consistent and empirically important, we analyze its *substantive importance*. The fifth question then for both necessary and sufficient conditions is whether the set relation is meaningful. At this stage, in order to interpret the set relation, we go beyond the technical aspects of the analysis and use external knowledge stemming from theory, concepts, and cases. For example, in Section 6.2 we discussed how we can compare the results against theoretical expectations to refute, extend, or confirm existing theoretical knowledge. Thus, we draw inferences from our analysis to more general abstract knowledge. Equally, conceptual knowledge can guide the analysis of substantive importance. For example, QCA can help researchers derive or refine typologies. Moreover, we can 'give names' to sufficient terms and necessary disjunctions (Mahoney and Goertz, 2006) and thereby relate QCA results to more abstract, underlying concepts. For instance, when detecting necessary disjunctions as supersets of the outcome, we will ask whether the SUIN conditions are functional equivalents of some underlying higher order concept (Section 3.3.2; Mahoney et al., 2009). Similarly, sufficient INUS configurations can be seen as representing specific types of cases, and the researcher could name them accordingly. Finally, we saw in Section 6.3 how case knowledge importantly informs the interpretation of QCA. This can help us make sense of complex configurations in the real world, test the causal nature of our set relations, and highlight limitations and scope conditions of the analysis (Rohlfing and Schneider, 2018).

Based on these steps, researchers are able to answer the sixth question: What can the results eventually tell us about the complex and contextually specific nature of social reality (Misangyi et al., 2017; Møller and Skaaning, 2019)? The protocol that readers have learned in this book allows for a diversity of uses and variants of QCA.

7.3   The Diverse Uses of QCA

QCA is a remarkably flexible method that can be implemented in numerous variants for assessing research questions about necessity, sufficiency, and/or one or more aspects of (causal) complexity (see in detail Section 1.2).

7.3.1   Approaches to QCA

In this book, we have primarily dealt with QCA as a technique, a formalized data analysis based on dataset observations, involving truth table analysis and logical minimization. However, the QCA technique is embedded within a broader QCA approach, including 'the processes before and after the analysis of the data, such as the (re-)collection of data, (re)definition of the case selection criteria, or (re-)specification of concepts' (Schneider and Wagemann, 2012, p. 11). Figure 7.3 shows how there are eight different possible types of QCA approaches along three dimensions: the role of theory (mode of reasoning), the use of within-case knowledge in addition to cross-case patterns (approach to cases), and the criteria for a valid explanation (approach to explanation) (Ege et al., 2019; Thomann and Maggetti, 2020). Traditionally, QCA is seen as an exploratory, case-oriented, 'realist' approach (Type 1; Berg-Schlosser et al., 2008). Yet, as QCA has spread and evolved in different disciplines (see Section 1.2), several approaches to QCA have emerged (Thomann and Maggetti, 2020). Against this background, we now take a step back from the technical details of QCA analysis and reflect on the different uses of QCA.

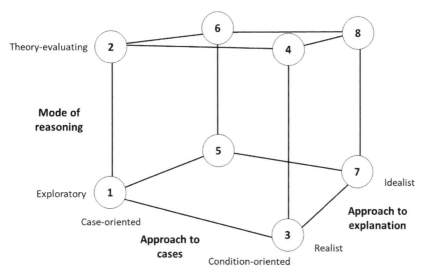

Figure 7.3 Approaches to QCA

The *mode of reasoning* is about drawing inferences from QCA results toward more abstract conceptual or theoretical knowledge. The mode of reasoning can either be exploratory or theory evaluating, but not both. QCA is often characterized as an exploratory approach (Berg-Schlosser et al., 2008, p. 16). Indeed, QCA is well suited for theory development. Here, the goal is to learn from the cases about new, hitherto unexplored or underexplored patterns, and derive some form of abstract lessons. However, we can also adopt a theory-evaluating mode of reasoning with QCA (Section 6.2). While the technical truth table analysis retains an inherently exploratory character, the goal of theory-evaluating QCA is to assess ex ante theoretical expectations in light of the new empirical findings: to see whether cases confirm prior knowledge, go against prior conventions, or whether they help us improve or refine existing theory (Ragin, 1987; Schneider and Wagemann, 2012, section 11.3).

The approach to cases can be either case oriented or condition oriented, but not both. These approaches differ in how they integrate inferences about specific cases. QCA was originally designed as a strongly case-oriented approach (Ragin, 1987; Rihoux and Ragin, 2009; Schneider and Wagemann, 2012). Intimate familiarity with individual cases is used to understand cases as complex 'wholes' and to ensure valid description and explanation (Berg-Schlosser and De Meur, 2009). However, with the emergence of large-N QCA, researchers have started to perform QCA in the absence of case knowledge. A condition-oriented approach to QCA aims to understand configurations of conditions and patterns between cases, but does not use any within-case information for establishing inferences. Here, the faithful representation of individual cases is not the aim; instead, the researcher seeks to gain conceptual knowledge about types of cases and the robustness and reliability of QCA solutions (Fiss et al., 2013; Greckhamer et al., 2013). The central difference between the two approaches is whether the researcher relies on within-case inferences to complement the cross-case QCA inferences in a systematic manner. This is independent of case numbers: large-N studies can also be case-oriented if they integrate knowledge and analyses of individual cases.

Finally, we can distinguish two *approaches to explanation* in QCA that adopt divergent criteria of what constitutes a good explanation based on what source(s) of inference: the realists and the idealists (Schneider, 2018). The goal of the traditional, 'realist' approach to QCA is 'to find meaningful super- and/or subsets of the phenomenon to be explained' (Schneider, 2016, p. 2) and to do so under the constraint of imperfect empirical information. Inferences are drawn on the foundation of case, conceptual, and theoretical knowledge in order to derive set relations that resonate with theoretical and substantive knowledge and do not entail empirically contradictory or logically untenable claims. QCA realists carefully justify the counterfactual assumptions made on logical remainders (Ragin, 2008b; Schneider and Wagemann, 2012). Necessary but not sufficient causes are analyzed separately. Conversely, the 'idealist' approach focuses on redundancy-free QCA models that only contain difference-makers (Baumgartner and Thiem, 2015, 2020). QCA idealists prioritize causal inference, thus conditions that are both minimally sufficient and contained in a minimally necessary condition for an outcome. Thus, they only causally interpret parsimonious solutions with a high coverage (indicating the necessity of the entire solution). Causal inference is drawn based on cross-case patterns, and within-case analyses can only serve to confirm, but not to establish, causal inference.

While any QCA study should ideally adopt one clear approach to cases, reasoning, and the mode of explanation, these three elements do not mutually exclude each other. For instance, QCA realists can adopt a case-oriented or a condition-oriented approach, in an exploratory or theory-evaluating fashion. In this book, we have emphasized the realist approach and argued that case-orientation helps strengthen inferences with QCA. Indeed, for many realists case knowledge is one of the sources of external knowledge that they use to determine if set relations are meaningful. and hence descriptive and causal inference should heavily rest on follow-up within-case analyses in the framework of SMMR. Idealists, conversely, tend to prefer condition-oriented QCA as they would typically see no major added value in going back to cases. In between the eight corners of the property space in Figure 7.3, we find the 'hybrids' which do not consistently adopt an approach on one or more of the three dimensions. These hybrids do not tend to coherently match the use of tools with the underlying approach. For example, some QCA researchers formulate hypotheses but do not systematically evaluate them in light of the results (hybrid mode of reasoning). In particular, a very high share of explanatory QCA studies do not adopt a consistent approach to explanation; this can mean among other things that they make causal claims although there is no methodological approach by which their results could be interpreted causally (Ege et al., 2019).

Users should explicitly adopt a suitable approach and be aware that some of the technical tools available may not fit very well the respective analytic goals of a given approach. To avoid the potential pitfalls facing hybrid QCA studies, in Table 7.2 we provide a non-exhaustive list of the main QCA tools (rows of the table) currently available and indicate their compatibility with the QCA approaches.[3, 4] On the one hand, some tools are particularly recommended for a given approach, while also being applicable for others (third column of Table 7.2). For example, set-theoretic multi-method research is ideally suited for a case-oriented approach where case-based inference is at the core, but it could also be adopted for any approach. On the other hand, some tools are clearly incompatible with a given approach, as indicated in the last column. For example, QCA idealists will never assess necessity and sufficiency separately because they cannot causally interpret necessary but not sufficient conditions; thus, the tools for analyzing necessity are not considered useful or even meaningful in this approach to QCA.

Before the analysis, checking the data for potential skewness and missing values is especially important for condition-oriented and large-N QCA where the data are not yet very well known to the researcher. During the analytic moment, as we have explained earlier, the main distinction is between realists and idealists. The protocol for analyzing necessity is only relevant for realists. Testing the necessity of specific conditions makes particular sense when there are theoretical expectations for necessity, while the `superSubset()` function identifies single or combined necessary conditions in an exploratory manner. Moreover, realists would usually derive intermediate solutions (Standard Analysis or Enhanced Standard Analysis), while idealists only interpret parsimonious solutions without considering potential counterfactuals involved in logical minimization. Condition-oriented large-N studies should pay particular attention to the problem of simultaneous subset relations, as case distributions

---

[3] Both the list of tools and the assessment of compatibility may be subject to future methodological developments.

[4] Along the three dimensions, there are six approaches: approach to cases (case-oriented or condition-oriented), approach to explanation (realist or idealist), and mode of reasoning (inductive/exploratory or theory-evaluating). Combining them results in $2^3 = 8$ possible types of approaches; see Figure 7.3.

Table 7.2 Matching tools with QCA approaches

Analytic step	Tool	Particularly recommended for approach(es)*	Not applicable for approach(es)
		Before the analytic moment	
Data management Chapter 2	Describing & inspecting data; Dealing with missing values	Condition-oriented	–
		During the analytic moment	
Necessity Chapter 3	Single necessary conditions	Theory-evaluating	Idealist
	SuperSubset function	Exploratory	Idealist
	Relevance of Necessity	–	Idealist
Sufficiency Chapter 4	Simultaneous subset relations	Condition-oriented	–
	Single sufficient conditions	–	Idealist
	Parsimonious solution	Idealist	–
	Conservative solution	Realist	Idealist
	Intermediate solution	Realist	Idealist
	Standard Analysis	Realist	Idealist
	Enhanced Standard Analysis	Realist	Idealist
	Identifying counterfactuals	Realist	Idealist
		After the analytic moment	
Diagnostics Chapter 5	Robustness tests	–	Idealist
	tQCA	–	Idealist
	Two-step QCA	–	–
	CNA	Idealist	–
Post-QCA Chapter 6	Formal set-theoretic theory evaluation	Theory-evaluating	Exploratory
	Set-theoretic multi-method research	Case-oriented	–

*Note: Tools particularly recommended under one approach (column 3) are not precluded for use under other approaches unless specified in the last column.

strongly influence them. Of the tools for use after the analysis, we have discussed that some have special affinity with certain approaches. However, QCA idealists would deem the use of CNA as superior to tQCA or two-step QCA in modeling causally interpretable temporal patterns. Idealists would also see no major added value in going back to cases, whereas for realists descriptive and causal inference should heavily rest on follow-up within-case analyses in the framework of SMMR. Moreover, the use of formal theory evaluation makes little sense for an exploratory research question.

In summary, QCA is a flexible method that can be and is implemented within a variety of different research approaches. This does not mean that 'anything goes' with QCA. On the contrary, it is important to coherently adopt one mode of reasoning, one approach to cases, and one to explanation in order to choose tools in line with analytic approaches and to adhere to good practices.

7.4   Recommendations for Good Practice

Researchers today have sophisticated analytic tools available to perform QCA in the R environment. At the same time, many methodological developments have not yet made their way into broad QCA practice (Emmenegger et al., 2013; Wagemann et al., 2016; Ege et al., 2019; Møller and Skaaning, 2019; Verweij and Trell, 2019). Naturally, its proper use is a necessary condition for QCA to meaningfully enrich the toolkit of social science methods. Therefore, it is crucial that QCA researchers adhere to good practices when conducting and documenting QCA and presenting its results. Schneider and Wagemann (2010) have formulated recommendations for good practice. Wagemann and Schneider (2015) and Koivu et al. (2020) have added standards of transparency for QCA (see also Greckhamer et al., 2018; Rubinson et al., 2019). Here we summarize and update or differentiate good practices where warranted, considering recent methodological and technological developments and the aforementioned diversification of approaches to QCA.

Box 7.2 Good Practice – General Recommendations

1. QCA should be used for suitable analytic aims.
2. QCA should be applied together with other data analysis techniques in a research project.
3. Familiarity with cases is beneficial before, during, and after the analytic moment of a QCA.
4. The appropriate QCA terminology should be used.
5. A given QCA approach should be chosen and followed consistently, in line with its analytic goals.

QCA as a multi-method approach. QCA has always been intended for application within research designs that complement the QCA-based inferences with other techniques of data analysis (Ragin, 1987). Within the 'original', case-oriented approach to QCA, this has usually meant combining QCA with qualitative case studies. Therefore, familiarity with individual cases when performing a QCA has been seen as a requirement. However, with the emergence of condition-oriented and large-N variants of QCA, QCA has been complemented with other techniques of cross-case comparison (e.g., Meuer and Rupietta, 2017). Arguably, not all multi-method applications of QCA require researchers to possess in-depth case knowledge – at least not of all cases. For example, set-theoretic multi-method research also allows QCA analysts to follow up only on selected cases (Section 6.3). Nevertheless, we take the opinion that qualitative insights into specific cases are best suited to clarify the extent to which QCA results can be interpreted causally (Rohlfing and Schneider, 2018; for a different argument, see Baumgartner, 2015). Familiarity with cases will also greatly facilitate many analytic decisions.

Terminology. Terminology helps to avoid confusion and establish clarity about methodology and findings. For example, in Chapter 2 we saw that sets differ in important ways from variables. Conditions are not independent variables, nor are outcomes dependent variables. Similarly, with QCA we cannot engage in traditional 'hypothesis testing', but we evaluate theoretical expectations instead (Section 6.2). It is recommended to use the established QCA vocabulary as documented, for instance, in the glossaries in Rihoux and Ragin (2009) and Schneider and Wagemann (2012).

Coherence of the analytic approach. The proper use of any research method is usually a question of stringent research design that coheres with the overarching analytical goal of the given methodology (King et al., 1994). The diversification of approaches to QCA in recent years might lead to incoherent applications of QCA. To avoid these pitfalls, users should always choose their technical tools for QCA in line with the analytic goals of the overarching approach guiding their QCA analysis (see Table 7.2).

7.4.1   Before the Analytic Moment

Box 7.3 Good Practice – Before the Analytic Moment

6. There should always be an explicit and detailed justification for the (non-)selection of cases.
7. The number of conditions should be kept at a moderate level.
8. The conditions and outcome should be selected and conceptualized on the basis of adequate prior theoretical knowledge, as well as empirical insights gained throughout the research process.

Box 7.3 (Cont.)

9. The calibration of set membership scores should be discussed and reported in detail.
10. The pitfalls associated with skewed set membership scores should be avoided.

Selecting cases. Designing case-oriented QCA research (see Section 7.2 and Table 7.1) follows essentially the same principles as designing a comparative case study. This means, among other things, that the selection of cases needs careful justification. As we outlined in Section 1.2, this entails; (a) defining the unit of analysis; (b) defining the scope of the research (Goertz and Mahoney, 2009) (c) defining the universe of cases (Ragin and Becker, 1992); and (d) if applicable, defining criteria for selecting specific cases from this universe (Gerring, 2008). Part of this process is also to reflect on cases that are not relevant for the analysis (Mahoney and Goertz, 2004; Mikkelsen, 2017), and to justify why potentially relevant cases were not included. Also, for condition-oriented QCA, researchers need to carefully justify the sampling strategy. These justifications are vital for clarifying the scope and potential generalizability of the results. This is necessary to draw inferences, even if they are modest, for a potential wider universe of cases. Selecting cases is an iterative process.

Selecting conditions. In Chapter 4, we saw how limited empirical diversity may pose serious challenges to QCA inferences. Thus, we want a big enough share of truth table rows to be populated with cases. While there is no fixed threshold for this, adjusting the ratio of case numbers to condition numbers (as proposed by Marx and Dusa, 2011) may not in itself be a solution. High levels of limited diversity can also be the result of highly clustered data, such as when the case numbers are (at least) as high as the number of logically possible configurations (Schneider and Wagemann, 2012, pp. 151–177). The safest way to avoid overly large truth tables is by keeping the number of conditions at a moderate level. To avoid potentially missing out on important explanatory factors (Radaelli and Wagemann, 2019), an informed selection of relevant conditions should consider the state of theory and empirical evidence in the given field. If the number of potentially relevant conditions is too large, several strategies can help further reduce limited diversity. For example, in Chapter 2 we learned how to combine different conditions into 'meta-conditions' (Goertz and Mahoney, 2005). Two-step QCA (Section 5.4) splits the analysis into the necessity of so-called 'remote conditions', and the sufficiency of more 'proximate' conditions (Schneider and Wagemann, 2006; Schneider, 2019). And cluster diagnostics (Section 5.3) allows for post hoc tests of whether the exclusion of potentially relevant conditions is warranted. Again, the process of selecting conditions is iterative.

Conceptualizing and calibrating sets. It is good practice in QCA to use both theoretical and empirical insights to conceptualize and calibrate sets, and to refine these decisions based on preliminary insights gained in the research process. In Chapter 2, we outlined good practices for set calibration. Calibration decisions are highly consequential for the subsequent analysis. Therefore, researchers should at least partly base them on criteria external to the data at hand. They must establish the highest possible transparency about the criteria and reasons why calibration anchors were chosen. In particular, the justification of the anchor that established the difference in kind needs to be discussed in detail. Decisions on calibration anchors can and should be subjected to robustness tests, as described in Section 5.2.

Skewed data. As Schneider and Wagemann (2012) show, situations when cases have skewed membership in the outcome or condition sets can lead to manifold analytic pitfalls at all stages of QCA. Indeed, the majority of the practical problems surrounding QCA that we have discussed throughout the book can be framed as problems of skewed data. For example, when (almost) all cases are members or non-members of the outcome set, we cannot distinguish necessary from sufficient conditions (Section 7.2). Skewed membership in the condition or the outcome set can produce trivial necessary conditions (Section 3.2.3). Similarly, the problem of simultaneous subset relations manifests itself when most cases are non-members of the condition set (Section 4.2.2). Moreover, the inclusion of one or several skewed condition sets will directly aggravate the problem of limited diversity, as, inevitably, fewer truth table rows will be populated by empirical cases (Section 4.4). Finally, especially with large-N QCA skewed set membership scores also contribute to misleadingly high or low parameters of fit, making it very hard to interpret these. This is why users are well advised to diagnose and avoid such potential problems throughout the analysis: by applying the method of difference, avoiding overly skewed set scores when calibrating sets (Section 2.3.1), considering RoN and PRI scores, making careful counterfactual arguments in the face of limited diversity, and graphically visualizing set relations rather than only relying on parameters of fit (Chapters 3 and 4).

7.4.2   During the Analytic Moment

Separating analyses. As we have demonstrated in Chapters 3 and 4, the analysis of the outcome and the negation of the outcome should be dealt with in separate empirical analyses. Due to the asymmetric nature of set relations, it is impossible to conclude from sufficient conditions for an outcome the sufficient conditions for the negated outcome. Moreover, as soon as our empirical data display limited diversity or inconsistencies, De Morgan's law (Chapter 2) will not be directly applicable to them. It is certainly legitimate for researchers to focus their analytic interest only on one outcome. For a 'realist' approach emphasizing substantively interpretable results, it is also recommended to perform the analysis of necessity and of sufficiency separately. Here too, researchers can legitimately focus their analytic interest only on necessary conditions, or only on sufficient conditions. However, if both are done, necessity should be analyzed first, in order to avoid analytic pitfalls, as we explained in Chapter 4.

Box 7.4 Good Practice – During the Analytic Moment

11. The outcome and the negation of the outcome should always be dealt with in two separate analyses.
12. Necessary and sufficient conditions should be analyzed in separate analytical steps, with the analysis of necessary conditions going first.
13. The choice of appropriate levels of consistency and coverage are research specific and need to be supported with arguments.
14. Contradictory truth table rows should be resolved prior to minimizing the truth table algorithm.
15. The treatment of contradictory rows (in csQCA) and of inconsistent truth table rows (in fsQCA) in the logical minimization process should be transparent.
16. Set relations should be identified with the help of appropriate, formally cited computer software.
17. The existence and treatment of logical remainders should be reasoned, made transparent, and documented.
18. Based on one truth table, several solution formulas of different complexity should be produced.

Appropriate thresholds. Parameters provide one indicator for the empirical consistency and importance of the results. Earlier in this chapter, we provided the reader with some indications of what the acceptable thresholds for necessity and sufficiency could be. The values the parameters of fit take on are highly research specific and may conceal important information. Therefore, we advise caution when applying such thresholds automatically, without considering the clustering of individual cases, the presence of skewed data, and the existence of simultaneous subset relations, and without providing a reasoned argument for the choice of a given threshold.

Dealing with inconsistencies. Rather than mechanically applying thresholds, it is important to identify inconsistencies in truth table rows prior to logical minimization. Otherwise, configurations might be considered as sufficient for the outcome for which the evidence suggests otherwise. Researchers can either exclude inconsistent rows from logical minimization (at the cost of lower coverage) or include them (at the cost of lower consistency). They can try and resolve the contradiction by changing the case selection or calibration, adding conditions, and/or reconceptualizing the outcome. Whichever option is chosen, researchers need to be transparent about how they treat contradictions (in csQCA) and inconsistencies (in fsQCA) during the construction of the truth table and its logical minimization.

Logical minimization and treatment of logical remainders. Logical minimization should be performed using appropriate software, rather than by hand. It is good practice to formally cite the software that is used. Researchers have different options for dealing with logical remainders during logical minimization (Section 4.4). To ensure replicability and transparency, researchers adopting a realist approach to explanation should specify the extent of limited diversity, the nature of the empirically unobserved configurations, the nature of the assumptions made on logical remainders, and the resulting conservative, intermediate, and parsimonious models (see Section 4.4). Much of this information can be reported in an online appendix, and in the text typically only one of the solution formulas is interpreted substantively.

7.4.3   After the Analytic Moment

Box 7.5 Good Practice – After the Analytic Moment

19. Different presentational forms of QCA results should be used in order to depict both the case- and variable-oriented aspects of QCA.
20. Solution formulas should be linked back to the cases, preferably through graphical representation tools.
21. QCA should always be related back to the cases, concepts, and/or theory, using post-QCA tools, rather than being applied in a mechanical way.
22. Individual conditions of a conjunctural and equifinal solution term should not be (over)interpreted.
23. The researcher should always provide explicit justifications when one (or more) of the paths toward an outcome is deemed more important than others.
24. Solution formula alone should not be taken as demonstrating an underlying causal relationship between the conditions and an outcome.
25. The researcher should specify scope conditions for the results.

Presentation of results. The presentation of results should do justice to the three overarching aims of QCA: understanding single or groups of cases, unraveling set relations, and assessing the fit of the results with the underlying data structure (Schneider and Wagemann, 2010b). To reflect all these aspects, the presentation ideally includes various graphical, tabular, and numerical elements. Table 7.3 summarizes some of the most common tools for visualizing

Table 7.3 Prominent tools for visualizing sets and set relations

Tool	Description	Differences captured	Frequencies of cases visible	Type(s) of sets	R command
Histogram	Distribution of raw and calibrated data	In kind or degree	Yes	Multi-value, fuzzy	hist()
Scatterplot	Distribution of raw and calibrated data	In degree	Limited	Fuzzy	plot()
Euler/Venn diagram[a]	Set relations, complex combined sets	In kind	No	Crisp, multi-value, fuzzy	venn()
2 × 2 table	Set relations	In kind	Yes	Crisp	xy.plot(), pimplot()
Enhanced XY plot	Simple set relations	In kind and degree	Yes	Fuzzy	xy.plot()
Enhanced XY plot	Complex set relations	In kind and degree	Yes	Fuzzy	pimplot()
Radar charts	Complex combined sets	In kind	No	Crisp, multi-value, fuzzy	QCAradar()
Path diagram[b]	Complex combined sets	In kind	No	Crisp, fuzzy, multi-value	–
Necessary conditions table	Necessary conditions with parameters of fit	In kind	Not usually	Crisp, fuzzy, multi-value	–
Solution table	Sufficient solutions with parameters of fit and single case coverage	In kind	Yes	Crisp, fuzzy, multi-value	stargazerSol()
'Fiss-style' table[c]	Different sufficient solution types with parameters of fit and single case coverage	In kind	Yes	Crisp, fuzzy, multi-value	–

[a] See Mahoney and Vanderpoel (2015).
[b] See Goertz and Mahoney (2005).
[c] See Fiss (2011); Ragin (2008b, chapter 8).

sets; where we have not treated them in this book, we point the reader to relevant sources. The second column shows the descriptive purposes we can use the tool for. The third column specifies whether the tool visualizes differences in kind, or differences in degree between cases, or both. Fourth, some tools help us see the frequencies of cases, whereas with others we cannot see or count the cases. The last two columns specify which kinds of sets we can visualize using these tools, and where applicable, what the corresponding R function is to produce the graph. Researchers should choose the presentational tool best suited to reflect the aspects of the set or the set relation they seek to demonstrate. In Rubinson (2019) and Mahoney and Vanderpoel (2015), readers can find a more detailed discussion of these and additional tools.

Doing justice to the QCA epistemology. The interpretation of complex QCA results is a very demanding analytic exercise. The results should be related back to cases, rather than mechanically running computer algorithms over the data. In case-oriented QCA, this can mean relating QCA results to individual cases. Condition-oriented QCA tends to focus on types or classes of cases. Once a necessary condition or a sufficienct solution is derived, its interpretation needs to do justice to the logic of conjunctural causation (see Chapters 3 and 4). We can never interpret the role of an individual SUIN and INUS condition in isolation. Instead, its role has to be understood in combination with the other conditions that form part of the configuration. External knowledge coming from cases, concepts, and theory can inform and facilitate this process. Similarly, QCA results do not tell us anything about the size of the effect of an individual condition.

Importance of results. Often, applied researchers find some aspects of their results more interesting or important than others. At the same time, in a truth table analysis equal weight is given to truth table rows irrespective of how many cases they are populated with. Every case counts and can provide valuable insights, including, for instance, rare cases that hitherto have remained deviant or misunderstood. Thus, researchers should give explicit justification for why some results are deemed more important than others. Criteria could, for instance, be empirical weight (coverage), theoretical relevance, or the specific research interests underlying the given research question. Finally, set relation does not equal causation. Set relations indicate a cross-case pattern in the data which the researcher needs to interpret. It is not usually possible to directly attribute causality to QCA results of necessity and sufficiency based on observational data. Such interpretations should only be made cautiously and by resorting to both theoretical reasoning and within-case analysis of causal mechanisms (Rohlfing and Schneider, 2018; Schneider, 2018).[5]

---

[5] It can be argued that it is a necessary (but not sufficient) condition for a QCA solution to be causally interpretable that it is redundancy-free (Baumgartner, 2015).

7.4.4   Transparency and Replicability

Box 7.6 Good Practice - Transparency and Replicability

26. If several equally plausible analytic choices exist, robustness tests should be performed.
27. The raw data matrix should be accessible for replication.
28. The truth table should be reported.
29. All logical unions that passed the threshold for consistency, coverage, and Relevance of Necessity should be reported.
30. In the presence of model ambiguity, all alternative models should be reported and the model choice should be justified.
31. Every QCA must contain the solution formula(s).
32. The parameters of fit should always be reported.

For the results to be replicable and traceable by the readership, it is essential to establish the highest possible levels of transparency about the analysis, much of which can be done via separate online appendices. This entails making the raw dataset accessible for replication. If data protection or funding rules prohibit publishing raw data, the calibrated dataset should be published. Publishing the truth table helps the reader understand decisions on coding truth table rows. Limited diversity and assumptions made on logical remainders should also be reported. Moreover, researchers should establish full transparency about all results yielded. For the analysis of necessity, this means reporting all conditions – both single and unions of conditions – that pass the thresholds for consistency, coverage, and Relevance of Necessity. For the analysis of sufficiency, in the case of model ambiguity, researchers should report all alternative models and justify the choice of the model they choose for interpretation (Koivu et al., 2020).

In summary, researchers should adhere to good practices when implementing QCA. At the same time, a number of developments are likely to shape what happens next in the field.

7.5   Outlook

To conclude this book, we will selectively and non-exhaustively map what we consider the most exciting current methodological developments at the interface with applied QCA.

Diversification of QCA

Thanks to QCA's remarkable flexibility, in recent years we have seen a notable diversification of its use. QCA continues to be used in new disciplines (Rihoux et al., 2013). Data suggest that there have been sizable expansions of QCA use in recent years in the fields of business and management (Misangyi et al., 2017), as well as in various subdisciplines of environment and health research (Roig-Tierno et al., 2017).

As discussed earlier in this chapter, we have also seen a diversification of approaches to and associated uses of QCA. The most notable development is undoubtedly the increase of large-N QCA associated with a more condition-oriented approach. Although QCA is often seen as particularly suited for comparing a small to medium sized number of cases, there are no technical obstacles to applying QCA to larger samples. The development of both more refined methodological tools, such as robustness checks or set-theoretic MMR described in Sections 5.2 and 6.3, and of sophisticated R packages for QCA (Dusa, 2018; Oana and Schneider, 2018) now makes it possible to process and meaningfully analyze massive datasets with QCA. Large-N QCA appears to be particularly popular in organizational research with its predominant focus on meso-level data and the existence of prominent theories that postulate causal complexity (Fiss, 2011; Greckhamer et al., 2013, 2018). It also opens up the possibility of using QCA for the analysis of micro-level data, for example, in survey research (e.g., Thomann et al., 2018) – a level of analysis where QCA has traditionally been less frequently applied (Rihoux et al., 2013).

Robustness Tests

One question that repeatedly sparks controversy is the extent QCA results can be considered 'robust', given that the method is case sensitive and relies on a configurational logic (Thiem, 2014b). On the one hand, scholars discuss the various analytic choices that can affect the robustness of QCA results, such as difference in sampling, the choice of conditions, measurement or calibration, consistency thresholds, and the assumptions on logical remainders (Section 5.2; Schneider and Wagemann, 2012, pp. 284–294). On the other hand, scholars discuss what it actually means for QCA results to be 'robust': does the result have to be unchanged, or is it enough if a subset relation between the results is maintained. The approach introduced in Section 5.2 offers an integrated and comprehensive Robustness Test Protocol.

So far, sensitivity and robustness test for QCA results have rarely been applied in practice. In principle, performing robustness tests is particularly important under a condition-oriented, large-N approach (Meuer and Rupietta, 2017; Thomann and Maggetti, 2020). Clearly, robustness tests should (only) be implemented for meaningful possible alterations and in a manner that does justice to the overall QCA approach of a given study (Wagemann and Schneider, 2015).

Multi-Method Research

Complementing QCA with other methods of data analysis can strengthen QCA inferences (Kahwati and Kane, 2018). However, there has been little guidance available to users on performing multi-method research with QCA. In recent years, this has been changing. On the one hand, proposals have emerged to combine QCA with other methods of cross-case comparisons under a condition-oriented approach, including social network analysis, matching techniques, and econometric methods such as hierarchical linear models or bootstrapping (Fischer, 2011; Fiss et al., 2013; Cooper and Glaesser, 2016a; Meuer and Rupietta, 2017). On the other hand, sophisticated protocols have been formulated for combining QCA with qualitative case studies and methods, such as grounded theory (Jopke and Gerrits, 2019) and process tracing (Beach and Rohlfing, 2018; Schneider, 2022). The fact that set-theoretic multi-method research (Schneider and Rohlfing, 2013, 2016, 2019; Rohlfing and Schneider, 2013, 2018) can now be easily implemented with R paves the way for a more widespread application of systematic set-theoretic multi-method research.

Software Development

Recent years have seen massive progress surrounding the implementation of QCA in different software environments. Several 'traditional' pieces of QCA software have been relaunched with improved functionality, including fs/QCA (Ragin and Davey, 2016) and Tosmana (Cronqvist, 2019), alongside other software for implementing QCA (see http://compasss.org/software/).

As Table 7.4[6] illustrates, the R environment currently offers the most advanced functionality for performing QCA and the implemention of related analytic tools: prominently, the packages QCA (Dusa, 2018) and SetMethods (Oana and Schneider, 2018) that we have introduced in this book. Thanks to these developments and, recently, the integration of a graphical user interface (GUI) (Dusa, 2018), performing QCA with R has become more user-friendly and easier to learn. Future software developments are likely to include fuller functionality in the GUI for users who do not want to work with codes; improved tools for visualization; and an easier export of solution tables and other presentational forms.

Translating Innovation into Applied QCA

Arguably one of the major tasks ahead is to translate the sophisticated methodological state of the art of QCA into applied QCA. The afore mentioned innovations and software developments are major and necessary steps in this

---

[6] Tools not introduced in this book are not part of this table. Procedures that do not require dedicated functionalities (for example, two-step QCA) are also not included in the table.

Table 7.4 Comparison of functionality of fs/QCA, Tosmana, and R as of late 2019

Analytic step	Tool for	fs/QCA 3.1	Tosmana 1.6.1	R: QCA 3.7, SetMethods 2.6
	Before the analytic moment			
Calibrating & combining sets Chapter 2	Recoding	✓	✓	✓
	Direct calibration (logistic and other functions)	(✓)	(✓)	✓
	Indirect calibration	(✓)	(✓)	✓
	Threshold setter		✓	
	Boolean calculations	(✓)	(✓)	✓
	During the analytic moment			
Necessity Chapter 3	Single necessary conditions	✓	✓	✓
	SUIN combinations (predefined and inductive)	(✓)	(✓)	✓
	Relevance of Necessity			✓
Sufficiency Chapter 4	Single sufficient conditions	✓	✓	✓
	Edit OUT in truth table	✓		✓
	Show PI chart	✓		✓
	Parsimonious solution	✓	✓	✓
	Conservative solution	✓	✓	✓
	Standard Analysis	✓	✓	✓
	Enhanced Standard Analysis	(✓)		✓
	Identifying counterfactuals			✓
	After the analytic moment			
Diagnostics Chapter 5	Robustness tests			✓
Post-QCA Chapter 6	CNA			✓
	Set-theoretic theory evaluation			✓
	SMMR			✓
	General features			
Visualization	XY plots	(✓)		✓
	Set diagrams		(✓)	✓
Variants of QCA	csQCA	✓	(✓)	✓
	fsQCA	✓	✓	✓
	mvQCA		✓	✓

Note: ✓ = full functionality; (✓) = partial functionality.

direction, but not yet sufficient on their own. While the dissemination of QCA via textbooks and student training is steadily expanding, it would also be desirable to integrate set-theoretic techniques with their distinct epistemological underpinnings and areas of application into the standard undergraduate methodological curricula of universities. Moreover, although we have seen clear improvements in technical aspects of applied QCA, good practices in QCA relating to research design need to be emphasized and taught more extensively. Improving applied QCA requires focused efforts by QCA users, reviewers, editors, and instructors in conveying, enforcing, and adhering to good practices and coherent research designs before, during, and after the analytic moment in QCA studies.

Our book should be seen as one contribution to this joint effort.

References

Adcock, Robert, and Collier, David. 2001. Measurement validity: a shared standard for qualitative and quantitative research. *American Political Science Review*, **95**(3), 529–546.

Arel-Bundock, Vincent. 2019. The double bind of Qualitative Comparative Analysis. *Sociological Methods & Research*, DOI. 10.1177/0049124119882400.

Bara, Corinne. 2014. Incentives and opportunities: a complexity-oriented explanation of violent ethnic conflict. *Journal of Peace Research*, **51**(6), 696–710.

Barrenechea, Rodrigo, and Castillo, Isabel. 2019. The many roads to Rome: family resemblance concepts in the social sciences. *Quality & Quantity*, **53**(1), 107–130.

Basurto, Xavier, and Speer, Johanna. 2012. Structuring the calibration of qualitative data as sets for Qualitative Comparative Analysis (QCA). *Field Methods*, **24**(2), 155–174.

Baumgartner, Michael. 2008. Uncovering deterministic causal structures: a Boolean approach. *Synthese*, **170**(1), 71–96.

Baumgartner, Michael. 2009. Inferring causal complexity. *Sociological Methods & Research*, **38**(1), 71–101.

Baumgartner, Michael. 2013. Detecting causal chains in small-N data. *Field Methods*, **25**(1), 3–24.

Baumgartner, Michael. 2015. Parsimony and causality. *Quality & Quantity*, **49**(2), 839–856.

Baumgartner, Michael, and Thiem, Alrik. 2015. Identifying complex causal dependencies in configurational data with coincidence analysis. *The R Journal*, **7**(1), 176–184.

Baumgartner, Michael, and Thiem, Alrik. 2017. Model ambiguities in configurational comparative research. *Sociological Methods & Research*, **46**(4), 954–987.

Baumgartner, Michael, and Thiem, Alrik. 2020. Often trusted but never (properly) tested: evaluating Qualitative Comparative Analysis. *Sociological Methods & Research*, **49**(2), 279–311.

Beach, Derek, and Rohlfing, Ingo. 2018. Integrating cross-case analyses and process tracing in set-theoretic research: strategies and parameters of debate. *Sociological Methods & Research*, **47**(1), 3–36.

Berg-Schlosser, Dirk, and De Meur, Gisele. 2009. Comparative research design: case and variable selection. Pages 19–32 of: Rihoux, Benoit, and Ragin, Charles C. (eds.), *Configurational Comparative Methods: Qualitative Comparative Analysis (QCA) and Related Techniques*. Thousand Oaks/London: Sage.

Berg-Schlosser, Dirk, De Meur, Gisele, Rihoux, Benoit, and Ragin, Charles C. 2008. Qualitative Comparative Analysis (QCA) as an approach. Pages 1–18 of: Rihoux,

Benoit, and Ragin, Charles C. (eds.), *Configurational Comparative Methods. Qualitative Comparative Analysis (QCA) and Related Techniques*. Thousand Oaks/London: Sage.

Brady, Henry E., and Collier, David. 2010. *Rethinking Social Inquiry: Diverse Tools, Shared Standards*. Lanham: Rowman & Littlefield.

Braumoeller, Bear F. 2017. Aggregation bias and the analysis of necessary and sufficient conditions in fsQCA. *Sociological Methods & Research*, **46**(2), 242–251.

Caren, Neal, and Panofsky, Aaron. 2005. TQCA: a technique for adding temporality to Qualitative Comparative Analysis. *Sociological Methods & Research*, **34**(2), 147–172.

Cooper, Barry, and Glaesser, Judith. 2016a. Exploring the robustness of set theoretic findings from a large n fsQCA: an illustration from the sociology of education. *International Journal of Social Research Methodology*, **19**(4), 445–459.

Cooper, Barry, and Glaesser, Judith. 2016b. Analysing necessity and sufficiency with Qualitative Comparative Analysis: how do results vary as case weights change? *Quality and Quantity*, **50**(1), 327–346.

Cronqvist, Lasse. 2019. *Tosmana [Version 1.61]*.

Cronqvist, Lasse, and Berg-Schlosser, Dirk. 2009. Multi-value QCA (mvQCA). Pages 69–86 of: Rihoux, Benoit, and Ragin, Charles C. (eds.), *Configurational Comparative Methods. Qualitative Comparative Analysis (QCA) and Related Techniques*. Thousand Oaks/London: Sage.

de Block, Debora, and Vis, Barbara. 2019. Addressing the challenges related to transforming qualitative into quantitative data in qualitative comparative analysis. *Journal of Mixed Methods Research*, **13**(4), 503–535.

Dusa, Adrian. 2018. *QCA with R*. New York: Springer.

Ege, Jörn, Thomann, Eva, and Paustyan, Ekatarina. 2019. Approaches to Qualitative Comparative Analysis (QCA) and standards of good practice: a systematic review. Paper presented at the ECPR General Conference, Wroclaw, November 4–7, 2019.

Emmenegger, Patrick. 2012. How good are your counterfactuals? Assessing quantitative macro-comparative welfare state research. *Journal of European Social Policy*, **21**(4), 365–380.

Emmenegger, Patrick, Kvist, Jon, and Skaaning, Svend-Erik. 2013. Making the most of Configurational Comparative Analysis: an assessment of QCA applications in comparative welfare-state research. *Political Research Quarterly*, **66**(1), 185–190.

Emmenegger, Patrick, Schraff, Dominik, and Walter, André. 2014. QCA, the truth table analysis and large-N survey data: the benefits of calibration and the importance of robustness tests. COMPASSS Working Paper 2014-79.

Fischer, Manuel. 2011. Social network analysis and Qualitative Comparative Analysis: their mutual benefit for the explanation of policy network structures. *Methodological Innovations Online*, **6**(2), 27–51.

Fischer, Manuel, and Maggetti, Martino. 2017. Qualitative Comparative Analysis and the study of policy processes. *Journal of Comparative Policy Analysis: Research and Practice*, **19**(4), 345–361.

Fiss, Peer C. 2011. Building better causal theories: a fuzzy set approach to typologies in organization research. *Academy of Management Journal*, **54**(2), 393–420.

Fiss, Peer, Sharapov, Dmitry, and Cronqvist, Lasse. 2013. Opposites attract? Opportunities and challenges for integrating large-N QCA and econometric analysis. *Political Research Quarterly*, **66**(1), 191–197.

Freyburg, Tina, and Garbe, Lisa. 2018. Blocking the bottleneck: internet shutdowns and ownership at election times in sub-Saharan Africa. *International Journal of Communication*, **12** (2018), 3896–3916.

García-Castro, Roberto, and Arino, Miguel A. 2016. A general approach to panel data set-theoretic research. *Journal of Advances in Management Sciences & Information Systems*, **2**, 63–76.

Gerring, John. 2000. Case selection for case-study analysis: qualitative and quantitative techniques. Pages 645–684 of: Box-Steffensmeier, J., Brady, Henry. E., and Collier, David (eds.), *Oxford Handbook of Political Methodology*. Oxford: Oxford University Press.

Gerring, John. 2011. *Social Science Methodology: A Unified Framework*. Strategies for Social Inquiry. Cambridge: Cambridge University Press.

Goertz, Gary. 2006. *Social Science Concepts: A User's Guide*. Princeton: Princeton University Press.

Goertz, Gary. 2012. *Social Science Concepts: A User's Guide*. Princeton: Princeton University Press.

Goertz, Gary, and Mahoney, James. 2005. Two-level theories and fuzzy-set analysis. *Sociological Methods & Research*, **33**(4), 497–538.

Goertz, Gary, and Mahoney, James. 2009. Scope in case study research. Pages 307–318 of: Byrne, David, and Ragin, Charles C. (eds.), *The Sage Handbook of Case-Based Methods*. London: Sage.

Goertz, Gary, and Mahoney, James. 2012. *A Tale of Two Cultures: Qualitative and Quantitative Research in the Social Sciences*. Princeton: Princeton University Press.

Goertz, Gary, and Starr, Harvey. 2003. *Necessary Conditions: Theory, Methodology, and Applications*. Lanham/Boulder: Rowman & Littlefield.

Greckhamer, Thomas, Furnari, Santi, Fiss, Peer C., and Aguilera, Ruth V. 2018. Studying configurations with qualitative comparative analysis: best practices in strategy and organization research. *Strategic Organization*, **16**(4), 482–495.

Greckhamer, Thomas, Misangyi, Vilmos F., and Fiss, Peer C. 2013. The two QCAs: from a small-N to a large-N set theoretic approach. Pages 49–75 of: Fiss, P. C., Cambre, B., and Marx, A. (eds.), *Configurational Theory and Methods in Organizational Research*. Somerville: Emerald Publishing Ltd.

Haesebrouck, Tim. 2016. The added value of multi-value Qualitative Comparative Analysis. *Forum Qualitative Sozialforschung* [Forum Qualitative Social Research], **17**(1).

Hug, Simon. 2013. Qualitative Comparative Analysis: how inductive use and measurement error lead to problematic inference. *Political Analysis*, **21**(2), 252–265.

Jopke, Nikolaus, and Gerrits, Lasse. 2019. Constructing cases and conditions in QCA-lessons from grounded theory. *International Journal of Social Research Methodology*, **22**(6), 599–610.

Kahwati, Leila C., and Kane, Heather L. 2018. *Qualitative Comparative Analysis in Mixed Methods Research and Evaluation*. Thousand Oaks: Sage.

King, Gary, Keohane, Robert O., and Verba, Sidney. 1994. *Designing Social Inquiry. Scientific Inference in Qualitative Research*. Princeton: Princeton University Press.

Koivu, Kendra, Schneider, Carsten Q., and Vis, Barbara. 2020. Set-analytic approaches, especially Qualitative Comparative Analysis (QCA) Final Report of QTD Working Group III.4, in Jacobs, Alan M. et al. (eds), Transparency in qualitative research: an overview of key findings and implications of the deliberations. *Perspectives on Politics* **19**(1): 171–208.

Krogslund, Chris, Choi, Donghyun Danny, and Poertner, Mathias. 2014. Fuzzy sets on shaky ground: parametric and specification sensitivity in fsQCA. *Political Analysis*, **23**(1), 21–41.

Lazarsfeld, Paul. 1937. Some remarks on typological procedures in social research. *Zeitschrift für Sozialforschung*, **6**(1), 119–139.

Lazarsfeld, Paul Felix, and Barton, Allen H. 1957. *Qualitative Measurement in the Social Siences: Classification, Typologies, and Indices*. Redwood City: Stanford University Press.

Lebow, Richard Ned. 2010. *Forbidden Fruit: Counterfactuals and International Relations*. Princeton/Oxford: Princeton University Press.

Legewie, Nicolas. 2017. Anchored calibration: from qualitative data to fuzzy sets. *Forum Qualitative Sozialforschung/Forum: Qualitative Social Research*, **18**(3), 24.

Levi-Faur, David. 2006. A question of size? A heuristics for stepwise comparative research design. Pages 43–66 of: Rihoux, Benoit, and Grimm, Heike (eds.), *Innovative Comparative Methods for Policy Analysis*. New York: Springer.

Mahoney, James. 2010. After KKV: the new methodology of qualitative research. *World Politics*, **62**(1), 120–147.

Mahoney, James, and Goertz, Gary. 2004. The possibility principle and case selection: choosing negative cases in comparative analysis. *American Political Science Review*, **98**(4), 653–669.

Mahoney, James, and Goertz, Gary. 2006. A tale of two cultures: contrasting quantitative and qualitative research. *Political Analysis*, **14**(3), 227–249.

Mahoney, James, Kimball, Erin, and Koivu, Kendra L. 2009. The logic of historical explanation in the social sciences. *Comparative Political Studies*, **42**(1), 114–146.

Mahoney, James, and Vanderpoel, Rachel Sweet. 2015. Set diagrams and qualitative research. *Comparative Political Studies*, **48**(1), 65–100.

Marx, Axel, and Dusa, Adrian. 2011. Crisp-set Qualitative Comparative Analysis (csQCA), contradictions and consistency benchmarks for model specification. *Methodological Innovations Online*, **6**(2), 103–148.

Mello, Patrick A. 2021. *Qualitative Comparative Analysis: Research Design and Application*. Washington: Georgetown University Press.

Meuer, Johannes, and Rupietta, Christian. 2017. Integrating QCA and HLM for multi-level research on organizational configurations. *Organizational Research Methods*, **20**(2), 324–342.

Mikkelsen, Kim Sass. 2017. Negative case selection: justifications and consequences for set-theoretic MMR. *Sociological Methods and Research*, **46**(4), 739–771.

Mill, John Stuart. 1872. *A System of Logic*. 8 ed., vol. 2. London: Longmans, Green, Reader.

Misangyi, V. F., Greckhamer, T., Furnari, S., Fiss, P. C., Crilly, D., and Aguilera, R. 2017. Embracing causal complexity: the emergence of a neo-configurational perspective. *Journal of Management*, **43**(1), 255–282.

Møller, Jørgen, and Skaaning, Svend Erik. 2019. Set-theoretic methods in democratization research: an evaluation of their uses and contributions. *Democratization*, **26**(1), 78–96.

Oana, Ioana-Elena, and Schneider, Carsten Q. 2018. SetMethods: an add-on R package for advanced QCA. *The R Journal*, **10**(1): 507–533.

Oana, Ioana Elena, and Schneider, Carsten Q. n.d. A Robustness Test Protocol for Applied QCA: Theory and R Software Application. Under review.

Paykani, Toktam, Rafiey, Hassan, and Sajjadi, Homeira. 2018. A fuzzy set Qualitative Comparative Analysis of 131 countries: which configuration of the structural conditions can explain health better? *International Journal for Equity in Health*, **17**(1), 10.

Przeworski, Adam, and Teune, Henry. 1970. *The Logic of Comparative Social Inquiry*. 8 ed., vol. 2. New York: Wiley-Interscience.

Radaelli, Claudio M., and Wagemann, Claudius. 2019. What did I leave out? Omitted variables in regression and Qualitative Comparative Analysis. *European Political Science*, **18**(2), 275–290.

Ragin, Charles C. 1987. *The Comparative Method: Moving beyond Qualitative and Quantitative Strategies*. Berkeley: University of California Press.

Ragin, Charles C. 1994. *Constructing Social Research. The Unity and Diversity of Method*. Thousand Oaks: Pine Forge Press.

Ragin, Charles C. 2000. *Fuzzy-Set Social Science*. Chicago: University of Chicago Press.

Ragin, Charles C. 2008a. Measurement versus calibration: A set-theoretic approach. Pages 174–198 of Steffensmeier, J., Brady, Henry. E., and Collier, David (eds), *Oxford Handbook of Political Methodology*. Oxford: Oxford University Press.

Ragin, Charles C. 2008b. *Redesigning Social Inquiry: Fuzzy Sets and Beyond*. Chicago: University of Chicago Press.

Ragin, Charles C. 2008c. Qualitative Comparative Analysis using fuzzy sets (fsQCA). *Configurational Comparative Methods: Qualitative Comparative Analysis (QCA) and Related Techniques*. Pages 87–122 pf Rihoux, B., and Ragin, C. C. (eds), Configurational Comparative Methods: Qualitative Comparative Analysis (QCA) and Related Techniques, vol. 51. Thousand Oaks: SAGE Publications, Inc.

Ragin, Charles C., and Becker, Howard Saul. 1992. *What Is a Case?: Exploring the Foundations of Social Inquiry*. Cambridge: Cambridge University Press.

Ragin, Charles C., and Davey, Sean. 2016. *Fuzzy-Set/Qualitative Comparative Analysis 3.0*. Irvine: Department of Sociology, University of California. Available at: www.socsci.uci.edu/~cragin/fsQCA/software.shtml.

Ragin, Charles C., and Fiss, Peer C. 2016. *Intersectional Inequality. Race, Class, Test Scores, and Poverty*. Chicago: University of Chicago Press.

Ragin, Charles C., and Strand, Sarah. 2008. Using Qualitative Comparative Analysis to study causal order. Comment on Caren and Panofsky (2005). *Sociological Methods and Research*, **36**(4), 431–441.

Ragin, Charles C., Shulman, David, Weinberg, Adam, and Gran, Brian. 2003. Complexity, generality, and Qualitative Comparative Analysis. *Field Methods*, **15**(4), 323–340.

Rihoux, Benoit, Alamos, Priscilla, Bol, Damien, Marx, Axel, and Rezsohazy, Ilona. 2013. From niche to mainstream method? A comprehensive mapping of QCA applications in journal articles from 1984 to 2011. *Political Research Quarterly*, **66**(1), 175–184.

Rihoux, Benoît, and Ragin, Charles C. 2009. *Configurational Comparative Methods: Qualitative Comparative Analysis (QCA) and Related Techniques*. Thousand Oaks: Sage Publishing.

Rohlfing, Ingo. 2015. Mind the gap: a review of simulation designs for Qualitative Comparative Analysis. *Research & Politics*, **2**(4), 1–4.

Rohlfing, Ingo. 2016. Why simulations are appropriate for evaluating Qualitative Comparative Analysis. *Quality & Quantity*, **50**(5), 2073–208.

Rohlfing, Ingo, and Schneider, Carsten Q. 2013. Improving research on necessary conditions: formalized case selection for process tracing after QCA. *Political Research Quarterly*, **66**(1), 220–235.

Rohlfing, Ingo, and Schneider, Carsten Q. 2018. A unifying framework for causal analysis in set-theoretic multimethod research. *Sociological Methods & Research*, **47**(1), 37–63.

Roig-Tierno, Norat, Gonzalez-Cruz, Tomas F., and Llopis-Martinez, Jordi. 2017. An overview of Qualitative Comparative Analysis: a bibliometric analysis. *Journal of Innovation & Knowledge*, **2**(1), 15–23.

RStudio Team. 2019. *RStudio: Integrated Development Environment for R*. Boston: RStudio, Inc.

Rubinson, Claude. 2019. Presenting Qualitative Comparative Analysis: notation, tabular layout, and visualization. *Methodological Innovations*, **12**(2), 1–22.

Rubinson, Claude, Gerrits, Lasse, Rutten, Roel, and Greckhamer, Thomas. 2019. Avoiding common errors in QCA: a short guide for new practitioners. COMPASSS Working Paper, available at https://compasss.org/wp-content/uploads/2019/07/Common_Errors_in_QCA.pdf.

Sartori, Giovanni. 1970. Concept misformation in comparative politics. *American Political Science Review*, **64**(4), 1033–1053.

Schneider, Carsten Q. 2016. Real differences and overlooked similarities. Set-methods in comparative perspective. *Comparative Political Studies*, **49**(6), 781–792.

Schneider, Carsten Q. 2018. Realists and idealists in QCA. *Political Analysis*, **26**(2), 246–254.

Schneider, Carsten Q. 2019. Two-step QCA revisited: the necessity of context conditions. *Quality & Quantity*, **53**(3), 1109–1126.

Schneider, Carsten Q. 2022. *Set-Theoretic Multi-Method Research: A Guide to Combining QCA and Case Studies*. Cambridge: Cambridge University Press. Under contract.

Schneider, Carsten Q., and Maerz, Seraphine. 2017. Legitimation, cooptation, and repression and the survival of electoral autocracies. *Zeitschrift für Vergleichende Politikwissenschaft*, **11**(2), 213–235.

Schneider, Carsten Q., and Rohlfing, Ingo. 2013. Combining QCA and process tracing in set-theoretic multi-method research. *Sociological Methods and Research*, **42**(4), 559–597.

Schneider, Carsten Q., and Rohlfing, Ingo. 2016. Case studies nested in fuzzy-set QCA on sufficiency: formalizing case selection and causal inference. *Sociological Methods & Research*, **45**(3), 526–568.

Schneider, Carsten Q., and Rohlfing, Ingo. 2019. Set-theoretic multimethod research: the role of test corridors and conjunctions for case selection. *Swiss Political Science Review*, **25**(3), 253–275.

Schneider, Carsten Q., and Wagemann, Claudius. 2006. Reducing complexity in Qualitative Comparative Analysis (QCA): remote and proximate factors and the consolidation of democracy. *European Journal of Political Research*, **45**(5), 751–786.

Schneider, Carsten Q., and Wagemann, Claudius. 2010. Standards of good practice in Qualitative Comparative Analysis (QCA) and fuzzy-sets. *Comparative Sociology*, **9**(3), 397–418.

Schneider, Carsten Q., and Wagemann, Claudius. 2012. *Set-Theoretic Methods for the Social Sciences: A Guide to Qualitative Comparative Analysis*. Cambridge: Cambridge University Press.

Skaaning, Svend-Erik. 2011. Assessing the robustness of crisp-set and fuzzy-set QCA results. *Sociological Methods & Research*, **40**(2), 391–408.

Thiem, Alrik. 2014a. Membership function sensitivity of descriptive statistics in fuzzy-set relations. *International Journal of Social Research Methodology*, **17**(6), 625–642.

Thiem, Alrik. 2014b. Mill's methods, induction, and case sensitivity in Qualitative Comparative Analysis: a comment on Hug (2013). *Qualitative & Multi-Method Research Newsletter*, **12**(2), 19–24.

Thiem, Alrik. 2014c. Unifying configurational comparative methods: generalized-set qualitative comparative analysis. *Sociological Methods & Research*, **43**(2), 313–337.

Thiem, Alrik, and Dusa, Adrian. 2013. QCA: a package for Qualitative Comparative Analysis. *R Journal*, **5**(1), 87–97.

Thiem, Alrik, Spöhel, Reto, and Duşa, Adrian. 2016. Enhancing sensitivity diagnostics for Qualitative Comparative Analysis: a combinatorial approach. *Political Analysis*, **24**(1), 104–120.

Thomann, Eva. 2015. Customizing Europe: transposition as bottom-up implementation. *Journal of European Public Policy*, **22**(10), 1368–1387.

Thomann, Eva. 2019. Qualitative Comparative Analysis (QCA) as a tool for street-level bureaucracy research. Pages 370–391 of: *Research Handbook on Street-Level Bureaucracy: The Ground Floor of Government in Context.* Cheltenham: Edward Elgar.

Thomann, Eva, and Maggetti, Martino. 2020. Designing research with Qualitative Comparative Analysis (QCA): Approaches, Challenges, and Tools. *Sociological Methods & Research*, **49**(2), 356–386.

Thomann, Eva, van Engen, Nadine, and Tummers, Lars. 2018. The necessity of discretion: a behavioral evaluation of bottom-up implementation theory. *Journal of Public Administration Research and Theory*, **28**(4), 583–601.

Toth, Zsofia, Henneberg, Stephan C., and Naude, Peter. 2017. Addressing the 'qualitative' in fuzzy set qualitative Comparative analysis: the generic membership evaluation template. *Industrial Marketing Management*, **63**, 192–204.

Verweij, Stefan, and Trell, E.-M. 2019. Qualitative Comparative Analysis (QCA) in spatial planning research and related disciplines: a systematic literature review of applications. *Journal of Planning Literature*, **34**(3), 300–317.

Wagemann, Claudius, and Schneider, Carsten Q. 2015. Transparency standards in qualitative comparative analysis. *Qualitative & Multi-Method Research*, **13**(1), 38–42.

Wagemann, Claudius, Buche, Jonas, and Siewert, Markus B. 2016. QCA and business research: work in progress or a consolidated agenda? *Journal of Business Research*, **69**(7), 2531–2540.

Index